# THIS BOOK COULD VITALLY EFFECT YOUR MARRIAGE

DO YOU AND YOUR MARRIAGE PART-
NER KNOW ALL YOU *MUST* ABOUT SUCH
CRUCIAL ASPECTS OF YOUR INTIMATE
RELATIONSHIP AS THE SEVEN MYTHS OF
FEMALE ORGASM, THE ZONES OF LOVE,
WHAT REALLY HAPPENS DURING INTER-
COURSE, UNEXPECTED SEX PROBLEMS
CAUSED BY THE PILL, NEW WAYS TO
OVERCOME IMPOTENCE AND PREMA-
TURE EJACULATION, WOMEN WHO
CAN'T REACH ORGASM, SEX DURING
PREGNANCY, THE SECRETS OF LOVE-
MAKING, AND HOW TO INCREASE SEX-
UAL DESIRE?

RESULTS OF THE LATEST SEX RE-
SEARCH, AS DISCUSSED FRANKLY, IN
PLAIN LANGUAGE, BY DISTINGUISHED
DOCTORS, PSYCHOLOGISTS, AND MAR-
RIAGE COUNSELORS, COULD VERY WELL
MAKE A GREAT DIFFERENCE IN YOUR
MARRIED LIFE. YOU OWE IT TO YOUR
HUSBAND OR WIFE—AND TO YOURSELF
—TO READ

## SEXUAL FREEDOM IN MARRIAGE.

## Other SIGNET Marriage Manuals

# SEXUAL FREEDOM IN MARRIAGE

*edited by*
Isadore Rubin, Ph.D.

*with an Introduction by*
John E. Eichenlaub, M.D.

A SIGNET BOOK from
NEW AMERICAN LIBRARY
TIMES MIRROR

SIGNET TRADEMARK REG. U.S. PAT. OFF. AND FOREIGN COUNTRIES
REGISTERED TRADEMARK—MARCA REGISTRADA
HECHO EN CHICAGO, U.S.A.

SIGNET, SIGNET CLASSICS, MENTOR AND PLUME BOOKS
*are published by The New American Library, Inc.,*
*1301 Avenue of the Americas, New York, New York 10019*

FIRST PRINTING, SEPTEMBER, 1969

PRINTED IN THE UNITED STATES OF AMERICA

# Contents

# II. UNDERSTANDING THE OTHER SEX

# III. IMPROVING YOUR SEX ENJOYMENT

## IV. PROBLEMS THAT INHIBIT SEXUAL FULFILLMENT

# V. OVERCOMING IMPOTENCE AND FRIGIDITY

# INTRODUCTION
## John E. Eichenlaub, M.D.

When Isaac Newton was asked how he had made his great scientific discoveries, he answered: "By standing on the shoulders of giants." How fortunate for the world that he operated under different "ground rules" than those prevailing in the field of sex! Every recent generation has started its quest for knowledge in this sphere almost from scratch because of widely observed taboos. Until Masters and Johnson began research on sexual excitation and orgasm, this area was almost entirely closed, even to physicians. You can still vainly search through physiology texts (which describe digestion, urine production and reproduction in lavish detail) for such data.

*Sexology* magazine, from which these selections were made, stood alone for many years as a medium of informational exchange in this sphere. In many ways it was ahead of its time, so that material from back issues remains quite current today. Certain attitudes present throughout this volume stem from the unique oposition this "beacon in the wilderness" has occupied, and add considerably to the value of this book.

Every article in this book gives practical guidance. Almost every one singles out a matter of deep concern to many readers (or to the people they try to help) and explores it in sufficient depth to provide useful remedies or reassurance. The few exceptions have practical implications for individuals and for communities—the lead article, "What Happens During the Sex Act," abstracts virtually all material of practical interest to nonmedical people from Masters and Johnson's important work, for instance, and pleads eloquently for an end to the taboos which have restricted such research in the past. *Sexology*'s editors apparently ask themselves over and over: "What *useful facts* will the reader find in this material, and how can they be brought to the fore?" In the articles presented here, they have generally come up with several good answers pertinent to each topic considered.

Articles in this volume leave no loose ends. The crucial importance of this policy revealed itself to most sexologists after a recent television program which dealt rather well and frankly with the problem of frigidity, but failed to define its terms. Many women were left with the impression that failure to reach an orgasm in virtually every incident placed them squarely in the pathologically inadequate group. Over the next few months, marriage counselors spent many hours reassuring women whose undue concern about feminine adequacy had been precipitated or aggravated by this program, and nobody knows how many anxious females are still beset with such concern. *Sexual Freedom in Marriage* immediately lays any ghosts and specters it raises. Since a few of them arise fairly frequently, this leads to occasional redundancy— but that is the lesser evil.

Books about sex generally encounter two barriers to clarity, both of which this volume has avoided. Some (among which I would number *Ideal Marriage* and possibly *Human Sexual Response*) lean over backwards to avoid salaciousness and in the process become obscure. Actually, the clear, bright light of totally frank clinical discourse has much less prurient appeal than the shadowy dimness of suggestion. Full "clinical" presentation has no sexually stimulating action at all, as has been proved in many of my "technique-teaching" couple sessions. When first one and then the other of a married couple are thoroughly draped as if for genital examination, then used as "anatomical models" for discussion of the areas of sexual sensitivity, appropriate caresses, etc., both anatomical and intellectual exposure are at peak. Yet not one of these sessions has led to male erection, either during the "his" or the "her" section of the discourse. The clinical, intellectual-understanding-directed approach throws cold water on sexual excitement one hundred per cent. This book's articles hit a similar tone—totally frank and therefore intellectually stimulating, not suggestive and therefore emotionally exciting.

The other common barrier to clarity which this book also avoids, is esoteric language. Established disciplines develop their own words or attach special shades of meaning to familiar words, and thus set many traps for the uninitiated reader. Freud, for example, uses "sex" for all physical attraction between people and for all pleasurable or fulfilling physical contact. With this definition, homosexuality has a vastly different meaning than that commonly attached to it, and resulting misunderstandings sometimes have been immense. Since the articles in this book were prepared for readers of varied background, the editors have carefully avoided such "special meaning" terms, and you can read without fear of semantic traps.

Practicality, thoroughness, clarity—all the qualities needed to get problem-solving ideas through from the authors to the reader—are to be found here. You will certainly "get the idea" from any article in this book. But is "the idea" worth getting? Is it sound, and does it apply fully to *you* and *your* sex life?

On basic soundness, I would argue with only one point (and since several authors agree on it, I'll admit that I'm in the minority even there). A number of these articles refer to parental concealment of sexual activity as totally natural and totally desirable. If they limited their injunctions to *privacy* —to avoiding actual observation of intercourse and advanced sex play—I would agree with them one hundred per cent. However, the cult of *secrecy*—of taking vast and substantial steps to conceal or deny the existence of continuing sexual activity in the thirties, forties and fifties—seems to me both unnatural and extremely harmful for three different reasons.

First, youngsters' awareness of continuing sexuality gives them perspective which most of their generation sadly lacks. A young adult who thinks that sex is virtually over at age twenty-five acts with reckless haste. He feels as if he has a season ticket to a series of attractions which will soon be over, so he has to "get in there and pitch." Youngsters who become aware of parental sexuality realize that sex is a long-term phenomenon and that a year or two of sacrifice to keep it meaningful over several decades really adds up to a good investment.

Second, youngsters' awareness of their parents' relationship is certainly much fuller for their appreciation of its physical element. You can serve much better as models for your children's later relationships because of this, and fulfill a very important role which phony concealment of continuing sexuality would certainly warp or abrogate.

Third, you reveal that you are "with it" instead of "has beens," and greatly improve the likelihood that your youngsters will call on you for counsel. Awareness of continuing couple activity accomplishes much more toward opening channels of communication than any number of "heart-to-heart" talks.

If you would argue that such disclosure—or really simple and deliberate failure to conceal—is "unnatural," we might review the housing arrangements of other cultures and other generations. Do Eskimos kick their children out of the igloo into the forty below whenever the urge for couple communion strikes? Did Grandpa sleep so soundly in the attic of his parents' pioneer cabin that he never heard a murmur of endearment or the rustling of a pine-bough bed? Twentieth century America is one of the only cultures in history where youngsters can pass the age of sophistication without any inkling of what their parents do in bed. Our phony, mass attempt at sexual denial is unnatural warpage and unwholesome obstruction of a normal learning channel, in my opinion, and I dispute the lip service several authors in this book pay to this "prevailing norm."

Granted this one exception, I would agree with the material presented here. "Standard reservations" apply to this book as to everything you read in fields involving intimate personal relations. Let me leave you two such "grains of salt" with which to take these messages:

First, "facts" which concern human relationships can never be more than prevailing current opinions. Even what is right today, among people who grew up with X taboos and Y inhibitions, may be wrong tomorrow for a (hopefully) more liberally reared generation. And at least some ideas with which most experts agree might be wrong.

Second, all pronouncements in this sphere assume "standard" sociologic and psychologic background, which may make them unsuited in some particulars to your own highly individual (or unique couple) circumstances.

These limitations are not too great. You can read on with confidence and hopeful expectation—there is a great deal of guidance, reassurance and aid in this volume for virtually everyone. But cull out those notions which seem unsuitable to you or which seem likely to produce substantial couple conflict. Take the ideas presented here as suggestions, not as gospel, so far as your particular couple adaptations are concerned. Used in this way, this volume can enhance your knowledge, probably ease unwarranted feelings of inadequacy or guilt, and constructively attack some truly basic problems.

# I.

# DESTROYING OUTWORN MYTHS AND TABOOS

# 1. What Happens During the Sex Act?

### Isadore Rubin, Ph.D.

It is not surprising that the work of Dr. William H. Masters and his research associate, Virginia E. Johnson, described in their book *Human Sexual Response,* should be the subject of widespread interest and discussion as well as heated and vigorous controversy. For this research was undoubtedly one of the most controversial projects ever undertaken.

These two scientists went far beyond Kinsey and his associates in their sex research. Instead of merely asking questions about sexual behavior, they actually observed, photographed and measured what happened to human beings in the acts of sexual intercourse and masturbation.

For eleven years they had carried on their researches—little known except to a comparatively small number of professionals—among men and women in a laboratory in St. Louis. Now, for the first time, a shocked world was to learn of their work.

In their book, Masters and Johnson reported on the sexual responses of 382 women and 312 men, ranging in age from eighteen to eighty-nine. In all, they observed anywhere from ten to fifteen thousand orgasmic cycles, a number that staggers the imagination.

The orgasms were obtained through intercourse as well as masturbation, in pregnancy as well as nonpregnancy, and even—in seven cases—by women who because of developmental errors had to have artificial vaginas created. In some cases, special plastic artificial penises were used, through which observations could be made and photos taken.

The result is a wealth of data that presents professionals for the first time with a solid body of knowledge about the physiology of sexual response that will prove invaluable to everyone who must counsel couples about sex.

The first question most people ask is, "How could they possibly have gotten persons who were willing to take part in research of this kind? How could normal people actually respond in a laboratory situation like this?"

When the research started, no one knew the answer to either of these questions. In fact, Masters and Johnson themselves assumed at the beginning that the only persons they would be able to get would be prostitutes. For the first twenty months of the project, they studied only this group. None of the findings about prostitutes, incidentally, are contained in their book.

However, they later decided that they had to get a group that would allow them to establish a secure baseline of anatomic normalcy. They found it possible to get volunteers (whom they paid) from the students at the university-hospital complex they were associated with.

As knowledge of the project spread, many couples came to volunteer their services, many in the hope of getting help for various sexual problems.

It is important to remember that the persons taking part in the experiments were given a number of orientation sessions to make them feel at home with the laboratory equipment. It might take nine to twelve such sessions before the couple were ready to take part in the full-scale experiments.

*Just what did this research accomplish?*

First of all, the investigators were able to establish the patterns of sexual response that were found in the subjects they tested. This provided important data about physiology which enabled them to compare response in the younger and older years to help resolve the still-puzzling question of what takes place during sexual aging.

By getting data on blood pressure, heart, and lungs, physicians are now in a much better position to counsel patients who may have high blood pressure or who have had a heart attack.

One of the most dramatic findings was the identification of the source of lubrication of the vagina when sexual arousal takes place. According to older medical belief, this lubrication is provided primarily by the Bartholin glands, on either side of the front part of the vagina, and by the glands of the cervix, or womb neck.

By actual photographs, however, Masters and Johnson found that the Bartholin glands provide only a small amount of lubrication late in arousal. The primary source of lubrication is in the vagina itself, which undergoes a process of sweating during sexual arousal. This is an important medical discovery.

For many years prior to the publication of the early findings of the Masters-Johnson research, one found in marriage manuals and in counseling journals a vigorous debate going on about the "clitoral versus the vaginal orgasm." That debate has become more or less academic in view of the findings by Masters and Johnson that physiologically exactly the same thing happens during orgasm, regardless of the source of stimulation.

In other words, biologically, "orgasm is orgasm," whether it results from manual stimulation of the clitoral area or other sensitive parts of the body, or whether it results from intromission of the penis into the vagina. This is not to say, of course, that the psychological or emotional satisfaction from different kinds of stimulation may not vary considerably.

Many of the older marriage manuals had also counseled the husband about the importance of continuing to stimulate the clitoris itself for women who may have had difficulty in reaching a climax. However, the Masters and Johnson research showed clearly that this was an actual impossibility.

During sexual arousal, it was discovered, the clitoris retracts and it is impossible to stimulate it directly. Stimulation takes place indirectly through manipulation of the clitoral area or other forms of pressure.

Masters and Johnson point out that many inexperienced men—led by a "textbook" approach to try to maintain manual contact with the clitoris—may cease active stimulation when retraction takes place, and spend time looking for the clitoris, with considerable sexual frustration for the female partner.

One of the things that seems to bother innumerable men is their feeling that their penis is too small to satisfy their wives. A preponderance of men seem to feel that the larger the organ, the more effective is the male in satisfying his partner.

This belief is a complete fallacy, Masters and Johnson showed. It is a delusion, they found, to believe that sexual adequacy is related to penis size.

They also found, by measurement of some eighty men, that it is a mistake to assume that the larger flaccid penis necessarily achieves significantly greater size in erection than does the smaller flaccid penis. They found that the smaller penises practically doubled their size in full erection; in contrast, the organs that were larger while flaccid did not increase nearly as much, so that size in erection did not end up essentially different.

They also discovered by careful examination that penis size bore little relation to the man's general body size. The smallest penis, they found, was possessed by a man 5 feet, 11 inches tall, and weighing 178 pounds.

In another experiment, they found that there is no difference in sensitivity of the glans penis of circumcised, as contrasted with uncircumcised, men.

They found, too, that there is no clinical evidence to support the common belief that intercourse during menstruation will lead to acute physical distress on the woman's part.

One of the most important gaps in our theoretical knowledge and clinical experience is found in the area of sexuality of older persons. Here, Masters and Johnson made a significant contribution in helping break down the taboos on discussion of sexual response in this increasingly numerous section of our population.

They found that, although the intensity of physiologic and anatomic response to sexual stimulation is reduced with advancing years, healthy aging men and women are fully capable of sexual performance, up to and beyond eighty years old. This is true particularly if they continue a regular sex life.

One of the most important findings of Masters and Johnson—and perhaps the one that will end up with greatest significance—was the discovery in 1959 of what they called a "lethal factor" in the vaginal lubrication of some of the women.

This was the finding that, for some as yet unknown reason, there was some substance in this lubrication which killed or immobilized sperm. If this factor can finally be isolated, it may offer the most effective birth control agent yet devised.

One brief report cannot exhaust all the findings of this epoch-making report. It will take a long time for sexologists to digest all the findings.

"Are the people studied typical enough for us to be sure we're getting normal findings?" many people ask. One can only reply that no studies of physiology or internal anatomy are based on the average person.

One does not go around operating on the bodies of a cross section of people to find out how the body works. Doctors have to make their observations on those persons who enter the hospital for surgery, or on the few cadavers available for dissection. They assume that the physiology or anatomy will not be too different from that of the average.

Kinsey got his foot firmly in the door of sex research, say Masters and Johnson; we have tried to open it completely. Their research not only tells us much about what happens during the sex act. It also helps us destroy many outworn myths and taboos.

# 2. Misconceptions Which Hinder Sex Enjoyment in Marriage
## Robert A. Harper, Ph.D.

The patient before me was a very attractive woman of twenty-three. She had just told me that she was very unhappy with her husband after one year of marriage, that he was similarly miserable, and that sex was at the root of their trouble.

"Tell me in what way sex is a problem in your marriage," I said.

"Well, it's so easy and so superficial and so omnipresent that deep and meaningful love has no chance to grow," she replied. "All he has to do is touch me, or sometimes just look at me, and I respond. I have orgasms—many of them—very easily.

"Well, I must be a freak. All the marriage books say that women are slower to arouse than men, and yet I am aroused before my husband or anyone else who is normal. True and meaningful love cannot be so superficially lustful as mine. I can't really love him or he me."

Hard as it may be to believe, it took a fair amount of emotional reeducation for this couple to come to accept the wife's sexual prowess, and to enjoy thoroughly their sexual relationship. The husband, as well as his wife, had swallowed the belief that her sexual responsiveness was somehow abnormal, superficial, and otherwise undesirable.

Wasn't this a quite unusual case? Yes, but after having practiced psychotherapy and marriage counseling for many years, I am always seeing and hearing new and unusual things from almost every person who consults me.

Despite the individuality of each person's problems, however, certain patterns of self-defeat are discernible among troubled people. One of these recurring themes is the tendency to keep themselves from really enjoying sex. Some people, like the couple mentioned, have to work pretty hard *not* to enjoy sex. Others seem to have no difficulty at all in making their sexual lives miserable.

Although the puritanical influence in our society is probably gradually declining, there is still a strong underlying belief among many Americans that it is really wrong to enjoy sex, even in marriage. Not a little of my practice consists of convincing people that it is fully desirable (and "normal" and "healthy") to go ahead and experience sex in the ways that they feel inclined. So long as they are not exploiting or violating the rights of others, I point out, any way is the "right way."

A type of common belief that often interferes with sexual enjoyment is that full satisfaction can be achieved only by simultaneous orgasms. Couples have sometimes acquired this conviction from marriage manuals and other writings on sex. I have investigated this matter, however, and have never found any basis for the assertion other than the bias of the writer or other person who is doing the asserting.

Excerpts of an interview I had with Mrs. B. may bring out further points about this kind of unnecessary interference with sex enjoyment. Mrs. B. had informed me that her sex life with her husband was "horrible" because they could not achieve simultaneous orgasms, and I had stated that I thought it was absurd to think that they were missing some marvelous experience.

**Mrs. B.:** But I've read several places that simultaneous orgasm is the *supreme* union of husband and wife and an experience several levels above anything else in sexual life. I am suspicious that you are just reassuring me so I won't feel so bad about what my husband and I have in our sex life.

**Therapist:** That is not true. For reasons I'll give in a moment, I don't think simultaneous orgasms are great levels of spiritual joy above other orgastic experiences. But it is also true that I believe it to be undesirable for "experts" to assert that one type of sex experience or feeling is preferable and that anything else is automatically second-rate or worse.

**Mrs. B.:** But is it foolish to struggle to achieve simultaneous orgasms?

**Therapist:** Yes, in two ways. One, we know that any sort of struggle, or determined effort, to achieve orgasm practically guarantees that it will not be achieved. The reason is that it distracts the person or the couple from the process of experiencing pleasurable sexual sensations and leads them to concentrate on the orgasm. This distraction is usually sufficient to *prevent* climax, which derives from a buildup of the pleasurable sensations thus being ignored.

Secondly, it seems to me that a considerable case can be made for a couple's having separate orgasms and enjoying each more. The wife is able to savor her orgasm while her husband vicariously experiences her enjoyment; then the husband can concentrate on his while the wife empathizes with his enjoyment. At best, simultaneous orgasms are simply *one* way of having sexual enjoyment. To strive constantly for this one way as all-important not only downgrades other methods of satisfaction, but can lead to distraction, frustration, confusion, and conflict. These results have apparently been experienced by you and your husband.

Another closely related way that some couples reduce their sexual enjoyment is by coming to believe that certain types of sexual activity are second-rate or abnormal compared with some other types. Any procedure that satisfies the husband or wife and does not bring pain or displeasure to the partner can be considered first-rate, normal, and in every way desirable for them and, hence, to be thoroughly enjoyed by them. How any such procedure might be rated by others (including "experts") is of no consequence.

People also sometimes reduce their sexual enjoyment by having various kinds of comparisons in mind. They may read, for example, that the "average couple" (whatever this is) has sexual intercourse two or three times a week and get worried if they have more or less than that. The only pertinent point is how often do *they* enjoy sex activity and not any statistics on the subject.

Similarly, I have had more than one husband insist on caressing his wife's breasts because of a rigid belief on his part that "all women enjoy this," even though she has told him specifically that she does not like this, but enjoys other types of caresses instead.

I have had wives who themselves enjoy taking sex initiative (and whose husbands appreciate their doing so) stop doing it because they have read or heard that men are always supposed to be the aggressive ones sexually. Still other couples give up as "kid stuff" petting and other activities they not only enjoy in and of themselves, but which increase their pleasure in sexual intercourse.

A quite simple prescription for sexual enjoyment emerges from the hundreds of stories I have heard of how married couples interfere with their pleasure in sex: namely, each husband or wife is encouraged to develop spontaneity and freedom in their expressions of love for each other. If they proceed to do what occurs to them (without censoring their thoughts and actions), they will soon develop various ways of relating to each other sexually that are pleasing to both of them.

The whole idea, as nature set it up, is to enjoy sex. The only "abnormal" or "unnatural" sex pursuits and expressions of love in marriage are those that are inhibited and rigidly confined. "Doing what comes naturally"—that is, a free and open love relationship—is the route to sex enjoyment.

# 3. Anxieties About Sex Organ Size
## Hugo G. Beigel, Ph.D.

Every sexologist has heard some men embarrassedly refer to the so-called smallness of their genital organs. *Sexology* magazine has time and again received letters from readers who, for the same reason, expressed fear for the marriage they had planned. As a rule, such men are told that the importance attached to penis size is exaggerated and that the so-called shortness need not affect the happiness of a marriage nor sexual functioning.

This is the only reply one can give to such questions. But frequently, however, the man who is so advised feels that the issue is thus merely dismissed with a consoling phrase because nothing can be done about the matter anyway. This does not solve his problem, and it does not relieve him of his anxieties.

Yet, it is this anxiety that matters most. The alleged smallness may be completely unimportant. But the fear of being inadequate as a man, and of being judged so by others, often has a powerful effect on character and personality. Sometimes it leads to serious behavior disorders.

Many strange and irrational behavior patterns have developed under the big shadow cast by a small penis. In numerous cases of transvestism, for instance, awareness of the smallness of the sex organ has contributed to the desire to abandon the male role and to dress and behave like a woman.

I do not claim that a short penis causes transvestism. But I have found that many a child who feels uncomfortable in the face of the demands made on boys, or who is afraid of his future role as a man, takes the smallness of his sex organ not only as an additional proof of his inadequacy but also as a sign that actually he was meant to be a female.

Several cases of emotional impotence were traced to the same cause. The men were so tensely expecting failure, embarrassment, or ridicule, or so defiantly set on meeting the "challenge," that they either had no erection or ejaculated immediately. Yet when they were hypnotized into the belief that their organs were of normal size, they functioned satisfactorily.

Once a young woman sought advice because after almost three years of marriage, she was still a virgin. Her husband was sweet and kind, but he never attempted intercourse with her. He played and petted with her but never let her see him unclothed and never allowed her to touch his lower body.

It turned out that in this manner, he hoped to keep from her the secret that his penis was rather short. This did not prevent him, however, from having normal erections and ejaculations when he masturbated. He could not be persuaded to accept professional help and was very unhappy when finally his wife insisted on an annulment of the marriage.

The list of such irrational reactions could easily go on indefinitely. What is important is the fact that it is less the so-called smallness that causes trouble than the mistaken belief that penis size is the decisive factor in the sexual relationship. It is not. Nor does the length of the organ determine a man's masculinity.

What is short? What is large? What are the "advantages" of a big penis and the "disadvantages" of a small one?

One of the ways in which short and long are established is the statistical average. Thus we learn that the average size for the erect male organ is six inches. But does this mean that six inches is the standard size below which the organ does not fulfill its purpose, does not reproduce, does not give pleasure to the man, fails to satisfy the female partner?

It means nothing of the kind. It is merely a statistical figure that describes the usual size found in the population. This average is made up of just as many men who have a smaller size than six inches as of men with a larger size. There is no such thing as a minimum requirement for size.

As a rule, the organ that is capable of erection is also capable of insertion in the vagina. I know two women, one of whom is a female pseudohermaphrodite living as a man.

They are living together as husband and wife and like any husband and wife they have coitus together. The "husband's" organ—an enlarged clitoris—measures two inches erect.

Erection and even insertion, however, are not the core of most sex organ size worries. Such men fear—or say they fear—that with a small organ, a man cannot satisfy a woman. They have in mind either depth (to which a short penis cannot penetrate) or width (which a relatively slender organ cannot fill). They forget that female sex organs, too, vary with respect to tightness or largeness.

A large vagina lacking in muscle tone may not provide the friction that aids a couple in bringing about an orgasm. But that would be so for bigger-sized men, too. It merely confirms what we know anyway, that not all people are "perfect fits" in this respect, even if their sex organs are of "normal" size.

Just as a middle-sized penis does not always find complete contact with a loose vagina, a woman may suffer pain if a man tries to insert an organ that is too big in relation to hers. Indeed, if the male organ exceeds the width of the sheath considerably—be it that he is "too big" or she "too narrowly built"—intercourse may be not only painful but actually injurious. She might well feel happier if her husband were not so large.

Another complaint frequently heard refers to depth penetration. Men believe that the penis must touch the cervix of the womb to give the woman pleasant sensations. This is incorrect. It is true that there are women in whom this contact brings an orgasm. But there are many others who disike so deep an entry. In some, the repeated hammering at the cervix has been responsible for inflammations of the womb. To a majority of females, probably, the contact with the cervix is unimportant either way.

Although nobody knows exactly how the so-called vaginal orgasm comes about, there is no doubt that, in general, it does not depend on the involvement of the womb. And sufficient contact with the walls of the vagina—apparently a stimulating factor—can be obtained not only by a short but also by a slender organ.

One case I know dramatizes how foolish these fears about a small penis may sometimes be. This was the case of a man who could not rid himself of his anxiety in spite of the fact that his marital relations with his wife were undoubtedly excellent.

Each time he had intercourse, he could not help asking whether she "really" enjoyed it. And however often she lovingly assured him that she did, he did not believe it. He tortured her with his doubts, assuming that she was constantly aware of his "deficiency."

He made her life so miserable with such accusations that she finally decided to break up the relationship. When I explained to her the cause of his behavior, she was taken completely by surprise. She had not even been aware of what he considered his terrible handicap—the allegedly "too short" penis.

What it all amounts to is this: intercourse between humans has its problems, and sexual intercourse is no exception. Real compatibility involves not only emotional but also physical elements. Eventually, any individual can find a proper mate, regardless of his sex organ size.

# 4. The Myth of Sex Organ Incompatibility

### Helen K. Branson, M.A.

Organic disproportion, a condition in which the sexual organs of husband and wife are physically incompatible, is much rarer than most people realize.

There are, of course, a few cases in medical records where the male penis is so underdeveloped as to make penetration, even if erection does occur, difficult or impractical. But this is exceedingly rare.

Similarly, there are some females in whom the hymen so nearly covers the vagina, or is so tough and inelastic, that penetration of the male organ is difficult or impossible without surgical help.

In fact, medical science records cases in which an unperforated hymen—one which completely covers the vagina and does not allow the escape of menstrual fluids—caused serious problems in which surgery was necessary. But these conditions so rarely occur that they are cause for medical curiosity.

In the rare case of the male with a penis of less than four inches, nothing can be done to make his organ larger once he has reached full maturity. But in fact this is entirely irrelevant to his sexual adequacy as a husband.

Marriage counselors, doctors, and other professional experts are constantly being besieged by men (it is almost always men; wives don't seem too concerned about their spouse's size) who suffer from feelings of inferiority because they think their penises are "too small." But in fact there is no such thing as a "too small" penis, since penis size has been found over and over again to have little to do with the sexual satisfaction of the woman.

Most recently, in the historic *Human Sexual Response* study by Dr. William H. Masters and Virginia E. Johnson, it was found by actual observation of human individuals in intercourse that penis size is unrelated to sexual adequacy.

The female, however, whose vagina is too small to admit the husband's erect organ, should consult a physician. An inelastic or unusually overgrown hymen can be remedied by simply cutting it away painlessly under a local anesthetic.

Much more often than not, however, what is suspected by the couple to be organic disproportion is not so at all. For example, the position of the vagina in some women may be somewhat lower, or the angle somewhat shallower, than the husband finds comfortable for insertion.

The manner in which the wife holds herself during coitus influences this matter considerably. If she lies on the back with her knees drawn up, this will make it simpler for intromission to take place. Sometimes a small pillow under the lower part of the back can be of assistance. The couple should experiment with various positions to determine which is best suited to their particular needs.

One fact which many women need to learn, because they have been improperly taught from childhood, is that the walls of the vagina are actually pleated in folds like an accordion. If this were not true, how could a full term infant's head—much larger than any penis—come through the vagina, or birth canal, and pass out of it?

True enough, a doctor often does an episiotomy in which he makes a small cut to prevent tearing of the vagina by the baby's head. But certainly the largest penis is not even one third the circumference of a baby's head.

Therefore, except in cases where the hymen is very tough or covers a large portion of the vagina, the size of the husband's penis should not be a great handicap in sexual relations. If the wife experiences considerable pain after the first month of marriage, or even before that, if pain is extreme, she should see a physician to determine the cause.

Most frequently, her problem will be emotional. It is normal in some cases for the wife to experience some pain the first few times the husband penetrates the vagina. Some women, however, even though they are virgins, experience no pain at all.

Sometimes, the pain of the first intercourse is overemphasized by mothers or other people anxious to preserve virginity before marriage. Then the wife comes to her first coital experience anticipating great pain. She ordinarily does experience some discomfort, and thus she tenses in anticipation of greater pain. This tension may be so severe as to cause the muscles of the vagina to contract to the point where entry of the male organ is very painful, difficult, and even impossible.

In such cases, the husband should make certain that lubrication is adequate. If the vagina of the wife does not provide enough lubrication to make entry easy, the use of vaseline or K-Y jelly before intercourse may be helpful. If painful intercourse persists, however, a physician should by all means be consulted.

Counseling or even psychotherapy may occasionally be required to assist the wife in overcoming her problem of anticipating pain. It may take her some time to convince herself consciously or subconsciously that her female organs are of sufficient size to accommodate her husband's penis.

Some gynecologists and family life educators have felt that encouraging young girls to use tampons during menstrual periods from the beginning of puberty would dispel this psychological feeling that the vagina is too small to accommodate the male organ. Tampons are made in various sizes to accommodate the needs of various girls and women, and they are not harmful in any way when properly placed and changed frequently.

There is, of course, the other side of the coin to be considered. Some husbands complain that after many childbirths, the wife's vagina is so loose as to make sexual relations less satisfying both to her and to him. When this is actually the case, the couple should not hesitate to take steps to remedy the situation.

If no more children are planned, the doctor can repair this situation in a few minutes under local anesthesia. There are also muscle exercises which can tighten up relaxed vaginal muscles.

Sometimes women whose sexual life has been satisfactory early in life develop a condition after change of life in which coitus is painful. This often occurs in women past fifty-five, and results from a thinning of the lining of the vagina, as well as a lessening in its secretions during sexual arousal.

These circumstances may cause intercourse to be painful or just unpleasant because of the feeling of friction. There are hormone ointments available which will help this problem. They should not be used, however, without a thorough physical examination to determine the cause of the pain.

Actual organic disproportion and anatomical problems are very rare in marriage. Since pleasant and fulfilling sexual relations are dependent on emotional as well as physical factors, these two aspects of sexual expression must be considered simultaneously in any given situation.

Couples worried before marriage about what they consider to be unusually small or unusually large sexual organs should be especially careful to have a thorough physical examination and talk with their doctor *before* marriage. This will eliminate any real physical barriers which might exist, and will give the bride and groom the reassurance that they are physically compatible.

# 5. Masturbation in Marriage
## Hugo G. Beigel, Ph.D.

It has become fairly well known by now that masturbation is harmless. But as soon as the question of masturbation in *marriage* arises, few persons are able to discuss it calmly and unemotionally.

A wife or husband's intolerance of such self-service is understandable. If the mate's masturbation becomes habitual, the other one is bound to resent it.

The wife who has so satisfied her needs is unwilling to receive her husband in her arms. The man who has just indulged his private fantasies is for some time thereafter usually incapable of further sex.

In the long run the situation creates difficulties. The man feels rejected and reacts with hostility. The normally-sexed wife feels deprived and takes the imposed continence as a reflection on herself. Even if the wife's sexual needs are extremely low, the discovery of her husband's masturbation usually upsets her.

Nonetheless, masturbation in marriage is not infrequent. Among the married men between twenty-one and twenty-five years of age, it is believed that about 42 per cent supplement their marital relations by this means at one time or another. The downward tendency of the trend leaves 11 per cent at the ages between fifty and fifty-five.

For the younger groups, the wife's pregnancy, abstinence after childbirth, and menstrual periods account for a great number of autoerotic activities. During the later years, alienation from the wife, or the wife's sicknesses, are often mentioned as reasons.

Young women frequently masturbate because sex relations arouse them but fail to produce the relief of an orgasm. As the mates adapt themselves to each other's needs, masturbation is used more sparingly. As the couple ages, the husband's sexual decline may compel the wife to resort to this means again.

In addition, however, there are circumstances that make masturbation not only an occasional but the main outlet for either the man or the woman. These circumstances become rarely known to the researcher. As a rule they are revealed only to the therapist or the marriage counselor, and then only after considerable resistance.

Women seem to resort to it mainly because they are unable to obtain an orgasm through intercourse alone. In several instances, the trouble could have been avoided if the man had tried to arouse his wife by caresses and foreplay. In others, either physiological or psychological adjustment is lagging.

Whatever the reason, whether a woman needs more intense stimulation or feels discomfort at penetration, whether the male ejaculates too soon or his penis loses rigidity in the middle of the act, she is left alone before her excitement has abated. For nervous relief, she continues the stimulation herself until she reaches orgasm.

There is obviously nothing wrong with this except that it is practically always done with a bad conscience and hence secretly. Shame and fear often make these women avoid intercourse altogether.

Similar sentiments are occasionally expressed by women who fear pregnancy but do not use contraceptives. Since they insist upon the husband's early withdrawal they become aroused but hardly ever satisfied.

Only some of these women resort to masturbation, but a great number of them force their husbands to masturbate by these measures. If this happens, or if it drives the husband to another woman's bed, they are deeply offended and quite upset.

Sleeping habits and sleeping arrangements also contribute to the development of the habit. For strong as the sex drive appears to be in some instances, in others it is not strong enough to get a man to roll over to his wife's side or to cross the gap between two twin beds.

The gap becomes even more difficult to cross if it stretches not over space but between the couple's sleeping and waking habits. A man may be very tired in the evening, but in the morning—especially the morning when he need not go to work—his appetite is wide awake. Unfortunately, the wife is up and about early and cannot be lured back to bed. With their imagination aroused, such men often choose masturbation as the way out.

This situation has its counterpart. The husband had a good day. His behavior in the evening clearly indicates that he is in an amorous mood. But the wife is too "respectable" for adventures of that sort. She can accept lovemaking only in bed and at night. Yet when night falls and he hopes that this will end his waiting time, then she has still to do her hair, to remove her makeup, to wash a blouse and to mend a stocking. Or there is a television show which she must listen to.

By the time she appears—presumably also ready for him—he has relieved his urge with a more "eager" fantasy female, and is asleep.

However, not always can the wife be blamed. There are men who do prefer masturbation to sexual intercourse. One, for instance, suffered from premature ejaculation.

His wife was frustrated. So was he, especially since she could not refrain from mocking remarks whenever he became affectionate. Instead of trying to have his condition remedied, he retreated to the solitary play of his bachelorhood.

In a second case, a man was so ashamed of his relatively small sex organ that he abstained from sex relations until he married at the age of thirty. During these many years he satisfied his sexual needs by masturbation. In marriage he hoped to change.

However, the sex relations with his wife proved unsatisfactory. This may have been—according to his description—because a vagina is less adjustable than a hand and because the exposure of his organ made him feel uneasy.

His wife was young and quite eager to erase one failure by a new try. But when she started caressing him, he pretended to be tired. Sometimes he looked forward to embracing her in the evening. But then he got so aroused that he masturbated in anticipation.

In his feeling of guilt, this man accused his wife of undue aggressiveness. Obviously, a young woman who after weeks of abstinence tries to lure her husband into intimacies cannot be called overly aggressive. However, both real and imaginary aggressiveness on the woman's part is a source of anxiety to certain men.

Some of them feel so endangered that they withdraw from sexual intimacies and masturbate. Thus they escape the threatening power of the mate.

A dozen additional causes, fears and disturbances could be enumerated that lead to masturbation in spite of an available mate.

Suffice it to say that masturbation in marriage, like masturbation outside of marriage, is entirely harmless and perhaps even helpful in some instances. But when it becomes a compulsive habit and a retreat from marital sex, one should consider it a sign of some difficulty.

# 6. "Undersexed" or "Oversexed"

## Donald W. Hastings, M.D.

For centuries, as he tried to understand what was "normal" sexually, civilized man has used labels such as "oversexed" and "undersexed." People whose sex lives seemed to differ to a marked degree from those of others were regarded as "abnormal," in the sense of being diseased.

Even today healthy people who are not suffering from physical or mental disease are often given such a label just because they have either more or less interest in sex than the majority of individuals.

The terms used to describe sexual behavior have become deeply ingrained in our thinking and one commonly hears even physicians use words like "undersexed." It has only been over the course of the past few decades that man has been able to straighten out his thinking on these matters. This depeneded upon the development of the branch of mathematics known as statistics.

This can be illustrated by a consideration of body weight. If I am 6 feet tall and weigh 180 pounds, is my weight "normal"? Actually, there is no possible way of answering this question unless, in addition to my height, I also list some other facts such as my age, sex, race, whether my frame is light or heavy, and so on.

I can then say to myself, "I am not quite so heavy as most men my age, height, race, etc., but there are men like me who are lighter than I am."

What I am doing is placing myself on a point along a mathematical curve, and this is called the "normal curve of individual differences" when used in this way. Because it looks something like a bell, it is often called a "bell-shaped curve."

This curve of normal distribution can be applied to any biological function. What it says at rock bottom are well-known truths: that people differ a great deal in any way one cares to measure them and that no two people are alike.

Let's apply these ideas to our sexual drive.

First of all, since it is a biological function, people will differ in the strength of their sex drive just as they will differ in body weight.

The fact that individuals are at different points of the curve does not mean that they are suffering from a disease. They are merely different from the "norm" or average.

Thus, the terms "oversexed" or "undersexed" are meaningless by themselves. A person is "undersexed" or "oversexed" only in comparison to a particular sexual partner.

However, the fact that people are different in their sex drive—sometimes tremendously different—can cause serious problems between a husband and wife. A psychiatrist often gets the impression that few marriages see people of about equal sexual drives get together. This sexual mismatching creates resentments and hostilities and undoubtedly often results in divorce, alcoholism, depression and symptoms of various kinds.

Take the case of a young physician of twenty-nine who had had very little sexual experience and who dated two girls frequently. One was from a socially prominent family. They did a good deal of petting and had sexual relations twice. Then he lost interest in her. He turned to the other girl, who was very pretty but rigid and perfectionistic and permitted no petting.

He was attracted to this girl and married her. On the honeymoon she was upset by his sexual advances and cried most of the two weeks. Two years later he discussed his situation with me: his wife was seldom interested in sexual relations. Her sexual needs were perhaps a tenth of his.

She was however a "good" wife in other ways and it made him feel guilty that he was entertaining private thoughts of divorcing her.

He told me that it took him about a year after his marriage to realize that he had married the wrong girl.

Another case concerned a married professional man of thirty-nine, whose wife was responsive sexually only about every six to eight weeks. At other times, she met his sexual advances by turning her back to him, saying that she was tired or didn't feel well. This pattern had persisted during the fourteen years of marriage. His religious beliefs kept him from considering a divorce, but he did take a mistress.

It is just as often the wife who needs more sexual intercourse. This was clearly the case of the twenty-five-year-old woman married to a man who pursued her ardently before marriage but who showed little interest in her physically after marriage. On the unusual occasions that the husband approached her sexually—two times in the past year—he had no trouble with potency.

They discussed the situation and he said that he simply wasn't interested in sex very often. At first she suspected that he must be having an affair outside the marriage but later felt that this was unlikely. As a result of her sexual frustrations, she developed sleeplessness, tension and headaches which brought her to the psychiatrist.

Husbands and wives must realize that people have varying sex needs, so that even as in these cases where sexual mismatching exists, the situation will not be aggravated by resentments, hostilities and charges of "abnormality."

Thus, if one describes a person as being "oversexed" or "undersexed," one must always ask, "in relation to whom?" If this were done, a much clearer understanding of the problem would result, and such unscientific words as "oversexed" or "undersexed" would tend to disappear.

# 7. Does Sex Come Naturally?

### Stephen Neiger, M.D., Ph.D.

One of the most amazing conditions observed by almost any sex expert is the persistent belief held by most people that "sex comes naturally."

Our grandparents, for example, refused to discuss sex with our parents not only because it was supposed to be a "dirty subject" in those days, but also because they were sure that, once the time of the wedding came, "things will somehow take care of themselves."

Perhaps such methods may have sufficed for most people at a time when getting babies was supposed to be the only purpose of sex in marriage. According to this moral philosophy, the husband, but *not* the wife, was allowed to derive some incidental pleasure in the process. Still, in those times of "expectation without preparation," quite a few became sexually crippled with such symptoms as impotence.

It is virtually certain, however, that knowledge of the sexual process is demanded in marriage from today's husbands and wives who are told even by their churches (to say nothing of movies, TV, books, magazines) that sex is a most precious (if not *the* most precious) means of expressing marital love and that wife as well as husband should fully enjoy marital relations.

Yet not even this knowledge is as available as one might think. Gynecologists and marriage counselors still report husbands who come to them for problems of "infertility" who think that intercourse consists of rubbing their penis between their wives' legs. Some have to be given diagrams of the female vagina and how to find it.

There is even a famous case of an attorney who came to his doctor after two years of childless marriage for treatment of his "sterility." This man had been trying to make sexual entry via his wife's navel.

And yet, we still insist that sex education is a matter of explaining the reproductive process without going into the de-

34

tails of sexual intercourse, and that any further facts and techniques would be luxury at best and corrupting at worst. Thus, so the theory goes, let the young couple "muddle through" and discover things for themselves.

It is questionable whether such minimal preparation enables more than a very tiny fraction of couples to make use of that wonderful potential which can enrich a marriage so much—if the emotion of love is combined with a well-understood and skillful technique of lovemaking. It is certain, however, that a large number turn up as victims of such "sex education" in the offices of the marriage counselor, the psychologist, or the psychiatrist after giving it a try for many wasted and frustrating years.

Less fortunate still are those who find themselves in divorce courts because their high expectations of marital sex turn into disappointment, bitterness and, all too often, into hatred. Between the two extreme minorities of those gifted in fantasy, who can teach themselves, and those who finally seek help or throw in the towel, lie the masses of couples who try to make the best of it but then conclude that "sex is probably a much overrated activity." They decide that "there are a lot more important things in life" or that "the whole thing just is not for me." This is a pity.

For the overwhelming majority of couples, sex can be one of the greatest sources of shared pleasure and one of the finest ways of creating the deepest affectional bonds between wife and husband provided, however, that it is realized that it does *not* come naturally. What nature *has* given us is the sexual *drive,* a mysterious longing for physical contact with the opposite sex. What it has *not* given us is the wisdom and the knowledge of *what to do with it.*

Instinct is indeed a reliable guide of action *in lower forms of life*—but in those only. Instinct in mammals, however, functions on a different principle. Here evolution seems to have experimented with instincts that are "imperfect," but for the same reason they are also adaptable to a much larger variety of conditions. Mammals—and we are all mammals—are much more dependent on another sort of guidance: previous *learning.*

Recent evidence in sex research, for example, tends to indicate more and more clearly that higher mammals must go through an intense period of learning before they are capable of performing (or being participating partners in) sexual intercourse.

Rhesus monkeys, for example, are quite unable to copulate at an adult age if, in addition to being deprived of proper mothering care, they are also not allowed to romp about during their childhood and engage in the type of rough and tumble play that promotes body contact and early sexual experimentation.

Dr. Harry Harlow, the researcher who staged this classic experiment, reports that adult male monkeys, if raised without the benefit of such learning, insisted on taking up all sorts of awkward positions with the females in which intercourse could not possibly take place. All the untrained females, in their turn, were uncooperative and some kept "defending" themselves fiercely against the male, even when the partner was a normally-raised, exceptionally patient and experienced male.

Male monkeys deprived of early learning opportunities thus remained "impotent" and the females "frigid" (as some would call these conditions in humans) in spite of all later opportunities. There are similar reports about the importance of early sexual learning in rats and cats.

We can see, therefore, that sex does *not* come naturally (if "naturally" is to mean sex *performance* without learning)—not even in animals.

Sexual learning is equally essential in human beings, who are mammals with the most imperfect instincts of all. The human sexual act cannot be performed without a complex process of learning, especially if it is expected that it be enjoyable to both partners.

Anthropologists describe a number of cultures in which children learn sex in the same way as Harlow's monkey babies. They engage in a great deal of body contact and rough and tumble play and at the same time they have the opportunity of observing adults in intercourse. Soon (and at a very early age) the body contact becomes sexual experimentation and not much later the experimentation becomes the act.

Our culture, of course, would not tolerate this. Most of us object to sexual experimentation and especially to sexual intercourse between children. Most of all, we treasure our privacy and would not consider opening our bedrooms for observation.

But this does not absolve us from the responsibility of providing an alternative to primitive sex education for our children. This writer believes that this alternative has to be much better than vague talk and dirty jokes, better than the half truths and distortions passed on in the schoolyard or on the street, better than initiations in houses of prostitution, better than the casual observations of animals, much better still than sanctimonious empty talk in the school class about the marvels of reproduction.

Until such an alternative has been found for a more sensible sex education of children and adolescents, perhaps the least that this society can do is to provide better educational opportunities for young adults looking forward to marriage.

# 8. Seven Myths About Female Orgasm
## Stephen Neiger, M.D., Ph.D.

Until recent years, when a few scientists began to investigate the mysteries of female orgasm, most thinking about it was dominated by myths based on armchair speculation or social prejudices. Unfortunately, such myths are hard to kill. Many of them are still around, causing difficulties of sexual adjustment to countless people. Husbands and wives are further encouraged in these false beliefs by quite a few outdated marriage manuals that still enjoy good sales.

It might be rewarding, therefore, to review some of the most dangerous half-truths and untruths about female orgasm. Along with these still-popular myths, we will also try to present the facts which are now slowly becoming available —but we will be careful to avoid easy answers to questions that are not yet clearly understood.

**Myth number 1:** "Like male orgasm, female orgasm is a universal trait in nature. It is found in all animals. It is found in all primitive societies. It is only our modern Western civilization and the stresses and neuroses produced by contemporary living that have inhibited this capacity in many women."

This is wrong on all counts. In contrast to male orgasm, female orgasm is very far from being "universal" in our biological ancestry, our own recorded history or, for that matter, in a variety of our *present* societies, whether "primitive" or "advanced." To what extent female orgasm is a "natural" trait is difficult to say, since its evolution is still not clearly understood.

The fact is that, in all species of animals that are related to man, only the males seem to achieve a climax with any consistency. *Orgasm among mammalian females appears to be rather an exception.*

While the famous Indian classic *Kama Sutra* presents eloquent testimony that female orgasm was well known in at least parts of India some 3000 years ago, we know that there also were (and are) a number of human societies which have entirely denied even the possibility of a female orgasm. In these societies, a woman capable of orgasm was (or is) considered a deviate, as in the fairly recent Victorian era of our own Western society.

Dr. Margaret Mead, a well-known anthropologist, found similar "Victorian" and "puritanic" attitudes among certain primitive tribes she studied. According to her, the woman's ability to achieve orgasm is a "potential that may or may not be developed by a given culture."

**Myth number 2:** "If the wife cannot achieve orgasm, the husband's technique is to blame."

This is partly true in some cases, probably quite untrue in many. Female orgasm can depend to a large extent on social attitudes and on individual learning.

Although the husband can often do a great deal to help provide the atmosphere for his wife to catch up on some of the learning she has missed, it would hardly be fair to blame him for everything that has or has not taken place before he appeared on the scene.

Still struggling with the remnants of Victorian repression, our society is now slowly changing its values. While on the one hand it insists on equal enjoyment of sex for women, on the other hand it hardly provides the most encouraging climate for the development of free female sexuality. It cannot be expected that the wedding ceremony will be effective in sanctioning, now even demanding, responses from the woman which previously were surrounded with so much secrecy, guilt, and shame for the girl.

**Myth number 3:** "Since the roots of their inability to experience orgasm lie deeply buried in their childhood, nothing can be done for most 'frigid' women short of, perhaps, remaking their whole personalities in a tedious, expensive and uncertain process of psychotherapy that must last many years."

This is quite untrue. A woman may well have missed out on many learning opportunities in the past and may have acquired much "wrong learning" such as guilt, false shame, and fear instead of a positive response to sex. Nevertheless, treatment that spends little time with the analysis of childhood experiences but concentrates instead on learning or relearning *here* and *now*, is quite effective, as the experience of many marriage counselors and sexologists clearly shows.

In quite a few cases "home remedies" will be effective. They include the attainment of sexually positive attitudes through reading and frank discussions between the partners to replace anxiety, guilt and shame, and experimentation in order to discover the most pleasurable physical and psychological stimuli.

Couples who reach the point where consultation with a specialist appears desirable—a step that should not be delayed for too long if home remedies fail—will find that a great deal of added help is available for the woman who cannot attain orgasm. It need not cost thousands of dollars or take years to work.

**Myth number 4:** "The woman who cannot attain orgasm suffers from constant physical pain; she tends to be sterile; and she is bound to have an unhappy marriage."

The first statement is at best a partial truth only. Recent research indicates that a woman who is *continually aroused* without having a regular opportunity of release by orgasm may indeed suffer pain. This results from the engorgement of blood vessels of the pelvic organs. There is no evidence to show, however, that *in the absence of arousal,* lack of orgasm produces any physical discomfort at all.

There is even less connection between female orgasm and sterility. The average woman will conceive quite easily whether or not orgasm takes place, if she and her husband are normally fertile.

There is also no absolute need for the woman without an orgasm to fail in her marriage, although her *statistical* chances for a happy marriage are possibly somewhat reduced. Some studies indeed indicate that, among broken or unhappy marriages, a higher rate of "poor sexual adjustment" is found. However, this finding can hardly be ascribed to lack of female orgasm alone.

Many of the wives (and husbands) in these marriages have all sorts of negative attitudes towards sex as well as towards other important aspects of marriage. These destructive attitudes are far more responsible for the poor sexual adjustment and the resulting breakdown of the marriage—and they certainly need not follow from lack of orgasm. Maturity, love and mutual respect are very likely to overcome the barrier of the wife's lack of orgasm on the road towards marital happiness.

**Myth number 5:** "There are two types of orgasm: 'clitoral' —achieved by stimulation of the clitoris—and 'vaginal'—produced by intercourse. Only vaginal orgasm is true orgasm; clitoral orgasm is immature, neurotic, and necessarily shallow."

This, perhaps the most harmful of all myths, can even prove "scientific" origin. Sigmund Freud, the father of psychoanalysis, originated the theory by observing that little girls, when masturbating, rub their clitoris and surrounding parts of their vulva. He believed masturbation to be an immature practice and argued that grown women must somehow learn to transfer sexual sensations to their vagina before they are capable of enjoying intercourse.

This hypothesis was uncritically accepted and fiercely defended by many of Freud's followers. However, it was just as vehemently contradicted by other authorities who pointed out that the vagina is largely devoid of the nerve endings that conduct sexual sensations while the clitoris and the surrounding area are full of these. The clitoris, therefore, must remain the major center of sexuality for the female through life, argued the second group of experts.

Only now, thanks to the most important work of Masters and Johnson, will it finally be possible to bury this unhappy controversy. Their studies found that, in terms of physical responses, orgasm was the same phenomenon no matter how it was induced.

**Myth number 6:** "Like most men, women prefer to have only one orgasm on most occasions. It is certainly not possible for a woman to have many orgasms during the same act of lovemaking."

Again quite wrong. Even earlier investigators like Terman and Kinsey reported that 13-14 per cent of the women in their samples were quite capable of achieving multiple orgasms, that is, several climaxes on the same occasion. The research done by Masters and Johnson indicates that probably a far greater percentage of women have at least the *capacity* (and frequently the desire) for multiple orgasms.

**Myth number 7:** "To be really satisfying, female orgasm must be 'simultaneous' with male orgasm. This means that her climax is 'really good' only if it always occurs at the same moment, or very nearly at the same moment, as his does."

Simultaneous orgasm is *one* beautiful variety that a couple at a relatively high level of sexual competence can try. But, since it is not equally easy for all couples to achieve, there is certainly nothing wrong in substituting for it some of the other coital or non-coital variations in lovemaking in which the partners will be satisfied "successively," that is one after the other. This is especially true for situations in which the worry about achieving orgasm simultaneously may prove to be a chore which actually interferes with the abandon and pleasure.

Couples who can free themselves from such myths are likely to discover surprisingly pleasant new dimensions in their lovemaking.

# 9. Do Beautiful Women Make Good Lovers?

## Ben N. Ard, Jr., Ph.D.

If a woman is beautiful, does that mean she will be a superior sexual partner.

The relationship between beauty (that is, sexual attractiveness) and sex has been commented upon by poets, philosophers and novelists since time immemorial. Probably every man and every woman has some assumptions about beauty and sex which influence their behavior. What actually is the relationship between sexual *attractiveness* (or beauty) and sexual *performance*?

An old saying claims that "beauty is in the eye of the beholder." Translated into plain language, this means that what one person sees as "beauty" will not necessarily be seen as "beauty" by another. Another related saying is that "love is blind." Perhaps it is good that love is blind, since not all people are beautiful.

Many men have different preferences in what they desire in a sexually attractive woman. We hear men on the street refer to themselves as "leg" men or "breast" men. The basic assumption underlying many a man's looking at a woman from a sexual point of view is that a woman with a "sexy" figure will be more sexually satisfying and therefore a better sexual partner.

But the facts are that superior sexual performance does not necessarily go along with beauty. In fact, many very beautiful women have difficulty in their sexual performance *because* they are beautiful, that is, because of their reactions, and those of men, to their beauty.

One of the most beautiful women I ever had as a patient in group therapy was frigid. She had "slept around" with lots of men but had never had an orgasm. She even denied that women had any such thing as an orgasm. Many men pursued this strikingly attractive woman but were disappointed in sexual relations with her. Her *attitudes* toward sex were what interfered with her sexual performance, despite her beautiful body.

In the same group therapy session another female patient, a hauntingly lovely Negro girl who had won several beauty contests with her beautiful figure, stated that she had never experienced an orgasm either, despite considerable sexual experience. These two beautiful women compared notes and confronted me with questions regarding women having an orgasm.

They both had all the necessary "standard equipment" and in addition were very beautiful. They had lovely hair, beautiful skin and gorgeous figures, and yet they could neither satisfy themselves nor their male partners in sexual relations. Their *assumptions* about themselves, men, and sex interfered with their adequate sexual performance.

A common assumption among many men that beautiful women make better sexual partners can be broken down into specifics. The belief that because a woman has certain measurements she will therefore perform better sexually, is just one of those notions that "ain't necessarily so." And vice versa. A woman who assumes that merely because a man is handsome he will therefore be a more adequate lover will often be sadly disappointed if she acts on this belief.

The fact that a man is tall and handsome really tells one very little about his sexual abilities. In fact, many a handsome man, just because he is handsome, is so pursued by women that he may become very careless, thoughtless, and sloppy in his sexual performance. I have had many such handsome men in my private practice who thought they were great lovers but many women discovered that was not the case.

Most people are *not* beautiful or handsome, and yet they have "standard equipment" as far as sexual capacity is concerned. *They therefore need not worry about their sexual performance merely because they are not "handsome" or "beautiful," as the case may be.* More important than "beauty," as far as sexual performance is concerned, is attitude.

Attitude is what makes the difference. The beautiful woman sometimes assumes that all she has to do is just "be beautiful," whereas a plainer girl may be warm, responsive and loving. The attitude toward sex is thus much more basic than measurements or configurations of bone and flesh.

What can be said that's positive about the relationship between beauty and sex?

Although different men seek different attributes of beauty in women, particularly the women they want for sexual partners, it would seem to be the case that a minimum of some kind of "beauty" is necessary for some men. Otherwise they will not be attracted enough to respond sexually, that is, have an erection. It certainly does help the sexual response of a man if a woman dresses attractively and pays attention to her hair and figure.

Cleanliness is also important to some people, both male and female. A certain minimum of cleanliness is helpful in making one sexually attractive to the other sex.

Since "beauty" means different things to different people, as does sex for that matter, the relationship of beauty and sex varies in each person. Therefore general conclusions are difficult to draw which will have very wide application.

But perhaps we can say that beauty seems more necessary for the man (in order to have the minimum sexual response for sexual performance) and handsomeness is not as pressing a matter for women. Of course attractiveness enters into sexual selection for both men and women. But attitudes toward sex are more basic and a better indicator of possible sexual performance than mere beauty.

Standards of beauty are largely culturally determined. Each culture develops its own special set of values. There are some authorities, however, who maintain that there are some universal standards of beauty that operate all over the world.

Good-sized buttocks and breasts are frequently cited as perhaps universally approved standards of beauty. But we know that different men have different tastes in such matters.

One fact is certain: in most regions of the world, men tend to place too great an emphasis on the more shallow or physical aspects of womanly beauty.

We need to get away from such shallow conceptions of beauty. These lead to self-defeating behavior. They frequently lead up a blind alley because they are based on false assumptions. Beauty obviously plays some part in sexual functioning, but *attitudes* would seem to be more basic than beauty.

# 10. Sex Tryouts Before Marriage

## Robert A. Harper, Ph.D.

Many couples feel that if they have sexual intercourse before marriage, this is a reliable way of testing their sexual compatibility after marriage.

Silly as it sounds, I have told couples who have had premarital counseling sessions with me that they could not be absolutely sure that they would be sexually compatible in marriage just because they both now found sexual intercourse fully enjoyable.

Most couples find it very difficult to accept this, as did the following young man and woman who came to me for counseling.

"I realize," the girl said, "that as a professional counselor you do not want to be in the position of *advocating* premarital sexual intercourse as a means of testing sexual compatibility before marriage. But when we, even before we talked with you, have *already* frequently had sexual intercourse and find ourselves fully compatible, I don't see why you can't admit we have passed the test, so to speak."

"I am only saying what I believe as a result of my experience," I said. "The main reason I cannot assure you that you'll have no sexual difficulties in marriage is that you have not lived together day in and day out over a considerable period of time.

"Sex is not all of marriage. It is an important and central part. But marriage is a pattern of many things, a total relationship between two very different individuals. One part affects another part, and each part is affected by the pattern as a whole."

"Frankly," the young man said, "that sounds pretty vague to me. Are we not much more *likely* to be sexually compatible in marriage when we know darn well we are sexually compatible *before* marriage?"

"If," I answered, "you're talking about the odds, I'll agree that your chances are greater. But I have known a great number of couples who enjoyed sexual satisfaction before marriage, but who saw their sexual enjoyment fade away after a few years of living together as legally wedded spouses."

"Well, we don't want that to happen," the girl said. "What can we do to see if we have the kind of sexual compatibility that will last in marriage?"

"The best answer to that question," I replied, "is to test your general attitudes about the marriage relationship and about each other. We know that you do not have basic sex problems as such. What we need to test for is whether or not there are other trouble spots in your relationship that might lead to an undermining of marital happiness in general, and sexual satisfaction in particular."

This couple and I went on to talk about the kinds of things that make for marital compatibility and about the attitudes each of them had toward each other. As I told them, a happy sex life enhances general marital compatibility, but sex, in turn, is strengthened, maintained, and improved by things going well in other aspects of the relationship.

Marital compatibility is not something which automatically follows upon being in love, and it cannot always be willed into existence by all-out effort. But there are certain things that can be done to increase a couple's ability to get along well together maritally in and out of bed.

First, it is desirable for both the man and woman to talk about and think through the realism and reasonableness of their expectations and standards. Some people are quite unrealistic. They anticipate a kind of heavenly or storybook sort of relationship. Both sexually and nonsexually, married life will not be an uninterrupted delight. There will be problems, difficulties, and differences.

Happiness is a balance between what you expect and what you get. If, in marriage, you expect your mate to do everything you want, to be everything you would like him or her to be, you are bound to be disappointed. If your marital expectations are reasonable, disillusionment with your spouse will be unlikely.

Second, incompatibilities can be worked at and changed. When the habits of one partner grate upon the attitudes of the other, both the habits of the one and the attitudes of the other are subject to modification. In sex relations and other aspects of the marriage, a couple who will talk things over in a friendly and nonblaming way can reach some kind of compatibility.

A wife who is careless about putting away her underthings, for example, may be tactfully induced to retrain herself in such matters. The husband, on his side, could learn not to be so irritated by her lapses. The husband who is too rough and abrupt in his sex approach can learn a more gentle and romantic set of procedures. If the wife is overly sensitive, she can learn to enjoy a greater amount of vigorous sexual activity.

Third, an excellent way to test for general compatibility is for the courting couple to de-emphasize romance. They ought to spend a good deal of time together in situations which take romance out of the spotlight. Lovemaking is the most enjoyable of recreational activities. But if couples spend most of their time making love, they will learn relatively little about each other's personality traits—those all-important details that will loom large in close day-by-day living.

Fun-spoiling as it may sound, couples who are seriously thinking about getting married would often do well to budget their lovemaking time and, instead, spend considerable time and effort getting to know each other in a wide variety of social experience.

Fourth, nonsexual compatibility can best be tested for in action rather than words. Although two romantically attracted individuals can maintain many pretensions in words, it is more difficult for each to fool himself and the other in action. If Linda, for example, is interested in drama and if Edgar professes great pleasure in reading Shakespeare aloud by the fireside, it would be desirable for Linda to get Edgar to start reading, rather than to take his word for it.

Fifth, another old-fashioned but fairly effective aid in testing for potential compatibility in marriage is time. Time works well in exposing character traits and habit patterns that may cause serious trouble—including sexual trouble—in marriage. Even young romance cannot perpetually maintain a blinding razzle-dazzle of best company behavior.

Finally, still another method of gauging compatibility prior to marriage is to get to know each other's family and friends. This is revealing of personality traits in several ways:

● The individual as been molded by his family and friendship associations; something of what the prospective marital partner sees in the family and friends is likely to appear in the future spouse (but may be temporarily hidden by the clouds of romance);

● In the pre-romance friendships of the individual, real interests and personality preferences are open to inspection;

● Families and friends bring out the relaxed habits and manners of persons; those who are consciously or unconsciously putting on company manners usually have their disguises removed in association with family members and friends.

If Bill's family and friends seem to be the steady beer-drinking, TV-watching, horse-betting types, the chances are good that similar interests and activities will continue with Bill. If Esther's family and friends are largely the gossipy, superficial, beauty-parlor talk and dress chitchat sorts, there is no reason to suppose Esther will be much different from them after marriage.

Marriage is the most intimate relationship, and it involves great amounts of time spent in each other's company in a wide assortment of dull, routine, and even unpleasant situations. It is important, therefore, to know well—not just *sexually* well—the person with whom we enter this partnership.

# 11. Intercourse During Menstruation
## Stephen Neiger, M.D., Ph.D.

Peter and Joan are a fairly average American couple and they have a problem—or so they think. As practicing Catholics, they must restrict their family planning to the rhythm ("safe days") method. It has worked pretty well so far. Being in their early twenties and having been married only two years, however, they would like to have intercourse more often.

Peter especially feels deprived. Joan's cycle is not a very regular one and this makes for very few "safe days." (The less regular the woman's cycle, the fewer are the "safe days" in the rhythm method.) To make matters worse, they lose still more of the few nights left to them because Joan's periods tend to last six days, sometimes even seven. "And, of course, I wouldn't want anything to happen to Peter by having intercourse during *those* days," she adds with genuine concern.

The belief that "menstrual blood" is poisonous is deeply rooted in our primitive past, in times when monthly bleeding was an awe-inspiring mystery. Strict rules still prohibit intercourse with a menstruating woman in practically all known primitive cultures today. In fact, in many societies even her touch has to be avoided. She is considered dangerous not only to people, but also to animals and plants.

Like all religions that originated before the advent of modern science, Judaism and Christianity (which had taken over much of the Judaic heritage) could not avoid incorporating such primitive beliefs.

During the Middle Ages, a Catholic woman was not admitted to church while menstruating and her husband was forbidden to have intercourse with her. Intercourse with a menstruating woman is still strictly taboo in the Orthodox Jewish family.

Superstitions do not die easily. The average "modern" man and woman, enlightened as they may be in other matters, still lack the knowledge that would help them distinguish between fact and myth in the matter of menstruation. From my experience as a marriage counselor, I know that there are many couples who would benefit from a survey of the known facts.

What are these facts? What should I say to Peter and Joan? Is intercourse during menstruation dangerous to husband and wife? Or can couples who so desire make love during this time, just as at all other times?

The fact is, millions of American couples do have intercourse during the wife's menstrual period. Chances are, too, that their number is increasing. As early as 1938, Terman reported that about one in ten women in his (middle class) sample said that they had intercourse during menstruation. He estimated that the actual number was probably larger, because the whole question was still surrounded by so much taboo and shame. Many women would have hesitated to admit to this type of "perversion," especially a generation ago.

Medical science knows of no dangers to the average husband and wife who wish to have intercourse during days of the menstrual flow. None of the substances discharged—a small amount of blood, mucus and discarded fragments of tissue from the lining of the womb—are "poisonous" in any way or otherwise harmful. Practically all modern medical and sexological authorities agree, therefore, that intercourse during menstruation is harmless. It is entirely a matter of taste and other personal factors.

What are some of the *possible* disadvantages for *some* couples in having intercourse during menstruation?

Some women report increased sensitivity of the vagina (and sometimes the vulva), especially during the day of the heaviest flow. Many women experience this condition as pleasant and sexually arousing. Other women complain, however, of irritation and even pain, if intercourse is attempted. If a couple finds that the wife belongs in the latter group, it may be wiser indeed to abstain.

Another complaint voiced by some women is that intercourse during menstruation tends to prolong their periods by stirring up the menstrual flow. This is questionable. Kinsey and his co-workers claim that erotic stimulation *slows down* the menstrual flow, although the physical activity associated with intercourse might be expected to increase it. In both situations, the Kinsey group remarks, the flow will tend to *return to normal* after intercourse.

Just as some wives experience irritation of the vagina through coital friction, a few husbands also complain about irritation of the penis. Both these complaints are due partly to changed conditions in the vagina during menstruation. Natural lubrication of the vagina may be decreased and replaced by menstrual substances, which do not make a good lubricant. Sometimes anterior urethritis (a slight inflammation of the portion of the urethra that passes through the head of the penis) will occur in the male.

These difficulties can be avoided, however, through the application of artificial lubricants, such as surgical jelly and, if necessary, by the use of a well-lubricated *condom*. If the couple prefers, the woman may wear a vaginal diaphragm during intercourse on the days of the heaviest flow, instead of, or in addition to, the man wearing a condom. The diaphragm is one of the best means of keeping the vagina free from menstrual discharge during intercourse. Of course, it must be removed just as soon as intimacies are over.

Even a vaginal douche (generally frowned upon by many gynecologists when used habitually) in order to remove the irritating substances, is permissible as an *occasional* measure before intercourse as well as after intercourse to remove lubricants, if they have been used. With a combination of some or all of these measures, most couples should find intercourse during menstruation not only completely harmless but also enjoyable.

Of course, the most common objection that couples voice is not on "medical" but on "esthetic" grounds. "It is such a messy affair," one tends to hear husbands say just as often as wives. Most often it is those who have never tried it.

It is a well-known fact among gynecologists that most women (and even some husbands under their wife's influence) overestimate the total amount of blood shed during a typical menstruation. Just how much do you think is lost? A pint? A cupful?

In most cases no more than an ounce and a half of blood is lost during a menstrual period. This is three tablespoonfuls! While more blood may be shed by some women, it seldom exceeds five ounces. In addition to blood, about one quarter to one half as much discharge will leave the vagina in the form of tissue fragments, etc.

Few couples stop to consider this significant fact: in most women, the largest amount of the total discharge is usually shed within a few hours of a particular day (usually the second), or of two days at the most. This hardly constitutes a compelling reason for a week's abstinence. The remainder of the "flow" (more precisely, often hardly a trickle), absorbed by tampons during the day and, if necessary, held in check by a diaphragm at night, will certainly not make for the large bloodstains most couples see as an inevitable consequence of sexual intimacies during *all* the nights the period lasts.

Of course, the esthetic sensibilities of some people will not allow them to accept even the slightest amount of strongly diluted "blood" on their genitals. They will not permit even a few traces of soft pink on their bedding. Whether or not *you* choose to remain in this group is a matter only you and your spouse can settle, guided by your feelings and by occasional special circumstances.

It is a good idea always to respect enduring sensitivities and esthetic objections of *either* partner in such matters.

Nevertheless most couples do not have an aversion to intercourse during menstruation that is deeply rooted. It is maintained unthinkingly, mainly because of false traditional beliefs (as in the case of Joan), or out of natural feminine modesty that will yield readily to reassurance by an affectionate husband. Such couples, if they have a strong desire, will be pleased to see how easily their inhibitions can be overcome if they also possess a spirit of experimentation.

One particular advantage to having sexual intercourse during the menstrual period, especially for couples who rely on the rhythm method, is that these are among the "safest" days. The most widely appreciated advantage that freedom from menstrual taboos offers lies in the additional opportunities to express marital love sexually. Sexologists and marriage counselors realize increasingly that a gain of additional nights per month can be of importance for some couples.

Joan and Peter left my office relieved and happy. They learned that they need not fear health hazards if they wish to have intercourse during Joan's menstruation. Fortunately, they had the courage to ask, to challenge their fears, their ignorance, their traditional beliefs. However, I cannot help wondering how many Peters and Joans there are who remain victims of superstition, who go on assuming that this prolonged, and often most unwelcome, period of abstinence is absolutely unavoidable, just because no one told them otherwise.

# 12. How to Enjoy Sex During Pregnancy

## Renee and Conrad Adams

How disappointed were you with the chapter on pregnancy in your marriage manual? When it mentioned sexual relations and "adapting your positions for the expectant mother's changing figure," was it so vague that it was very little help at all? Ours was.

We notice that marriage books sometimes go into great detail about how to excite and delight each other right after marriage to build a close, lasting relationship. Does this lose its importance once the natural result of that delight occurs? We don't think so.

We believe any husband and wife of average intelligence with a strong desire to please each other and a healthy attitude toward their physical love, can arrive at very satisfactory compromises that don't even seem like compromises.

We are not experts who have studied the sexual lives of many, but we are a happy couple who have arrived at a very satisfactory marriage relationship, and for this reason we feel qualified to speak out.

In chapters on prenatal care, the authors seem to concentrate on the coming infant, forgetting that the lovers who conceived this infant still desire to be lovers without fear of harming mother *or* child. We are going to fill in where most reticent writers leave off. We do not believe that sexual pleasure is a nice "side effect" of the "main purpose" of procreation. We believe that it has a definite purpose of its own, to help cement the marriage and build lasting happiness and enthusiasm for family life.

To all couples we suggest that you check with your own doctor, after studying the positions described, as to their advisability for your case. When we spoke with ours, he said all the positions were perfectly safe for most normal pregnancies. A good measuring device for each position might be: if it is not uncomfortable, it is not harmful. The healthy majority are free from difficulties and need few restrictions on normal activities.

One doesn't need to be a doctor or a specialist in the study of human sexual relations to experiment and devise comfortable ways to enjoy physical love in marriage during advanced pregnancy, when the wife's abdomen is enlarged, and before the doctor has forbidden complete intercourse. The few new positions some couples have heard of for this time may be either uncomfortable or embarrassing for the wife, such as the knee-chest position, although many highly enjoy it.

When the wife declines for these reasons, being also too embarrassed to explain, the husband may think she no longer desires him, and is more interested in their child now. On the contrary, she may desire her husband very much and almost resent the child's interference, but she is too shy to suggest other ways to her husband even if she has thought of some.

Shyness should be locked outside the bedroom door. Both should feel free to communicate ideas about their desires for lovemaking and new or more comfortable ways, just as they are thoughtful of each other's preferences in other areas of life. It may take some effort to get over any inhibitions and talk freely of such an intimate subject, but the closer relationship you develop will be well worth it.

As you learn to discuss your ideas, you will find more ideas occurring to you. The following paragraphs are to be used as a guideline, and not considered the only ways there are. Your imaginations will take you on from there.

Whole books have been written about varying the ways couples can enjoy married love. We recommend one book in particular, which was advertised in a good family magazine. Written by Jerome and Julia Rainer, and published by Simon and Schuster, it is entitled *Sexual Adventure in Marriage*. It is an excellent manual for the truly married, truly in love, even those who feel completely satisfied that they have enough variety and joy in their physical love.

Before describing positions for intercourse, let us remind the husband that his wife may need longer, gentler foreplay than prior to pregnancy. He should patiently and lovingly provide all that is necessary to make her ready and eager for him.

For the wife who does enjoy the knee-chest position, with her husband accomplishing coitus from behind her, we suggest she have her knees together, and he place his on the outside of hers. This provides great pleasure for both without the danger of too deep intercourse. In another very satisfactory position for this time, the husband lies on his back. The wife kneels astride his hips. Intromission can be as deep or as shallow as comfort dictates.

If the wife sits farther back on her husband's thighs, this prevents deep penetration, while at the same time stimulating her outer area very effectively as she moves. This also gives her husband a pleasant view of her body, with the rounder, fuller breasts of pregnancy. Nor will any normal couple object to the sight of the swelling abdomen. On the contrary, they will probably feel increased happiness, thinking of the new life they have created through their deep love for each other.

Similar to the accepted "standard" is this one: the wife lies on her back, but the husband kneels between her thighs rather than lying over her. He can either hold onto her knees or leave his hands free to caress her as they prefer.

One posture that requires very little effort from the contented, sleepy wife is possible with her lying on her side with her upper leg bent and resting on the bed. Her husband kneels astride her straight leg and can easily find release as soon as he likes. Any considerate wife will cooperate with her husband's desires even when she's very tired, if it can be accomplished with ease and comfort. If the wife is too often very tired, a midday nap is suggested so that she can be more active to increase her husband's pleasure and her own.

In a favorite of ours, the husband lies on his left side (or right, depending on preference, but we will use left to keep description clear), with his knees bent. His wife lies on her back, legs together and places them over his right thigh as if sitting sideways on his lap. The husband's torso is at an angle to his wife. Although it is difficult for their faces to meet and kiss, in a softly lit room they can gaze lovingly at each other, or caress each other's faces and lips.

For stronger, closer movements, the above position can be changed slightly so that the wife's left leg is between her husband's thighs, her knee bent. In this way she can help with their motions, and they can both use manual love play simultaneously with intercourse. The responsive wife can easily be brought to orgasm this way.

Some "experts" believe that simultaneous orgasm is essential to perfect union. We disagree. When the husband helps his wife to climax first, her lingering desire for closeness is satisfied while he attains orgasm. Then she is ready to separate and fall asleep soon afterwards, as he is. Even after her orgasm, a conscientious wife can voluntarily keep moving to help bring her husband to completion. Such is not the case with some husbands, who are very tired immediately and wish to sleep. For those who like to fall asleep still united, the last position described is ideal.

In the last month of pregnancy, almost all doctors forbid intercourse for the patient, but few even hint at any way for her to keep her husband sexually happy for the next eight to ten weeks (until their baby is a month or six weeks old), unless the patient brings it up herself. However, shyness prevents many women from asking intimate questions. So many frayed nerves could be prevented, and contentment could still reign, if they would learn a few temporary substitutes.

There are several ways a thoughtful, loving, uninhibited wife can stimulate her husband to orgasm when intercourse —before and after birth—cannot be allowed.

We will assume here that both husband and wife keep their bodies very clean, either by daily bathing or carefully washing the genital parts each night before retiring. Now, any form of love play, either manual or oral, is very pleasant and not at all distasteful for the truly in love. As the wife lovingly excites her husband she may find herself becoming aroused, too. With very clean hands, her husband can also manually stimulate her external parts only, as much as she wishes, even on to climax.

[Editor's Note: When the physician prohibits intercourse for fear of bringing about miscarriage or labor, this prohibition should apply equally to any method of reaching orgasm such as by manual stimulation or masturbation. As Masters and Johnson's research showed, masturbation usually causes more intense contractions of the womb in orgasm than does intercourse itself.]

Some wives' desire continues until the end of pregnancy, and resumes soon afterwards. But for the wife whose sexual desire *does* diminish, it is still possible to show her love for her husband by happily cooperating with his desires until intercourse can once again be resumed. From him she will reap great appreciation and love as her reward. This is as important to some wives as the act of love itself, and may be very helpful in avoiding marital stress.

## EDITOR'S NOTE

The approach taken in this article accords with the new approach being taken by the medical profession toward sexual relations during pregnancy.

Professionals interested in reading more about this are referred to SIECUS Study Guide No. 6, "Sexual Relations During Pregnancy and the Post-Delivery Period," written by Dr. S. Leon Israel, Editor of *Obstetrics and Gynecology* and Dr. Isadore Rubin, Editor of this book.

The Guide is obtainable from the Sex Information and Education Council of the U.S. (SIECUS), 1855 Broadway, New York, N.Y. 10023, for the price of 50 cents.

# 13. The Virility Diet
## Leonard H. Gross

The Hollywood versions of Roman orgies always depict huge banquets, the men glutting themselves with whole roasts and chalices of wine. Salome-style dancing girls circle about, resting on a lap here, bestowing a kiss there, tweaking a beard and sharing a vessel of wine elsewhere. The men's eyeballs bulge and the blood vessels of their corpulent faces pop with supposed sexual eagerness.

Those who have feasted at an ordinary Thanksgiving or Christmas dinner know the lie in these depictions. After overeating, men usually burp and doze at the table. On these occasions, even their dreams are probably too leaden for sex.

According to Masters and Johnson in *Human Sexual Response*, overindulgence in food and drink is the great enemy of male sex functioning, particularly for men past forty.

Food can have this negative effect. But can it not also aid a man's potency?

Many men have asked this question and not long ago a book called *The Virility Diet* was published, receiving considerable attention. The author, Dr. George Belham, devotes the latter part of the book to problems of diet, which he claims has an important role to play in maintaining sexual activity.

To break the suspense in the beginning, let it be stated clearly that there is no such thing as a "virility" diet. That is, there are no specific foods which in themselves will create extraordinary potency. Which does *not* mean that one's diet is irrelevant.

What does contribute to virility is one's general good health, freedom from worry, and freedom from fatigue. So, in a broad sense, diet can contribute to virility by contributing to the overall health of the individual.

This relationship between general health and sexual potency has been noted by Masters and Johnson. Discussing the increase in potency in some older men given male hormone treatments, they suggested that this may be due to an improvement in general health rather than to any direct action of the hormones. The Kinsey group as well cites nutrition and general health as factors in deciding how frequently a man will engage in sex activity.

As mentioned, overeating and excessive drinking of alcohol are probably the greatest hindrances to an active sex life, especially for older men. This overindulgence tends to repress sexual tensions, as well as make the man less able to feel and act in other respects.

As a result of overeating, some men lose sexual feelings altogether. If the eating patterns are grossly excessive and kept up for a long period, the loss of sex desire and ability may be permanent.

Excessive drinking is an even more important factor. In men in the late forties and fifties, say Masters and Johnson, impotence is connected more directly with large consumption of alcohol than with any other single factor.

With age, there may be a tendency to obesity that may slow down sex drive. This is controllable. Men require less food once they are in their mid-twenties, since the body burns it less readily once past youth and also because such men exercise less. Yet men go on consuming the same immense quantities as formerly. So there is frequently a slow but constant gain of weight. The cumulative effect over the years is a fat man who is lethargic and lacking eagerness—which militates against a satisfactory sex life. Any physical exertion, including sexual, just doesn't interest them.

In order to stay in their prime, sexually and otherwise, men should curtail their appetites. However, there are definitely cases of metabolic disorder where food is not digested and utilized properly. These should be treated by a physician.

Other men, though, should learn which are the high calorie foods and avoid them. The average man who holds a desk job and doesn't get around a lot requires only about 2,500 calories daily. But most men eat closer to 3,500.

What about all the legendary super-foods? Goat's testicles and goat's milk for example? Or the special vitamins whispered of like a secret treasure? Or a meatless diet? Or the countless other magical substances one has heard of? Alan Hull Walton in his book, *Aphrodisiacs*, reviews many hundreds of ingested substances that have been used through the ages.

There is no special sexual value in these foods except to the extent that they provide good nutrition. Goat's milk is high in protein and quite nutritious, for example, as are many of the countless other recipes. A meatless diet can suffice if enough proteins and vitamins are gotten from other sources such as nuts and whole grain.

The many herbs and spices that have been touted as aphrodisiacs are somewhat different. They can work in a small way by irritating or slightly sensitizing the urethral tract. The internal tickling effect can help create erection, although some of these substances irritate the urinary tract to a very dangerous degree.

Oysters, clams, and other seafoods are legendary aphrodisiacs. And countless people are convinced they are. They feel this way because they have been told it's so, so there may be some psychological effect from eating seafood. Furthermore, they may feel active and spry after a raw seafood snack. This is because it is a source of energy and protein, yet it is not bulky. Many other foods fit this bill ideally, without being actual aphrodisiacs or virility foods.

All the vitamins are essential to general well-being and a notable lack of any of them hurts one's health in one way or another. When the body is suffering somehow, potency is apt to be affected because it is one of the most sensitive and easily disturbed bodily functions. This can be explained both on the basis of the interdependence of many of the body's functions, and because of the depressing emotional effect of any ailment.

There are certain pitfalls in modern day food supply which may render people poorly nourished even though they eat amply. Consumers Union reports that the processing and freezing of foods for the housewife's convenience often has the sad effect of destroying vitamins, and many preservatives may be harmful to the body over a long period.

Vitamin E deserves special mention, if only because it is the vitamin most frequently referred to as an aphrodisiac. It is a sex-related vitamin, since its absence can bring about abortion in the female and a degree of degeneration of the testicles. It is commonly acquired by eating raw egg yolks, green, leafy vegetables such as lettuce or spinach, beans as well as other foods.

An extreme deficiency of vitamin E can cause sterility in the man. Some doctors believe it may affect potency too, though this has not been established. But an abundance of the vitamin will not do anything more than the minimum requirement of the vitamin necessary for healthy bodily functioning. That seems to be the key with all other vitamins as well. A certain minimum amount is necessary. Excess will produce no wonders and may even be harmful.

Meals should be balanced to contain the gamut of vitamins. Caloric intake should be sensible. An overstuffed man is not ardent, nor is a starving one. Healthy living and as much freedom from worry as is possible enables a man to enjoy an optimal sex life. Despite technological advances, however, this prescription has not yet been merchandised.

# 14. Romance in the
# Later Years
## Isadore Rubin, Ph.D.

Sexuality is not the private preserve of the young. Some years ago, Dr. George Lawton suggested a "bill of rights for old age." A major plank in the program was "The Right To Be Romantic." In defense of this point, he argued that "faded and rheumatic oldsters get 'that way' about someone of the opposite sex because they want to participate in the great experiences of life. What youth believes to be its unique possession and privilege really belongs to the life force, whether that is twenty years old or seventy."

He added: "We don't ask the young to adopt the lovemaking style of oldsters or to believe that they can be romantic. What we demand is the right to be romantic, so long as we violate no law or city ordinance."

The right to be romantic and the right to the full expression of one's sexuality cannot be won by legislation. Since it exists in the minds of men and in the general climate of opinion, it can be won only by a long process of reeducation.

Dr. Mary Calderone, in her book *Release From Sexual Tensions*, tells of a meeting of women whom she had been invited to address on the subject of the menopause. Expecting to find an audience of older women, she was quite surprised to find almost all of them under thirty-five. When she asked why they had invited her to talk about the menopause, their reply was: "We thought you could help us prepare for it."

When the inevitable question came up as to whether or not a woman's sex life stops with the menopause, Dr. Calderone told the audience the story of a woman friend who had assured her that her sexual relationship with her husband, which had always been good, became increasingly better until they were both well into their seventies.

She also told about another woman who had failed to achieve sexual satisfaction with two husbands, the second of whom died when she was fifty-five. Fifteen years later, at the age of seventy, she fell in love with and married a man of her own age. With him, she reported, she experienced full satisfaction for the first time in her life.

When the doctor told each of these stories to the audience, their response was a burst of titters. These incidents led her to ask the women: "What is so funny about successful sex, or any sex for that matter, in a woman of seventy?" Of course, she received no satisfactory answer.

"No, sexual fulfillment is not the private preserve of the young," comments Dr. Calderone. "Indeed it should not be. What an opportunity we miss if we cut off, by our attitudes and beliefs, all possibility of continued fulfillment beyond the age of fifty. Our children grow up and venture forth into the world. What remains? Marriage, husband and wife, the greatest of all relationships, the relationship between a man and woman who are more important to each other than anyone else in the world, even the children they have borne and reared."

This desire for intimacy and friendship is made very apparent in any community of older people. "In St. Petersburg, Florida," for example, writes Pierre Boucheron in *How To Enjoy Life After Sixty*, "it is often said that there is more romance on the several thousand green benches of that paradise of the retired than any other spot in the United States. Here, a woman seated on a bench for a half hour or so is bound to be spoken to by a man she has never seen before and probably invited to lunch."

Those who have worked with "senior citizens" clubs report the large numbers of romances, affairs and marriages which occur in these groups. One woman of sixty confided to a club supervisor that, although she had been married for over thirty-five years to a man she still respected and loved, she would like to have a "romantic" affair with another man because her husband had never been romantic and now had lost interest in her physically. After several dates with men, she became convinced that the kind of love she was seeking would eventually destroy her home, but she still sought to attract men to her.

Some older couples who are in love with each other hesitate to marry because they are fearful that the money they possess would in some way be threatened or that their children would object because of the possible loss of an inheritance.

In some instances, the couple will decide to live openly with each other without being legally tied, although this action might be completely opposed to the ethical code they have lived by throughout their lives and one which they could condemn vigorously in their children. When such an arrangement occurs, it is generally accepted by others in the club without condemnation.

As Dr. Calderone told her audience, the importance of sexuality in life is not limited to the bearing of children nor to the release of a strong physical urge. The sexual relationship is more and more being recognized as a rich and vital aspect of human relatedness. It is "another language" by which couples share deep intimacies. It is an act that expresses the fullest emotional and physical relationships of the couple involved. As one doctor put it, nothing contributes more to the spiritual ties of a marriage than "the physical ecstasy attendant in a properly adjusted, equally shared and frequently enjoyed relationship."

This recognition of the importance of sex has only just begun in the case of younger couples. It has certainly not yet been adequately applied to older people. Preoccupation with the security needs of the aged has led most people to overlook their sexual problems altogether.

The mentally healthy older person, Dr. Alvin I. Goldfarb told an audience at the San Francisco Medical Center of the University of California, has needs that are not greatly different from the needs of younger persons. He desires friendships of varying types, and intimacy with both sexes.

Dr. Anna K. Daniels tells the story of a widow of fifty-eight who fell in love with a stockbroker of sixty-one and decided to get married. Her children however raised a terrific commotion. Their mother, they said, was making a fool of herself and of them. Imagine falling in love and getting married at her age!

After much hesitation, the widow finally decided to marry against the wishes of her children. Fourteen years later they were just as happy as at the time of their marriage, reported Dr. Daniels. In addition, the children found that their mother's happiness brought an added dimension to their own lives.

Remarriage undoubtedly has many psychological benefits to confer upon older people who are compatible with each other. Although it does bring with it many problems, it offers an important means of countering the loneliness, isolation, and lack of affection and intimacy that is the lot of so many of our aging population. Even for those who no longer are capable sexually, marriage has much to offer. Certainly, the popular prejudice against marriage in the later years should not be allowed to deprive individuals of their last chance for happiness.

Undoubtedly, love and sex in later years are far different from what they are in the earlier years of marriage, with the emphasis upon mutual affection, dependency, and companionship rather than upon sexual passion. But they are still for many persons major human experiences.

# II.

# UNDERSTANDING
# THE OTHER SEX

# 15. How Important Is Sex in Marriage?

## Robert A. Harper, Ph.D.

"You were right, Doctor," the young man said. "You told me two years ago that I was acting out of inexperience and immaturity when I said I knew that Judy and I could be happy without sex in marriage. Now I'm in love with another woman, and Judy is threatening suicide."

To have been right in such a situation as this brings little satisfaction to counselors or psychotherapists. We need to focus on how to help people with their problems, on where we go from here, and not on being right or wrong in predictions.

Judy was a very bright and pretty girl who had developed an extreme fear of sex as a result of an exceptionally prudish upbringing plus a quite shocking experience of attempted childhood rape. When she and Frank had seen me in premarital counseling, I had tried to convince both of them of the need for her to undergo intensive treatment.

Judy, who realized to some degree how tied up emotionally she was, could probably have been persuaded to get the help she needed prior to marriage. But Frank said that it was nonsense and that sex was overemphasized in marriage in any case.

Frank didn't really think that he and Judy could get along without sex in marriage. What I suspected he thought at the time (and what he was confirming in my office two years later) was that he, Frank, was charming enough and brilliant enough and sexy enough to get Judy successfully through her sexual problems into a happy sexual paradise with him.

This is the basic kind of conceit I find in many men and women: the delightful and wholesome and thrilling experience of being married to them will surely cure their prospective wives and husbands of whatever ails them, be it alcoholism, frigidity, impotence, compulsive gambling, laziness, or whatever. The reality of marriage is considerably less curative than such people expect. Marry to reform and expect to mourn.

So Frank did not really believe sex was unimportant in marriage, though before marriage he was saying something to that effect. He simply thought he could cure Judy of her sexual troubles.

Is sex, then, like money in the old saying, important only if you don't have any? Its absence, or its presence in poor quality and quantity, can certainly have a very negative (and often fatal) effect on marriage. But its highly satisfactory function can also create an atmosphere of happiness and good will which has a beneficial effect on the marriage as a whole. All of the thousands of cases I know of, both happy and unhappy marriages, point to the following answer to the question of how important is sex in marriage: of *central importance*.

When I have said something similar to the foregoing to many individuals, couples, and groups, I find that I have often been misheard. To say that sex is of central importance is not the same as saying that nothing else is important. Many other things are important in marriage.

It likewise is not the same as saying that if sex is satisfactory the marriage will automatically be successful. Marriages with satisfactory sexual relationships can fail. To say that sex is of central importance means that sex is the major focus, the hub, the heart, the keystone of the marital relationship. In marriage, as with the human body, it would be silly to say that nothing else is important or that a good heart automatically means a well functioning body.

It has interested me for some time how many people, including writers, argue against the importance of sex in marriage. I have collected and classified some examples of the incorrect reasoning on the subject and some of the motives which seem to underlie the downgrading of sex. Some of these follow.

*Sex in marriage has been exaggerated in importance.* Although this is the most frequent statement from the downgraders of sex, they are always quite vague about who is doing the exaggerating and in what way and degree. In and of itself, obviously, the statement has no content.

Closely related and often uttered in the same breath is the next contention that *sex isn't everything*. I have never found anyone anywhere who ever contended that it was.

*Other things are more important in marriage*. This is made as an assertion, but no evidence is offered. Sex, both from the standpoint of basic enjoyment and reproduction, is clearly the focus of the marital relationship and tends to distinguish it from many other types of relationship. The burden of proving something else *more* important in marriage would seem, therefore, to rest with the sex downgraders.

Sex as the centrally important aspect of marriage can adversley or beneficially affect other factors in the marriage, as we have already noted. The reverse is also true. Other difficulties can gradually have their desirable or undesirable effect on the sexual situation. But that in no way offsets the importance of sex as the major focal point of the marriage.

*Sex is discussed too much*. This is another one of those undefined assertions. Whose discussion is being referred to, and how much is too much? I have found with some people, *any* discussion automatically becomes too much. A person who makes this statement is simply revealing his own distaste for the topic (for whatever reasons) and says nothing whatever beyond that. It is comparable to saying that "I am sick of talking about preventing war." That may well be, but that does not mean it is not an important subject for discussion.

*Sex will take care of itself*. The greatest refutation of this point is the literally millions of marriages where it has taken care of itself very badly.

*Talking about it makes it a problem*. This is essentially the previous point in reverse. It is based on a kind of reasoning that says you don't have a boil on your face until you look at it in the mirror.

This by no means exhausts the sex-downgrading fallacies, but it gives the reader a fair sample. If we grant, then, that sex is centrally important in marriage, what can a husband and wife do to improve their sexual relations? Strangely enough, the very things the sex downgraders belittle: read and discuss.

There is an increasing supply of good books on sex which tackle every conceivable kind of sex problem encountered in marriage and describe practical solutions or alleviations for these problems from many different angles. With such written material as a guide, many husbands and wives can and do increase their sexual enjoyment by talking over and practicing changes in their relationships.

If a couple's own efforts with reading and discussion do not bring sufficiently favorable results, there are physicians, psychotherapists, ministers, marriage counselors, and other professional people prepared to help. Even if your marital sex life does not become ideal, it can be improved and made more enjoyable. Yes, sex is quite important in marriage, and denying it or hiding from it does not even slightly reduce this central importance.

# 16. How Women Really Feel About Orgasm

## Walter R. Stokes, LL.B., M.D.

In our folklore of sex, the attainment of sexual climax or orgasm by the female is surrounded by a swamp of treacherous myths and misunderstandings. All too often both husband and wife are likely to bog down in their efforts to achieve good marital sex adjustment.

The purpose in writing this is to point out the most serious of these myths and to offer the true facts as developed by recent professional investigation and by the testimony of honest, courageous women.

Foremost among all the myths about female sex orgasm is the traditionally accepted notion that most women really have little or no interest in genital sex and no capability of reaching climax in intercourse.

This view has no biological foundation. The fact is that all women, with the rarest of exceptions, are born with a powerful basic capacity to enjoy genital sex and to reach orgasm in intercourse if they are not blocked from doing so in the course of their emotional growth and development.

The widespread occurrence of inadequate female sex response in our society is largely a product of morbid sex puritanism in our traditions of child-rearing. The force of this puritanism is so great it has given rise to the myth that a large number of our women are sexually "frigid."

These women are not in fact truly frigid (that is lacking in basic sexual capacity). They simply have a powerful block against trusting their sexual feelings in the positive, enjoyable way experienced by uninhibited and responsive women.

Thus it is usually inaccurate to speak of a chronically unresponsive woman as "frigid." It would be better to say she is "sexually inhibited."

Another popular myth has it that the sexuality of women is somehow so different from that of men and so mysterious that it defies rational understanding by men.

According to this view, when a woman attains orgasm in intercourse, it is regarded as a romantic miracle rather than as the natural result of understandable forces.

This myth, born of ignorance and puritanical hush-hush, is rapidly being destroyed as modern scientific studies of sex are ever more clearly bringing out the facts and as women are better able to acknowledge honestly to themselves and others what they really feel and why.

As a result of their new sense of freedom about sex, women are now speaking up to scotch a number of sex myths mostly invented by men. One of these is the idea that the size of a man's penis determines the quality of a woman's sex satisfaction. Women are making it plain that this is not so, that what counts is the man's affection, ardor and dependable sex performance.

Many women are speaking out to debunk the notion that female response depends on highly sophisticated sex techniques employed by the man. They are saying that—given an affectionate, mutually warm relationship—they are likely to respond eagerly to very simple, direct sex stimulation, often with limited need for erotic preparation and no need for preliminary stimulation of the clitoris.

Emancipated women are able to acknowledge freely that they sometimes need several orgasms for full satisfaction. On other occasions they may deeply enjoy intercourse without being sufficiently aroused to reach climax. They protest that setting up precise and unchanging standards of sex response is unreasonable and unworkable.

I recall a case in which one of my patients, a warmly responsive woman, came in soon after her marriage, exasperated with her husband. When on some occasion she did not reach orgasm during intercourse, he would act hurt and give her an unpleasant "third degree" inquisition to find out what he had done wrong.

She could not get it over to him that he had done nothing wrong and that she was feeling affectionate and satisfied until he raised a rumpus. She observed to me, "There are just some times when I don't arouse strongly enough to reach climax but I am happy and content. I wish I could make my husband appreciate this."

The husband came in and, after a frank discussion, he accepted his wife's view and there was no further difficulty between them.

While mutual and simultaneous orgasm by husband and wife is particularly enjoyable and quite attainable for some, it should not be cause for disturbance if this does not always take place. Of greater importance is the adequate release of sex tension for both, whether singly or together.

A belief has grown up in recent sex literature that "orgasm is orgasm, however won." Many women deny this, stating that the quality and intensity of orgasm varies a great deal under differing circumstances. They state that orgasm resulting from insertion of the penis into the vagina is usually much more deeply satisfying than that reached solely through stimulation of the clitoris or through other forms of stimulation.

Also it is quite clear that for many women, clitoral stimulation is not at all a *must*, as suggested in some current sex literature. Clitoral stimulation *may* be desired, but for some is just an unnecessary nuisance when they are in a strongly aroused state.

In current sex literature it is frequently stated that sex problems between husband and wife are simply the result of difficulties about other things. Some women—although they admit some truth in this view—nevertheless state that sex maladjustment may be quite primary in itself and should be given the importance it deserves.

They are saying that sometimes refusal to do so is just a way of evading painful facts. This may be illustrated by failure to face honestly the sexual frustration and defeat imposed upon a woman by a husband with a chronic problem of quick ejaculation or very infrequent desire. I recall vividly the many cases in which sexually inadequate husbands have sought to evade responsibility for the effect of their behavior upon the wife's response.

It may be foreseen that, as women emerge more and more from the restrictions of puritanical sex inhibition, they will become increasingly able to express their sex feelings and needs and will do so both with pride and with a high sense of social responsibility. Very naturally they will tend to demand

of men an improved standard of affectionate, considerate, potent male sex behavior.

Some men may fear this. Personally I do not, for it seems
apparent to me that the new attitudes of women will lead to
improvement in man-woman understanding, to deeper satisfactions in marriage and to improved stability in family life.
Men with a mature outlook will profit from this new freedom
of women every bit as much as will women themselves.

# 17. What Men Should Know About Women

## H. K. Branson, M.A., and Ralph Branson, M.A.

What is the key to understanding a woman? What does she
need more than anything else to achieve complete sexual satisfaction?

On the surface, the answer seems simple: to be wanted and
loved. But a man also has this need. What then makes
women so difficult to understand?

For one thing, the wide difference in their sexual needs: a
man can find sexual release more easily than a woman,
whether he feels love for his partner at the moment of intimacy or not. Not so with a woman: she needs constant reassurance that the sexual interest of her husband is not just "a
passing thing of the moment," but is based on his special
affection for her.

So a man who really understands women will make sure to
show his feelings from time to time, even when he doesn't
have sex immediately in mind.

How ought a man show his feelings toward his wife? Let's
take a look at a case history in our files. We shall call the
couple Harriet and Mason.

His family seldom expressed much affection toward each
other. Except at certain times such as funerals, long separa-
tions, or in the marriage bed, they kept their feelings hidden.
Mason had seen his parents kiss only twice that he could remember: once, before his mother underwent surgery; again

when his father returned from overseas duty with the armed forces.

Harriet, on the other hand, came from a family where emotions were easily expressed from tears of joy to tears of anger. She assumed all married couples kissed each other tenderly before other family members.

Still, during courtship and engagement, Harriet admired Mason for his "coolness." No matter what they discussed, including sex and children, he never seemed tempted to carry his displays of affection "too far."

Then, during their honeymoon, Harriet began to notice disturbing little things: contrary to many other young couples on the beach, he avoided sitting close to her, or even holding hands in the presence of others. In private, he was affectionate, a good lover, a considerate husband. Yet Harriet could not escape a feeling of uneasiness. Mason obviously didn't want others to notice their strong feelings for each other.

When she started to mention the subject, Mason would tell her not to be silly, or he would change the subject. And soon Harriet noticed Mason becoming less and less attentive. When they finally wound up at a marriage counselor seeking help, her complaint was: "He never kisses me unless he wants sex. I can't understand why, but I like to play hard to get sometimes. Instead of his keeping after me, he just gives up and withdraws."

Mason told the counselor: "I have strong feelings, but I just can't express them."

Harriet, to feel adequate as a wife, desperately needed the reassurance of having others know her husband was fond of her. The counselor, in talking with Mason, suggested he start by going to a drive-in movie. There, in the privacy of their own car, Mason could bring himself to show affection.

He began by holding hands; then he forced himself to kiss her in front of their children. In time he was able to show affection not only for Harriet but his children as well. And as Harriet gained confidence from her husband's growing ability to express his feelings, she had less and less need for others to notice his attentions to her.

What this case demonstrates—and what most men fail to understand—is that a woman never loses her need for affectionate attention.

Does this mean the honeymoon should last the rest of a couple's life? Certainly not. On the other hand, after marriage the husband should not take his wife for granted. Yet this is exactly what often happens. He becomes preoccupied with getting ahead and making money for his family. And his wife usually fails to understand his preoccupations, taking his lack of interest as a personal rejection.

Usually, this is not true. Neveness, while she can hardly expect her spouse to keep up the high-pitched ardor of the moneymoon period, she does have a right to expect the feeling of being wanted and loved if she is to have a satisfactory sexual relationship.

Many husbands make the mistake of taking their wife's temporary lack of response as flagging interest or frigidity. This is not necessarily true. It may come from fatigue, preoccupation with the children and various other problems, or even from various hormone changes during the course of the month.

So the husband who notices that his wife seems less reponsive at some times than others should not interpret this as lack of interest in sex; nor as lack of ability on his part to satisfy his wife. What counts is not whether they have a perfect climax with each intercourse; the most important thing in a marriage is a satisfactory relationship in all areas—not only sex—over an extended period of time.

Another thing the husband should remember is that when his wife first enters marriage, she may find it difficult to change her role. During dating, courtship, and engagement, society has demanded she be continually on guard against the advances of the male. She has developed a strong habit of restraint.

Now that she is married, she may find these restraints hard to drop. She may wish to; she may know that she should; but often it takes months or even a year or more before she develops the ability to change a lifetime of saying "No" to "Yes."

Her mother's attitudes toward marriage and sex also may strongly influence her.

This much is certain: it takes time for women to reach the peak of sexual expression they are capable of. Another certainty is that intimacy between husband and wife does not end at some predictable year. It continues—and grows and changes—as long as the marriage lasts.

# 18. How Important Is the Wife's Orgasm?

## Walter R. Stokes, LL.B., M.D.

Just how important is the attainment of orgasm by the wife? The answer to this question is not simple. There is a strong difference of opinion even among expert marriage counselors.

Some of them tend to belittle the importance of sex enjoyment or to feel that it will automatically work out all right if the whole relationship between husband and wife is improved.

A few even go so far as to question whether orgasm in the wife is really of much importance to the success of a marriage.

Others see a high rate of passionate sex activity and orgasm as utterly essential to a good marriage, and view it as the touchstone to satisfactory married life.

Before discussing this question, it is necessary to get a few things straight. Living in a culture such as ours, we are enormously handicapped in our efforts to understand and to develop the best potential of either sex. We simply do not have much of a store of reliable information or experience about the expression of female sexuality at its guiltless, happy best.

In a great measure this is attributable to the unfortunate cultural heritage of sex in our society. Traditionally, there has been a basic assumption that enjoyment of sex is sinful, nothing more than bait in the Devil's cruel trap.

The effect of our traditional ideas upon the development of the female's capacity for orgasm in intercourse is painfully obvious. It is strikingly summarized in a story told me early in my practice by a cultured, elderly woman who had been reared in the strictest Victorian tradition, as a member of one of the First Families of Virginia.

She commented that up to the time of her marriage, her mother had never directly mentioned sex in any way. But as her wedding approached, the mother took her aside and grimly instructed: "You are about to be married and must be thinking of having children. To do this, a woman must submit to revolting physical contact with her husband. She must summon all her courage and endure this, as she does child-birth.

"It is said that there are women who enjoy sexual contact with a man but this has never been known in the history of our family. I am sure you will not enjoy the sex act but if you should, never let your husband know, for no decent man can respect a woman who does."

Many persons may justfiably point to the recent progress made by all three of our major religious faiths in moving away from the old sex puritanism. Insofar as this is really true I rejoice over the change. But I raise a serious question about the change that is taking place.

First, is the current image of the All-American girl actually much of an improvement over her grandmother? When I observe her superficial, empty glamor values, her cultivated self-love, her seductive use of phony sex appeal to win prestige and material awards, and her poor record in marriage, I wonder whether she is any closer to appreciating and expressing sex in a sound, functional way than was her grandmother.

My suspicion, backed by much observation in my medical practice, is that, just as in the old days, the family and society are still pretty much taken in by the ancient myths and are still hardly capable of giving children rational, humanly understanding support in the realm of sex development.

I would not wish to imply that there has been no progress in this century. But I suggest that much of the so-called progress is in the empty, unloving direction of glamor sex, thrill sex and pornography rather than coming more in tune with affectionate human relatedness or operating as the magnificent creative and social force which I deeply believe it should be.

Here I shall return to the question, "Just how important is enjoyment of orgasm in the personal and marital life of a woman?"

Judging from the testimony of the relatively few women of excellent orgasm capacity with whom I have explored this critically and carefully, I surmise that it is of overwhelming importance. Only through orgasm can woman know the fullness of life and the peculiar joys and satisfactions that are experienced in affectionately sharing her erotic emotions with a man of like capacity.

Mind you, I am not denying that a woman may find a good deal of pleasure and meaning in life without orgasm.

But I am led to believe that no other experience gives her so much happiness when enjoyed in an affectionate, genuinely mutual relationship.

It is my carefully weighed conclusion that although some women may endure marriage without orgasm, such a marriage is, at best, of poor quality compared with those in which the wife is erotically alive and regularly reaches orgasm in intercourse with her husband.

I am convinced that for a woman to function at her best as either wife or mother, she must have the rich emotional experience of guiltless capability to enjoy orgasm in intercourse.

I find something deeply significant in the fact that, during all of my practice as a counselor, I encountered only two instances in which a woman regularly achieving orgasm with her husband came to me contemplating divorce.

In each case there was a staggering discrepancy in the cultural backgrounds of the spouses and the husband was unable to provide enough financial security to undertake the responsibility of children. When divorce was finally decided upon, in each of these marriages the spouses wept bitterly and parted with reluctance. I am glad to report that it was not long before each entered a new and more suitable marriage.

Against these two cases, I have seen many hundreds of marriages break up in the face of poor sex response by the wife, even though in most instances the cultural backgrounds of the spouses were reasonably compatible.

I should not like to close without briefly noting one last point. Much as I value the experience of good sex, all my life I have felt that the mutually trusting, affectionate relationship comes first and that without it, sex is reduced to an unsatisfactory caricature.

# 19. Female vs. Male Sexuality

### Kenneth Walker, M.D.

There are certain differences in the attitude of men and women to sex and also in their emotional responses to sex stimulation. But before we start to discuss these differences, it has to be pointed out that no individual is ever one hundred per cent male, or one hundred per cent female. In every woman there lurk certain masculine characteristics, and in every man, characteristics of a feminine nature.

This preliminary statement about sexuality has been made in order that the reader may realize from the very start that the distinctions about to be made between the two sexes do not necessarily apply either to *all* men or to *all* women.

It would be true to say that the strength of sex desire appears to be more uniform in men than it is in women. While wide variations occur in the intensity of the sex drive of different individuals, women generally vary more greatly in their sex intensity than men.

Among women are to be found many examples of the two extremes of sexual feeling—namely the completely frigid woman and the so-called nymphomaniac woman. In men these extremes are less common.

Another difference between the two sexes is that sexual desire arises much more spontaneously in men than it does in women. It may occur in the absence of any emotional stimulation. A woman's sexual desires are much more dependent on some form of erotic stimulation, either caressing or a general emotional warmth, than are those of a man.

A woman's sexuality is more closely related to her emotions than is the sexuality of a man. Sexual intercourse for sexual pleasure alone is much less appealing to a woman than to a man. A woman requires that everything should be in keeping with her feelings and with those of her lover. A man is much less exacting about the setting of the sexual act.

He does not necessarily demand that the hour, the place and the emotional understanding existing between the two lovers should be entirely appropriate to the occasion. The reason for this difference between the two sexes is that a woman's sex is much more closely linked with her emotions than is a man's.

Even when a woman's sexuality has been stimulated by the presence of a man who is sexually attractive to her, the preliminary phase of the sex act, courtship, must never be omitted. It is an indispensable preliminary to what is about to happen.

"The way to my senses is through my *heart*," wrote Mary Wollstonecraft to her lover, Imlay. "But forgive me! I think that there is sometimes a shorter cut to yours." The different attitudes of men and of women to the act of love could not have been summed up more skillfully.

It has sometimes been said that while a man is essentially a polygamous (mating with many women) type of lover, a woman is, by nature, scrupulously monogamous (mating with one person) in her outlook. This has sometimes been used as an excuse for a husband's infidelity to his wife, but it is doubtful whether this statement expresses a truth. The more likely explanation of a woman's greater sexual restraint is that the sexual act may have much weightier consequences for her than it has for her partner. For this reason, a woman is likely to be slower and more careful in giving herself to another man.

For all these reasons courtship—and sometimes a prolonged courtship—may be required before a woman is psychologically and physically ready for engaging in sexual intercourse. This is particularly true of women who have previously had little or no experience of sexual intercourse. But the above statement is much less true of the unmarried woman of today than it was of the women of the past. Fifty years ago, it was exceptional for a bride to have had any sexual experience prior to her marriage. But this is not true of many of the brides of today.

It is highly important that a recently married man should be aware of the difference between the sexuality of men and of women. One of the most important of these differences was formerly that, whereas the husband had come automatically into possession of his sexual power and knew exactly what he wanted to do, his wife's sexuality had, up till then, remained entirely dormant in her. This being so, a bridegroom was faced with the responsibility of awakening in the bride her dormant sexuality. This threw a great responsibility on him, for if he awakened the bride's sexuality too abruptly, or unskillfully, he might interfere with the whole of his wife's future sexual development.

This may still remain true to a certain extent even though the wife may have had some previous experience of sexual intercourse. Sexual intercourse is really an art and in the majority of cases it is the husband who has to initiate his wife into the mysteries of that art. This does not mean that the wife should remain entirely passive throughout the sexual act, submitting to whatever her husband desires of her.

Lovemaking is a duet rather than a solo, and each of the players must learn how to play his or her appropriate part. The husband should of course take the lead in this duet, a duet which recapitulates, in miniature, their previous love-history.

The sexual act is usually subdivided into three phases, the

first being the love-play or courtship, the second the more active phase of sexual union, and the third the epilogue or what Van de Velde prefers to call the afterglow.

The husband plays the more active part in the love drama but, from time to time, the wife may take the lead, and may introduce some pleasing novelty into it.

The strength of sexuality is likely to be more rhythmic in women than it is in men. Investigations carried out, both in England and in the United States, show that the majority of married women recognize two cycles or peaks in their sexual desire. The first peak occurs just before the onset of the menstrual flow and the second just after it ceases. Unlike the animal's sexuality, man's sexuality is not bound to a seasonal rise and fall, although vestiges of this seasonal change still remain, and more especially in women.

Another difference between men and women is that for a man, a sexual relationship with a woman is only one among several other forms of relationship with people and things. It is undoubtedly an event of considerable importance to a man, but it is comparable with other nonsexual varieties of experience. But a woman is far more deeply embedded in her sexuality than is a man. Her sexual feelings are a part of her own being and in a sense are thus taken for granted.

It is so much an element in her existence that one single and particular act of sexual intercourse loses much of its intrinsic inportance for her. In contrast to this, for a man sexuality consists of a long series of *isolated* acts of love-making. All of these isolated acts seem very important. For this reason, a woman is much more able than is a man to bear a prolonged period of sexual continence that has been enforced on a couple by circumstances.

Another important difference between the sexual life of a man and of a woman is that the reproductive life of a woman comes to an abrupt end with the cessation of her menstruation and with the onset of the menopause. At a certain age women have to be relieved of the physical strains that are linked with pregnancy and with childbirth.

But psychologically, the menopause may prove to be a very difficult period for some women. Some are apt to feel that they have suddenly become old, and that they no longer have the capacity to excite admiration and love. The menopause, or what is called the "change of life," may occur in a woman at any time between the ages of thirty-five and fifty-five.

It is a debatable question whether or not a man also passes through a kind of climacteric. There is no need, of course, for a man to be relieved of his reproductive function, for whereas in the economy of a woman everything has been sacrificed to the purpose of her existence—reproduction—little or nothing has been sacrificed for this purpose in a man.

Women often experience an increase of sexual desire after the menopause. Many men retain their sexuality in an advanced age. A striking example of sexual vigor persisting into a green old age was provided by Goethe, who, at the age of seventy-five, fell so desperately in love with Ulrique, a girl of nineteen, that when he was rejected he wrote: "I am lost in unconquerable desire. There is nothing left for me but flowing tears. Let them flow, let them flow unceasingly, but they can never extinguish the fire that burns within me."

We are not certain as to what extent differences in men and women are inborn or are the result of the way in which they are brought up in society. Whatever the reason, there is a vast difference between the way men and women look at sex and express their sexuality. An awareness of this difference can prevent a good many of the marital problems that plague couples.

# 20. Respecting Your Mate's Feelings
## Edward Dengrove, M.D.

Sex relations between a man and his wife are much more than a device for achieving pleasure, or a means of relieving tension. They are not something one does to the other but—as the word *intercourse* means in its broadest sense—a form of *communication* between two individuals. In a good marriage the message that is communicated is one of love and respect. Unfortunately, a good many husbands and wives just can't seem to achieve the compromises that are necessary for this mutual respect.

The man who is brusque and hurried in his sexual relationship, for example, proceeding to his own gratification instantly but with only a token attempt, if any, to arouse or

satisfy his wife, is inconsiderate. His sexual behavior is an indication that he has no regard for her.

The sexual conduct of many women is somewhat similar to
that of the brusque male; like him, they hurry coitus. They
discourage every attempt on the part of the man to prolong
or vary intercourse, and thus reduce it to a routine, mechanical act.

Such women usually seize upon any excuse to avoid intercourse; they retire early and are asleep when their husbands
come to bed, or busy themselves with chores until their mates
are sound asleep. Nothing is more distressing to a normally
loving husband than having his affections thus constantly
rebuffed, and few things more seriously threaten a marriage.

Many wives are disturbed by their husbands' conduct during the menstrual period. Most couples do not participate in
sexual activity during this time, but some men seem to prefer
it.

Some women, too, find their sexual desires more stimulated
at this time, probably because there is the added lure of the
forbidden, but they are few. There is nothing essentially
wrong with intercourse during the menstrual period, but most
women shy away from it for esthetic reasons.

Some women are troubled when their husbands insist that
they display themselves completely nude before intercourse.
A good deal of the marital discord which arises on this score
is due to the lack of understanding men and women have
about each other's sexual psychology, needs, and responses.

Most men are greatly stimulated by seeing things which
have sexual connotations—most women are not. The male's
instinctive urge to look is often thwarted by his wife's refusal
to be seen. And far more common than one suspects is the
shy wife, the woman who never allows her husband to see
her in the nude. Her great need to hide her body is reflected
in other sexual inhibitions as well, which make the marriage
bed less attractive to her mate than it otherwise would be.

During or after the sexual relationship, some men mistreat
their wives in various ways. There are some who address
their wives in obscene language while making love to them, a
situation shocking and repelling to most women. Yet there
are also some women who insist that their mates speak to
them this way during intercourse.

Some men abuse their wives verbally; others do so physically. The man who must cruelly mistreat his wife after intercourse, or who ejects her from the bed once the act is completed, is one who has deeply-rooted feelings of guilt about

sex. Or he may see women as purely sexual devices, and not in any other way.

Some men mistreat their wives in still another way—by denying them the opportunity to experience orgasm. In rare cases, it is because the woman's climax arouses great anxiety within them, the result of an unconscious conflict about the nature of feminity; sometimes it is because they have feelings of hostility towards women, and deliberately deny the woman satisfaction to punish her.

More often, however, the man is unaware that his wife hasn't reached completion, or else he suffers from premature ejaculation and cannot delay his orgasm long enough to help her reach hers.

In some marriages, there is a great deal of conflict about the use of oral-genital contacts. While many married couples engage in it to some extent in the foreplay which precedes intercourse, there are some men and women who always insist upon it.

When a man prefers this activity to the exclusion of coitus, we may suspect that he is suffering from impotence to some degree. When it is the wife who shows a marked preference for such contact, it may be that she requires a great deal of clitoral stimulation to help her reach completion, and finds this activity superior in that regard to manual manipulation.

Some women complain that their husbands insist upon constantly changing the position used in intercourse. Too many wives feel that there are only one or two "right" postures; actually, a married couple should feel free to use any position which provides them mutual satisfaction.

The man who is in constant search for new postures, however, is probably the same man who is always chasing after new thrills and new sensations. His search for a different position in intercourse is really a search for increased sexual excitation.

Disturbing to many husbands is the wife who immediately following intercourse busies herself in the bathroom. This is the woman who regards intercourse as something so unclean she must hasten to cleanse herself of the products of the sexual act, and so hurries to douche. She is usually compulsive, overly-neat, and exhibits other phobias as well.

Though desiring intercourse, some women must be pursued and sometimes practically forced to submit. No wonder their husbands are often confused—it is frequently difficult for the man to know when her "No" means "No" and when it really means "Yes."

Actually, a woman who conducts herself in this way is acting out a rape fantasy. She believes the sex act is shameful and so does not want it to appear that she has entered it willingly; the man must always make it seem that she was forced into it.

There are many women who refuse to allow their husbands to make love to them if anyone else is in the house. If they are a couple who have children, the situation can be very difficult.

I know of one young husband whose wife refused to have relations with him while they were on an extended visit to his parents' home, but she was completely submissive in a parked automobile on a deserted country road. Behind this attitude, there lies the fear of being seen while performing the act of intercourse or preliminary lovemaking.

Each human being is a unique personality in his own right, and each has his unique sexual personality too, his own mannerisms and eccentricities. But a satisfying marital relationship is the result of the blending of these two personalities so that both partners are mutually gratified and neither disappointed. Such blending can only come about if husband and wife are considerate of each other's needs.

# 21. When Husbands and Wives Differ in Sex Drive
### Robert A. Harper, Ph.D.

It is not at all uncommon for couples who have a quite satisfactory marriage, including the enjoyment of sex relations when they occur, to differ considerably as to the frequency in which they want to engage in sex. This can become something of a problem.

Once in a while the counselor who talks with such a couple will find the sex drive differences more imaginary than real, as in the case of Wilma and Virgil. This couple, a twenty-year-old woman and a twenty-two-year-old man, had been married for two years at the time they saw me and reported great happiness together.

"There's just one problem," Wilma said, "but it is a really serious one. Virgil, you tell him."

"Well," Virgil said, "I'm oversexed. Wilma and I have done some reading, and we realize I am abnormal. I'm not only interested in sex at least once a day, but, if Wilma doesn't stop me, I proceed to make love to her every time I'm interested."

"Why do you stop him?" I asked Wilma. "Aren't you interested?"

"Oh, I *could* be interested," she said. "But I don't *let* myself be interested. I realize that to make love as much as once a day is not unusual during the first month or so of marriage. But we have read several places that after the first month or so, two or three times a week is considered normal. And here we have been married for two full years, and Virge, if I would let him, would make love every day and maybe three times on Saturday and Sunday."

"That's fine," I said. "There is no prescribed number of times per week or per day or per month which may be considered normal or healthy. If someone works out an average of, say, three times a week for coitus for a given number of married couples, there will undoubtedly be some couples who have sexual intercourse less than once a month, some ten or more times a week, and some at almost any figure you can mention."

Once both Virgil and Wilma were convinced that there was nothing immoral or abnormal about having sex as often as they had the time and inclination, Wilma turned out to be interested as frequently as Virgil. Up to that time, she had felt obligated to take the "strong character" role and to protect the marriage from Virgil's "abnormal lust."

Usually, though, differences in sex drive are deeper and more genuine than was the case with Virgil and Wilma. Sometimes, even though the couple reports enjoying marriage, there are problems—directly related to sex or not—which underlie differences in sex drives.

But what about differences in sex drives of husbands and wives which cannot be traced to problems of any sort? What about the instances where one marital partner is just plain and simply interested in sex much more often than the other?

Contrary to the folklore about the sex-eager male, I have found increasingly in my practice that it is the wife at least as often as the husband who complains about insufficiency of sex interest on the part of the mate. This does not mean that sex-eager males are not around. But among the couples I see, a good many men are ambitious, hardworking professionals and government and business administrators. They sometimes get so keyed up in their occupational lives that they have very little energy left for families and wives, including sex activity, except perhaps for vacations and occasional weekends.

The wives of these men, oftentimes, are leading relatively dull lives in their mother-housewife roles and are frequently much more desirous of love and sex than their fagged-out husbands.

Whether it is the husband or the wife who wants more sex activity than the other, what I said to one couple, whom I shall call the Clanners, seems to cover the possible solutions. In their case it was Mrs. Clanner who was much more often sexually interested than her husband. Mr. Clanner, however, did not fall into the ambitious, worn-out husband category. He just seemed to think that sex about once a week was quite enough, and Mrs. Clanner, whose preference was at least once a day, was willing to settle for about every other day.

"So far as we have been able to determine," I said, "there is nothing we can do to bring you closer together in frequency of sex drive. So, since you love each other and find the marriage otherwise very satisfactory and want to maintain it, we have four possible alternatives: (1) Mrs. Clanner just 'lumps it'—that is, she accepts the fact that she is going to be sexually frustrated several times a week; (2) she takes on one or more lovers to supplement what you provide her, Mr. Clanner, in sex satisfaction; (3) you masturbate as frequently as you want, Mrs. Clanner, to supplement your sexual relationship; and (4) you can exceed your own degree of drive, Mr. Clanner, by making love to your wife much more often than you feel personally inclined."

"How can I do that?" Mr. Clanner said. "You know a man can't engage in sexual intercourse if he hasn't got desire."

"Even if you have no erection," I answered, "you can make love to her in other ways, including manipulation and oral-genital sex activity."

"In any case," Mr. Clanner said, "I prefer that to what you call solution number two. You *and* she can forget that one."

"Yes," I agreed, "adultery is not a recommended solution to sex frustration for persons who want to maintain their marriages. And possibility number one—Mrs. Clanner's just living with her frustration—is unrealistic. She already shows willingness to compromise and not make a big deal out of her frustrations."

"And masturbation," Mrs. Clanner said, "is an *individual*

solution, in case I don't have a husband or in case my husband is away on a business trip. But masturbation is not a *marital* solution."

Mrs. Clanner was right. The marital solution in such cases as theirs is obviously number four. Here, as in most aspects of marriage counseling and psychotherapy, attitudes of both husbands and wives often have to be re-educated. In this instance, Mrs. Clanner's attitudes were quite healthy, but Mr. Clanner had to be dispossessed of the notion that lovemaking other than sexual intercourse is somehow an inferior breed of sex activity and that orgasms achieved other than in coitus are somehow inferior.

Mr. Clanner also felt "put upon" to make love when he was not particularly sexually driven. And often the more sexually interested partner feels, "I don't want him to do it unless he really wants to do so." But people are quite willing to please each other in all kinds of nonsexual ways in well-functioning marriages. Why do the rules have to be different for sex? They obviously do not, and people can change their attitudes in regard to it.

Couples who are willing to be re-educated along the lines of what we have called our number four solution often report the same results as the Clanners. About six months after I had last seen them, Mrs. Clanner phoned.

"You know what's happened, Dr. Harper?" she asked. "All this business of getting my husband to help satisfy me has gotten him all whipped up in *his* sex interest. It is now an open question as to who is helping whom."

# 22. How to Live with Someone You Love

### Clarence A. Tripp, Ph.D.

It is a commonplace saying that sexual attraction and love tend to come packaged together, and to work hand in hand in some way. When sexual attraction and love are combined, they produce what is probably the most dramatic and rewarding of human experiences. And when a love relationship begins to disintegrate, the pain and despair feels like the height of tragedy.

A love relationship can be divided into three consecutive parts: the establishment or courtship phase; the joys and problems of keeping it balanced and smooth; and the pains and problems of the end of the affair, if it comes. Most of the remarks to be made here will be limited to the "conflict" problems that arise in the middle period.

In the first stage, the high voltage of romance can swallow up the most outrageous errors committed by either partner. If later conflicts are managed fairly well, the relationship need not end unless you have made some gigantic error in mate selection, or unless some major change occurs in your partner or in yourself.

The trouble is that the intensity of high romance normally has a maximum life of a year or so, because it is based on an overevaluation of the partner, and frequently on various rather magical expectations.

When these illusions begin to fade, the affair either crashes immediately into oblivion, or translates itself into a continuing affectionate or tender relationship of some sort. Here in this second phase lie the most excruciating problems that can so torture the partners.

For the most part, these problems boil down to how to make complaints, and how to receive complaints from him or her.

You might ask, "Why do there have to be complaints?" Of course, there will always be complaints, and plenty of them.

Some of these arise from various conflicts of interest. Others are the natural consequence of two people living in close contact, each doing or neglecting things about which the other partner feels strongly. And there is an increased readiness for making complaints about a person whenever there is the slightest drop in the admiration one feels toward him or her.

The original romance, the part that lasts such a short time, is really based on three factors: (1) sexual attraction, (2) the other person's mysterious individuality, and (3) elements of high admiration one finds in the lover.

The sexual attraction eventually suffers a degree of fatigue. It may stay good for some time, but it does lose glory. And the delightful unraveling of the mysteries and intricacies of the other person eventually turn the mystery into the familiar, if not the disappointing.

At least parts of the admiration may stay in place for a

long time. For instance, physical beauty, longed-for social talents, a delightful wit, or precious little personal ways may keep their appeal, or even improve.

But these are only facets on a many-sided personality. Familiarity will show you many other qualities that are not glorious, or that may be painfully inferior to longed-for ideals.

Thus fatigue, disappointments, and unwanted qualities combine to poison the stream of magical expectations that were seen like a halo around the head of the lover when he or she was at that distance which romantic adoration requires.

Much of the bitterness and disappointment can be removed from later complaints if you know how to climb down from magical expectations (and help your lover do the same) before the first flush of attraction is at an end.

When you become aware of your first complaints, prepare to honor and make them. Do not heed advice like "forgiving" the other person or "tolerating" your own frustration. To do so is to live beyond your moral means and incubate the cat into a tiger.

When making a complaint, never hit a person's ego. Attack only the action, not the person who has taken the action. You can tell a person, for example, you feel neglected in a particular situation, but it is more sweeping and dangerous to say that he or she is an inconsiderate person.

In other words, make your complaint directly. Do not analyze, give verdicts, or ascribe motivation to his or her acts. When you are hurt, describe *yourself*, not your loved one's character or motivations.

You can say that you hate virtually any *act*, or any *feeling* in a particular situation; you can be very extreme about it too, if that is the way you feel. But you are asking for trouble, and for blood, if you say or imply that you dislike him or her.

You must never analyze actions you are objecting to, like "You did such and such just to hurt me," or "to get even with me," or "to make yourself feel better." The chances are very great that you will be wrong. In that case, you will look foolish or, if you are right, she will look foolish.

It is particularly dangerous for you to "win" in this sort of conflict, because the extent a person can like you is limited to the extent he (or she) likes himself (herself) as viewed through your eyes. To damage a persons self-image is to lower the ceiling on how much he can think of you. In short, by ascribing motivation to a person, you look silly if you are wrong, he looks silly if you are seemingly right, and you lose in either case.

You face the opposite side of the problem when your lover directs assaultive complaints against you. Chances are, he or she will make enormous errors and wrongly accuse you. Most accusations in this world have a grain of truth but are fundamentally wrong.

Probably the accusations heaped on your head will poorly describe you. You will have an urge to defend yourself, most particularly if you can seemingly rout the charge with one blow or one fact. Do not do it. There is no place in interpersonal relations where defense is an efficient move.

If you agree with your partner's complaint, say so and you will both feel much better. If the accusation is outrageous, agree with the part of it which you can, and then either make your point, or tell him or her how the rest of it makes you feel.

If your mate implies that you talk too much, or not enough, or rejects you for any other reason, then invite him or her to carry it further. Investigate the charge. Never attack the accusation itself. Remember never to defend yourself.

When you are the victim of a lover's hostility, you can easily make the error of thinking you are no longer loved. How utterly wrong this is. People are made of many parts, and not all of these are committed to any devotion.

Also, if someone is praising you to the skies, that person is exercising positive feelings toward you. If the praise is unqualified and too extensive, it is extremely dangerous. For by such action, the other person is building the muscles on the part of herself (or himself) that resents any such overcommitment.

You would be wise to say something like, "Yes, I am pleased at (what you have mentioned), but the trouble is that it isn't always true," or, "How nice of you to notice but I can't always do it," etc.

But perhaps the most important thing is to moderate the excesses of magical expectations—other people's as well as your own—those saccharine illusions that spin glorious images of hope and paradise, but which wear away rapidly in the face of reality and time.

# 23. How to Avoid Destructive Jealousy

## Ben N. Ard, Jr., Ph.D.

Jealousy has troubled relations between men and women for as long as recorded history. What causes jealousy? What can be done about it?

What one does about jealousy—and even one's feelings—depends to a great extent on one's assumptions. If an individual assumes that jealousy is a natural, normal, justified response to a given situation, that will lead to certain actions and consequences. If, however, jealousy is seen as not always justified or normal, then different reactions can be expected.

As an illustration of how one's *assumptions* influence behavior, consider the man or woman who assumes that unless their partner shows some jealousy now and then, it follows (in *their* mind) that the partner does not love them. They assume that jealousy must always accompany love.

Obviously this kind of assumption is incorrect. One man known to me in my practice as a marriage counselor was always very proud of his beautiful wife. When he was out of town (which was a lot since he was a railroad engineer), he never objected when his wife went out to dinner with men friends of theirs. He always said that he trusted his wife completely. Did this mean (since he wasn't jealous) that he did not love her? Not at all. He just defined acceptable behavior on the part of his wife in broader ways, perhaps, than other men might.

Other clients of mine have said, "I don't mind my spouse dancing, kissing, necking or petting with others, as long as he (or she) comes home to me at night. I want to be the one he (or she) sleeps with." Each person would probably draw the line of acceptable behavior for their partners at a different place.

There are no absolutes here, in the sense of limits that are universally agreed upon everywhere and at all times. The Eskimo practice of lending one's wife to the visiting guest should be sufficient to remind us of this.

But what is important for each couple (if they are to avoid unpleasant jealous reactions) is that they spell out for each other in explicit detail just what their assumptions are about the limits of acceptable behavior on the part of their partner and themselves with the other sex.

This should be done early in the game rather than late. Too often a person merely assumes that his partner agrees with him without ever checking it out. Then when behavior seems to violate the underlying (but unspoken) assumptions, all kinds of tragedies may result. People have been beaten up, shot and killed because of just these unspoken assumptions and the resultant jealous reactions.

When a person is dating casually, he or she may not like it if the date pays too much attention to others while they are out together, but usually does not feel entirely justified in making too much of an issue about it since obligations are fairly limited here.

As one progresses from steady dating into engagement and marriage, however, the limits of acceptable behavior narrow down considerably. Many difficulties that center around jealous reactions possibly could be reduced if couples were more explicit about their expectations as they move through various stages of commitment. What was acceptable during casual dating may not be equally acceptable during engagement or marriage.

Certainly by the time a marriage is contemplated, a certain basic trust would seem to be required. If marriage partners cannot trust one another, there is little hope for the future of the marriage. And partners who are really committed to one another should not have to (or feel the need to) continually check up on one another.

It might not be a bad idea to discuss possibly hypothetical situations ahead of time, just to check out each other's expectations. For example, what would you do if you walked into your home unexpectedly and saw your spouse kissing a stranger? Would you hit first and ask questions later? Go get a gun? Or would the thought occur to you that it just might be a long-lost kissing cousin returned from the foreign legion or the Far East?

Checking out the assumptions one has regarding acceptable behavior on the part of a partner probably is one of the best ways to avoid any unfortunate jealous reactions later on which one might regret. Easy ways to discuss such possible situations, for example, are after seeing movies, reading novels, or even observing other people's behavior at cocktail parties (where, perhaps, some hanky-panky is observed).

Talk it over first while it is other people's behavior that is involved, since it is usually easier to remain fairly calm and detached about their behavior than about one's own or one's partner's behavior.

Another example of how someone's assumptions can lead to trouble as far as jealous reactions are concerned is one that is very common: what happens when a husband looks with approval at some woman other than his wife and his wife "catches him at it."

Often the wife assumes that her husband would like to have sexual relations with the other woman (she might be right here); she then assumes that he must not love her any more (not necessarily true since he probably did not go blind when he got married); she may assume that "all men are polygamous by nature" (she might be right here); and that therefore no man can be trusted (a mistaken assumption that can lead to real trouble in a marriage).

It is a commonly held belief in our culture that it is just as sinful to lust after another man's wife (even if you don't do anything about it) as it actually is to commit adultery with another man's wife. And this very assumption often leads to jealousy and recriminations and even self-blame, none of which helps a couple to maintain good relations in their marriage.

The crux of the matter depends, as far as jealousy is concerned, on what actually is seen to be a threat to the relationship. All sorts of behavior may take place which one set of partners would not consider a threat at all, while another set of partners would break up their relationship immediately at the first occurrence of even one item of such behavior.

*Where* you would draw the line is not as important to the stability of the relationship as is the *explicit communication of expectations* to the partner. That is, clearly bringing to the surface and spelling out in detail the *underlying assumptions and expectations* about the roles each expects the other to play.

Merely "being in love" is *not* enough. Explicit communication of one's basic values, assumptions, and expectations is required. And it is so much easier to do this *before* situations have arisen in which one's jealous emotions are aroused.

# 24. Talking Out Sexual Conflicts

## William Zehv, M.S.

Most husbands and wives could resolve many if not all sexual conflicts if they would only talk about them frankly and openly with each other. So many men and women, however, are too inhibited to talk about the intimate details of their sexual relationship.

Mrs. E. consulted me after hearing me lecture. She complained that in foreplay her husband fondled only her breasts, sometimes pinching the nipples till she cried out in pain. "I'm not all breasts!" she exclaimed in anger and frustration. "I have other parts of the body."

I suggested, mildly, "Why don't you say so to your husband? Why don't you tell him precisely how you would like him to fondle you so that you would enjoy his caresses?"

Somewhat abashed, she whispered, "I'd like to. But I just can't seem to make myself do it, to get the words out of my mouth. I have thought many times of telling him, but I just can't get myself to say it. I'm afraid I'd feel like a hussy, like a woman who wants sex and not love. And I want sex to be love."

I explained to her that in marriage sex is a function of love and love a function of sex, that it was perfectly normal and socially acceptable for a husband and wife to discuss such intimate details of the sex relationship. Fortunately there was a book I could recommend which went into just such details. I suggested that she and her husband read the book and discuss it.

Mr. and Mrs. J. were in for marriage counseling. They had been married only a short time, but in those few months they had managed to build up a sex conflict of major proportion —and only because of misunderstandings, because they didn't talk it out.

Both Mr. and Mrs. J. worked. Since they were young and active, they usually went to bed fairly late. After a stimulating evening out, Mr. J. was often sexually aroused, while

Mrs. J. was tired and wanted nothing but sleep. When he was affectionate and fondled his wife, with intercourse in mind, she would snap at him, "Leave me alone. I'm tired."

Mr. J. felt hurt and interpreted it as a personal rejection. He would lie awake most of the night wondering if his wife loved him. All of the next day he would be grouchy; he would sulk and be sullen.

If it happened that perhaps that night his wife was relaxed and would welcome sex play, and coitus, he was so wrapped up in his misery and frustration that he wasn't aware of the opportunity. Or he felt that his wife would only reject him again. He became apprehensive about initiating intercourse on these occasions.

Now it is perfectly legitimate for a wife to be too tired for sex, or not in the mood, but it is important for her to learn how to communicate this without hurting her husband's feelings. As Mrs. J. said, she didn't mean to reject him, but she didn't know how else to say it.

In the course of counseling she had to learn that she could just as well take an extra minute to tell him that she loved him, that she appreciated his gestures of affection, but that she was too tired for intercourse that night. She even learned to add the phrase, "Perhaps in the morning. Or let's make a date for tomorrow night."

As for Mr. J., he had to learn that rather than stew in his frustration, it would be all right if the next day he talked to his wife about what happened the night before, how disappointed and frustrated he felt. Just talking it out helps more than people imagine; it clears the air of misunderstanding and hurt feelings.

Americans generally are not a talking people, particularly when it comes to the intimate details of their sex life. Husbands and wives, instead of talking out their petty grievances, harbor grudges day after day, week after week, until they pile up and there is an explosion. This was the case of Mr. and Mrs. T.

Mrs. T. was irritated with her husband over a period of years because, as she explained it, he had a habit of making sexual advances at the most inappropriate times. Just as she was bending over the stove, basting a turkey, Mr. T. would reach for her and make sexual gestures.

It rankled her that on a Saturday or Sunday afternoon, with the children running in and out, he would insist on having sexual intercourse. She felt that such behavior on her husband's part was vulgar and revolting.

Why didn't she mention it to her husband? Why didn't she

talk it over with him? She shook her head, saying, "How do you talk about such things? What words do you use?" The answer is that you just talk about it, and use everyday words. The difficulty is in broaching the subject the first time.

I have had many husbands and wives tell me that once they confronted the situation and talked about it, it was not as difficult as they thought it would be. And it became easier the next time and the next.

Mr. and Mrs. D. were in for marriage counseling. Mr. D. insisted that once in a while he would be pleased if his wife would initiate the sex act. "To show that she loves me, to show that she enjoys sexual intercourse."

Mrs. D. was obstinate. It was her contention that it was the obligation of the male to be sexually aggressive, that while she enjoyed coitus with her husband, it is not feminine for a woman to initiate it or to respond too actively. Mr. D. wondered if perhaps his wife was frigid and was only making believe that she found sex satisfactory.

This all came out in the consulting room. They couldn't talk like that at home, in the privacy of their bedroom. But with this as a start, they slowly and gradually began to discuss the intimate details of their sex life and began to understand each other better. It took a little time, but just talking erased a good deal of Mrs. D.'s inhibitions and her natural sexual impulses came to the surface.

Mr. D. was not only pleased but, as he later commented, it was no longer a relationship which he initiated to which his wife agreed. It was a mutual harmony of sexual desire.

The principals in the cases just cited were not neurotic people, nor individuals with insoluble sexual problems; the sexual conflicts were of the average type that occur in the homes of millions of couples across the country. However, such uncomplicated and petty misunderstandings and aggravations need to be resolved and worked through, or else they can become severe problems. With time they become magnified and build up from a molehill into a mountain. Talking it out not only saves much wear and tear, physically and emotionally, but instead leads to sexual harmony and satisfaction, to a sound marriage relationship and to peace of mind.

# 25. How Romantic Illusions Can Wreck Your Marriage

## Lee R. Steiner, M.S.

Marriage is our way of life. It is the way into which we divide society. A man, a woman, and some children live under one roof and try to make for themselves a good way of life. Some succeed. Some do not. It depends upon how much investment they make in the venture.

Recently, however, an increasing number of self-styled psychologists have added their seeming authenticity to the Hollywood and TV theme that marriage should and must be romantic—and that one should "live happily ever after."

As a result, an increasing number of individuals have grown to believe this and have severed what might be a workable marriage because it lacked "romance." Through this fiction, the attitude of what constitutes an adequate marriage has become so distorted that many people have accepted these false standards as a measuring rod for their own marital adjustment.

False notions of "masculinity" have given men who try to measure up to them a deep feeling of inferiority. How many men can identify with the brawny, tough, swaggering stud of current pulps? Although a marauder in the world at large, at home he must assume an entirely different personality because the sexual adjustment of his mate has now been laid at his door. With his mate he must be patient, gentle, loving and considerate. These are contradictory qualities. The great marauder cannot also be the gentle lamb.

The greatest burden, however, is that he must be able to experience full and lusty potency to keep his mate emotionally well-adjusted. This is entirely a fiction. No man is always potent or even adequate. Most men, even the lusty ones, experience periods of impotence.

And, biologically speaking, not everyone is capable of lustiness at all. We differ in our glandular makeup all the way from very weak to very strong. There are many good marriages that have little sex. Moreover, sex does not mean only intercourse. Many a woman would settle for a man who is weaker sexually if he were more loving generally. A pat, a kind word, a loving glance—this is also sex.

Nor is the modern woman, often college educated, able to measure up to the cliché of the good wife—basically dependent emotionally and financially, deriving her greatest delight from housework and child-rearing. Housework is a dreary, monotonous routine, generally delegated to those who have no other choice. And much as one loves one's children, the society of little ones all day long can be stultifying indeed.

The fact is, woman never was the dependent soul depicted in the literature. Even our grandmothers were entrepreneurs who dominated the household, their children, their husbands, and all who came into their orbit. The only difference is that today woman is asserting herself as a person. She no longer wants to pretend.

When one examines marriage honestly, one finds that woman is not always the passive one sexually. Many women must be the aggressors in sex if they are to have a sex life at all. In many, many homes (and these are often quite good marriages) the woman must do the wooing and stimulating of the man who is not too potent. Some women have learned that they must work hard for the sex life they have—and they feel it is worth the effort.

In a workable marriage, the man and the woman must appraise each other accurately, accept that reality as the working base, and make a good way of life out of it. False notions of romantic living or of goals for personality and behavior have little value and are harmful to that adjustment. Briefly, I refer to these four basic concepts as "romantic":

1. *That there is only one man for one woman; that destiny shall arrange their meeting; and that they shall remain "in love" forever.* This is nonsense. How and where we meet a mate is largely accidental. Certain people could be a good mate to any number of people and certain others could not make a good mate for anyone. After the first glow of glamour is over, the basic personality makes evident that these latter are not "spousable." Workable marriage depends upon the spouse's ability to appreciate and accept another person.

But many romanticists frown at my concept of "workable marriage." The realists, however, do not. They know that for two people to live harmoniously requires thoughtfulness, planning, and great regard for the personality ups and downs and the ebb and flow of sex desires.

No one is loving all the time. No one is stimulating all the time. It seems to be quite normal for two people to have no sexual desires for each other for extended periods without necessarily feeling that their relationship is a failure. Emotions are not something that can be tapped at will. Anything palls. So does sex with the same partner.

When this happens, we should be reassured that "this too shall pass." What makes me especially sad about a good part of the fan mail from my radio program is the number of letters from young people who, by the age of twenty, have already been married and divorced (often not only once, but twice) because he or she no longer found the mate "romantic."

2. *The second illusion is that it is possible to remain romantic throughout marriage.* Hectic emotions belong to youth. Love in maturity is made of different stuff. It consists of liking a person—which includes loving him—but it also includes those periods of dislike, when one does not even want him or her to touch one's body. To truly like a person is to like all of him, including his grouchiness and weaknesses.

This is a far deeper emotion than "being in love." Much of life and marriage is not pleasant—like child-bearing and periods of economic want and illness and misfortune. We should be telling young people that good, workable marriage is what they are seeing in their homes, so as to give them a pattern to conform to.

"Happy marriage" is as misleading a term as "romantic marriage." It is completely and totally impossible for any two people to be happy with each other and "in love" all the time. Anyone who professes this relationship is rhapsodizing, not confiding.

3. *The third fiction is that the partner in a good marriage never regrets his choice.* This seems inconceivable to me. A healthy person uses all of his emotions. He is not afraid to be angry or to dislike, for dislike is as normal and healthy an emotion as liking. In my many years of counseling, I have never encountered an individual who was not attracted to someone else during his or her marriage, at least once.

Factually speaking, would any wife want a husband who could no longer thrill to a shapely bosom? Or would any husband want a wife who had forgotten how to respond to an admiring glance? Spouses like to feel that others envy their choice.

In people of low sexual prowess, it is not uncommon that the spouse begins to blame the other for his deficiency and look to greener pastures. The straying might even have value to the marriage, if the individual learns that the weakness is within himself. He might then return to home base more content. Were he denied this verification, he might remain permanently restless.

4. *The corollary to the above is that infidelity is inexcusable.* If one is speaking Biblically, then of course it is. However, one does not need a Kinsey report to know that if the continuation of marriage were dependent upon complete fidelity, there would be few marriages that could survive.

What then is my thesis about marriage and my objections to the romantic concept? It is very briefly that romance in marriage is a fillip. A dessert. A high spot when something special happens or when we feel unusually expansive. There are many romantic moments or romantic spots in life. But there are no romantic marriages. At least, I have never been privileged to observe one.

In preference to this harmful notion, in preparing our young people for marriage we should teach them that what they see at home is probably normal marriage, that masculinity and femininity are whatever men and women are, and that a good marriage is what we make it.

# III.

# IMPROVING YOUR SEX ENJOYMENT

# 26. Zones of Love

### Richard Stiller, M.A.

Some years ago, when the so-called marriage manuals first became popular, a few super-sophisticated souls had great sport making fun of the various erotic techniques that were advocated. Some still do.

Of course it is easy to make almost anything look ridiculous. And there *is* something faintly silly about the image of the serious and conscientious bridegroom concentrating grimly on manipulating his bride as if she were some kind of complicated machine.

Most people like to think of sex as something that involves the whole person, and not just a case of each partner pushing the right "button" in the other person's anatomy. It is a matter of emotions as well as of mechanical skill.

And yet there is something on all sides of this matter of the zones of love—or what sexologists call the erogenous zones. There *are* parts of the body where sex nerves are most greatly concentrated, and where sex response is indeed quickly achieved by the proper amount of touching and stroking. These are quite naturally found in the sex organs and in a few other sexually significant parts of the body.

But that's not the whole of the story. Almost any part of the body can be sexually exciting when it is caressed and petted. And under certain favorable circumstances, the whole body can become one vast throbbing erogenous zone.

In addition, individuals differ so much among themselves that some of the most "unsexy" parts of the human anatomy can act like sexual triggers. Like eyebrows. Or hairs. Or teeth. Or ear lobes.

When the Kinsey investigators studied the sexual histories of almost 8,000 women, they found that some of them "(had) been brought to orgasm by having their eyebrows stroked, or by having the hairs on some other part of their bodies gently blown, or by having pressure applied on teeth alone."

Ear lobes, like the penis and the clitoris, "become engorged with blood during sexual arousal," they reported, "and become increasingly sensitive at that time. An occasional female or male may reach orgasm as a result of stimulation of the ears."

There is a reason why most discussions about the zones of love usually concern females rather than males. This is because there is a very important difference between the ways in which a male is aroused and the ways in which a female is aroused.

A man can be intensely aroused sexually without any physical contact at all. That is why pornographic pictures, or a girl with a sexually provocative walk, or any female nudity, draws such a dramatic response from men—especially young men.

Not so with women. For sexual arousal most women need bodily contact, specificially the kind of directly sexual caressing that all the marriage manuals talk about. This is not all they need, but it is an absolute necessity for most to receive sufficient stimulation by touch and by feel. Otherwise they will rarely respond sexually.

There are three important things to remember about the zones of love.

1. All people, men and women alike, are born with the same basic, physically-determined erogenous zones. These are the sex organs—penis, scrotum, clitoris, vaginal lips—and some other parts of the body such as the thighs, buttocks, anus, nipples, mouth, etc.

2. Human beings can be conditioned, and through habit and practice any part of the body can be sexually exciting if stroked and caressed. This kind of response—psychologists call it a conditioned reflex—is quite common.

3. Touching as a means of sex arousal is necessary—but it is not enough. Especially in the case of a woman, a general emotional attitude must be established before the caressing can mean anything. She has to at least like, if not love, her partner.

What are the physical factors that make a part of the body erogenous? *The number of nerve-endings that are found there.* We feel through the nerve-endings in our skin. Quite naturally we feel more intensely where there are a great many nerve endings, and less intensely where there are fewer.

Thus, the knee, the elbow, and certain parts of the back

are not too well supplied with nerve-endings. Hair and teeth don't have any at all. We don't feel pain or pleasure too well in those parts. (The pain we think we feel in our teeth when the dentist goes to work is really a transfer of the sensations of vibration through the enamel of the teeth to the nerve deep inside.)

But the tip of the penis, or the clitoris, or the nipples of the breasts are extremely rich in nerve-endings and are therefore very sensitive. Injuries to these parts are terribly painful. And by the same token, any caressing of them is intensely pleasurable.

The mouth, lips, and tongue are almost as rich in nerve endings. Next to the sex organs these are probably the most erogenous of zones.

Not surprisingly, the mouth is often used in direct sexual contacts. Oral-genital sex acts are quite common among human males and females and are practically universal among other mammals.

Incidentally, the human mouth has many more nerve-endings than the inside of the vagina, and may even be more erogenous. It is only the clitoris, lips and outer part of the vaginal opening that are sexually excitable in women. The special satisfaction that women receive from penetration of the vagina by the penis is believed to come from emotional considerations and generalized feelings of pressure, rather than from friction along the vaginal wall.

The penis, too, is not entirely erogenous. While the head or glans is very sensitive, the skin of the shaft is not too well supplied with the nerve-endings. It is probably very much like the inner wall of the vagina in this respect.

Males and females are alike in this distribution of nerve-endings. There are no real differences between the sexes, and areas which are erogenous in the man are usually so in the woman. Many people do not know that the nipples of the male are as sexually sensitive as those of the female, which is to say that they are not too important in either case. The female breast is really more erotic to the male than to the female. The anus is also rather erogenous in a good many people.

Sometimes—nerve-endings to the contrary—an out-and-out erogenous zone can be overruled by the prejudices and taboos of the mind. This is why in many parts of the world, the mouth is not considered erogenous at all. Kissing, for example, is looked upon with horror throughout much of Asia and Africa.

Even in our own country, say the Kinsey studies, many,

many people feel that only the penis and the vagina are "legitimate" erogenous zones and then only if they are in contact with each other and nothing else. Any kind of sex play, including kissing or caressing, is considered immoral and perverted by these people.

Nerve-endings or no nerve-endings, one man's sex pleasure can be another's disgust. The basic equipment is there in all of us, and most of us respond in much the same way. But there's no limit to what the mind and the emotions can do to turn almost any part of the body into a zone of love or a zone of revulsion.

# 27. How to Increase Your Sex Desire
## Robert A. Harper, Ph.D.

Most experts agree that a person's sex drive is largely an emotional matter. Of course one does need to have the necessary physical equipment. And such conditions as illness or fatigue can lessen sex interest considerably. But after physical problems have been ruled out, the man or woman with weak sex desires should consider some possible psychological causes of this.

Things that go wrong in a marriage, for example, that seem quite unrelated to sex, may cause a lessening of sex interest in one or both partners. The treatment that will renew sex desire might be some such apparently remote change as getting a baby sitter to give the wife some time away from home.

Take the case of Mr. and Mrs. G., for example. They were both tense, hardworking people. They tried to move right from some tedious task into lovemaking, and they were having considerable sexual difficulty and dissatisfaction.

I made the simple suggestion that they allow themselves a brief period of relaxation each evening, in which they lightly and pleasantly did something together. The idea was that they should not decide that they would or would not have sexual relations, but should let sex arise or not in a spontaneous fashion.

Well, arise it did with much greater frequency and enjoyment than it had formerly with their rather grim, tense, and routine approach to the whole matter.

In working with many married couples, I find that a lack of love and consideration is the most frequent cause of a loss of sex desire. This is especially (although not exclusively) true of women, who very often tie sex feeling in with love and consideration. Many (but not all) men seem able to have high sex desire even without much feeling of love, tenderness, and consideration.

Marriages which once were fine relationships based on affectionate understanding can run aground on these attitudes. Such feelings are often only sleeping and unnoticed rather than dead. Concentration on the reawakening of loving attention and considerate companionship between a husband and a wife, with or without the help of a marriage counselor, often brings about a remarkable rekindling of sex desire and activity.

Mrs. T., for example, was always finding fault with her husband's dress, his way of talking, his manners with guests, and any of a dozen or more other things she noticed daily. Mr. T. complained that he found little interest in sex. Neither of them had apparently made any connection between her nagging and his lack of sex desire.

I made the connection for them and literally trained Mrs. T. to give up her nagging. After several sessions in which she made progress in learning not to nag and criticize, Mr. T.'s sex desires began to show a marked increase. The last I heard, Mrs. T. had given up nagging for good, and Mr. T. had found that sex with his wife was a frequently enjoyable enterprise.

Sometimes the change that will bring about an increased interest in sex lies with the complaining wife rather than with the seemingly neglectful husband. Some wives have unrealistically high standards of what their husband should do in showing love and consideration.

Idealistic, perfectionistic expectations of the wife are the problem in such marriages. It is not the allegedly inadequate performance of the husband that is the cause of the marital and sex difficulties. Change in the wife's rigid attitudes can sometimes bring about remarkable improvements in the husband's sex desires.

In addition to these matters, individual emotional conditions can often be altered to bring about an increase in sex interest. Just as illness, fatigue, and other physical factors can interfere with sex desire and fulfillment, so also can such attitudes as anger, puritanical fears of sex, and worry. The most promising way of increasing sex desire is to practice dismissing distracting thoughts and developing one's ability to concentrate on sex and the husband or wife as a sex partner.

The general emotional atmosphere surrounding married sex can be improved, also. It is desirable to select a time when there is a minimum of strain and hostility between the mates, when both are relaxed and rested and unhurried, and when children and other distracting influences are least likely to interrupt.

Help in creating a sexually exciting atmosphere can be contributed by saying words of endearment, talking about sexually exciting situations, showing great interest in each other, recalling *aloud* previously stimulating experiences, showing confidence that each other can be aroused, and (for some people) providing photographic or written materials. All such efforts may help to bring into focus the enjoyment of the sexual act.

Sometimes sex desire may be increased from a long-run standpoint by temporarily cutting down on sex frequency. Usually, however, it is not that sex relations have been too frequent, but rather that either sex relations in particular or everyday life in general has become too humdrum and routine.

A vacation often helps stimulate sex desire. Physical and psychological novelties in sex approach may also step up lagging desire. Such things as having sex activities in the morning or afternoon instead of the evening or changing the form or position of sex relations, can have a stimulating effect from time to time on sex desire.

While it may seem obvious, loving and being loved are still the greatest stimulation to sex desire. Love not only releases sex inhibitions but it also reduces emotional insecurity and increases confidence. Sexual inhibition is really just another word for fear or anxiety. Fears disappear when we love our mates and feel loved by them.

An important thing to remember in the whole matter of increasing your sex desire is that you are really learning to achieve full use and enjoyment of the sex drive that you have. You are not in a sports contest to prove you are the sex athlete with the greatest desire. Getting the greatest amount of satisfaction from your existing sexual capacity—that is, using it to its fullest enjoyment—rather than trying to break some imaginary world's record should be your main goal.

# 28. Sex Positions and Your Sex Life
### Stephen Neiger, M.D., Ph.D.

Sex positions are one of man's oldest preoccupations, as is shown by early drawings found in caves. Love books from ancient India, Greece, Rome, and Arabia discuss positions in great detail. Repeated attempts have even been made to estimate how many positions there are. Some ancient writers counted hundreds by considering each minor change a new position.

From this preoccupation with positions, readers must have gotten the notion that this aspect is perhaps the most important source of pleasure in lovemaking. We know that this is not so. A person's attitude to sex in general, and to the partner in particular, are far more important factors. But skill in applying effective stimulation is also important. It is a valuable asset at any time and particularly essential under certain circumstances. The purpose of this article is to discuss the main reasons for a married couple to know several different positions for intercourse.

For one thing, different positions often permit novel and different types of physical stimulation. For example, the erogenous zones brought into play by face-to-face positions differ from those stimulated in vaginal entry from the rear positions.

This difference is not only due to the location of the pressures which the bodies exert on each other. The fact that the head and the hands are freed for different types of activities in some positions is just as decisive.

Thus, while the "conventional" face-to-face, man-above position permits excellent mutual stimulation of various parts of the face and the neck by kissing, most of its variations do not permit the man's hands to caress all parts of the female body, including the all-important region of the outer vaginal lips.

At this point, it is necessary to add that the often repeated belief that it is absolutely essential to stimulate the clitoris directly is no longer held to be crucial in sex play. The fact is, as the laboratory studies carried out by Masters and Johnson have shown, that the clitoris actually retracts, or draws back, during a high level of excitation. Attempts to stimulate it directly are often bothersome to the woman.

Also, it is quite unnecessary to go to extremes in seeking such contact because most wives receive clitoral stimulation *indirectly* during intercourse. This is due to the push and pull that the penis exerts on the vaginal lips. This friction is then communicated to the clitoris that sits in a special fold of the inner lips, the clitoral hood.

However, there still are good reasons for encouraging a couple to experiment with positions that promote closer contact between the pubic areas, as in the woman-above position, or in the conventional position when the woman places her legs on the man's shoulders or locks them on his hips (possibly with a pillow placed under the small of her back). Many couples enjoy such close contact because the labia (lips) are stretched and pressed most in this way. This area is richly endowed with "sex nerves" and this added "pull" brings more of them into play.

Psychological stimulation is perhaps an even more important factor in favor of experimentation with a variety of positions. Variety combats boredom. Also, there is a powerful *fantasy stimulus* that is inherent in many departures from the conventional position.

For example, all female-on-top positions (especially when the woman squats or kneels over the man) enhance physical stimulation for the woman by giving her the task of active pelvic motion. But it also provides a "summit" of *psychological* stimulation to both partners.

This is especially true for the husband. The man is freed from physical exertion and he has all the stimulation lavished upon him. Further, her body is all there both for viewing and for caressing.

For many couples, there may be fantasy-arousing elements in the "animal-like" quality of the "knee-chest" position (a variation of vaginal entry from the rear in which the woman is on "all fours" with her head lowered and the man approaches kneeling). Indeed, some couples dislike this position for precisely this reason. But all rear-entry positions can provide not only novel touch stimulation, but also completely new visual and fantasy qualities.

The visual-esthetic element is an important one to consider when discussing coital positions; yet it is often neglected. A woman with pendulous breasts, for example, which her husband is bothered by, will not look her best to him while above him in full light.

Health, in certain cases, may be the most important single aspect in choosing a position. In heart and circulatory ailments (such as high blood pressure or coronary conditions), or when a spouse is convalescing from a major illness or operation, "restful" positions are often recommended by the doctor in order to minimize the additional strain on the ailing spouse. There is an unavoidable exertion inherent in intercourse, even for a motionless partner. Generally speaking, the ailing or convalescing partner should assume the less active position.

Although seemingly trivial as compared with other health problems, obesity may also require special positional arrangements. Especially when the man is overweight, the female-above position will be found far more enjoyable than other arrangements. If the wife is obese (but still prefers to be below her husband), the couple will often find intercourse more comfortable when she places her legs on her husband's shoulders.

Partners whose sex organs are of disproportionate sizes may find little pleasure (and sometimes pain) in some positions. However, in most situations, a different position can be easily found that eases the difficulty and offers enjoyment.

For example, when a "large" penis is perceived as painful by an inexperienced bride, or when a long penis tends to irritate the womb neck, some rear-entry positions (e.g. side by side, or the woman lying on her stomach) may be successfully employed. This tends to prevent deep penetration. In the conventional position, the wife can also close her legs to provide an additional brake on her husband's movements. The female-above position also permits the woman to control penetration.

Conversely, if the penis is "too small" and/or the vagina "too large," positions which enable the greatest proximity of the pubic areas should be used.

As regards sex during pregnancy, the medical trend today is to permit intercourse up to very late stages of pregnancy (usually up to the last few weeks). This is, of course, provided that the wife has no tendency to habitual miscarriage and that positions assumed by the partners are those that will protect the unborn child. *It is important to avoid three things: acrobatics, too-deep penetration, and pressure on the female abdomen.* Positions in which the man's full weight rests on the woman's body and especially positions in which she lies on her stomach must be avoided. If the conventional position is preferred, the man should fully support his weight by his elbows and place his legs outside hers to avoid deep penetration.

Much can be found in marriage manuals about positions in which an unresponsive wife can be better stimulated. Most of what is said is quite true; I myself know many couples where the wife has experienced her first orgasm when she was above her husband and was, for the first time, freer to experiment with her own motions. In many cases, this has happened after years of unsatisfactory intercourse in the conventional position.

Men tending to *premature ejaculation* also often can be helped by the proper choice of position. Positions not requiring too much male activity are especially good for this purpose. For example, many men will find that the "passive" role they assume in the female-above position enables them to "last longer." This position, while allowing them sufficient stimulation by the woman's pelvic movements to keep them erect, tends to minimize friction on the sensitive tip of the penis.

As a general rule, applicable to almost all cases of common marital problems, it is advisable to select a position which allows the slower-reacting partner to be more active.

Coital positions definitely are not a cure-all for all situations and problems that are encountered in the bedroom. But even these few examples should suffice to illustrate that they can serve an important function. A sound understanding of at least a few basic positions and the situations in which they can (and often must) be employed will benefit every couple.

# 29. How Important Are Sex Positions?
### Richard Stiller, M.A.

Most of us are convinced that "our" sex ways are the only normal ones and that those of others are degenerate and perverse. People find it hard to believe that individuals can differ in their sexual behavior and still be "right" or "normal."

Take the matter of positions in sexual intercourse. Throughout much of the so-called civilized world—especially in Europe and America—it is largely assumed that the one position in which a man and his wife should have sexual intercourse is face to face, with the man above. This is usually referred to as the "conventional" or "traditional" position.

And yet in the classic cradle of western civilization, Greece and Rome, this sex position was almost unheard of if not unthinkable! It was customary, if we can believe the testimony of ancient art and culture, for the man to lie supine while the woman straddled him from above. The Roman poet Martial considered this so "normal and obvious," writes the famous sexologist Van de Velde in *Ideal Marriage,* "that he could not conceive of . . . married couples . . . in any other attitude."

As a matter of fact, the earliest known depiction of human coitus—unearthed in Iraq in 1936—portrays this position.

Even today there are many peoples, in the islands of the Pacific for one, who consider the conventional sex posture somewhat ridiculous. Anthropologists who have studied these people say that they describe the man-above approach with great humor as "the missionary position."

If one wishes to speak of a so-called "normal" coital position, one should consider the only position that is usual among mammals. Although one or two of the great apes are believed to use the conventional human position occasionally, in almost all mammals the male makes vaginal entry from the rear while the female crouches below and faces away from him. But this natural "animal" position (we are after all animals ourselves!) was used by only 11 per cent of the better educated couples interviewed by the Kinsey researchers, and fewer than 8 per cent of the less educated.

Right from the start, the Jewish and Christian sexual codes which determined our traditional sex attitudes frowned upon any sexuality in marriage which separated pleasure from procreation, or which seemed to emphasize sexual satisfaction in any way. Thus the matter of sex positions—as much as matters of frequency of coitus, masturbation, birth control, etc. —was an early concern of Jewish and Catholic authorities.

In the early days of the Catholic Church, any sex position except that of the woman prone with the man above was considered a matter for confession, and sometimes punishment. According to G. Rattray Taylor in *Sex in History,* the rear approach, which was believed to be the most pleasurable, was regarded with special horror and called for seven years' penance.

Modern Catholic interpretations have modified this view

considerably. A recently published official Catholic marriage manual, *Fundamental Marriage Counseling*, by Dr. John R. Cavanagh, lists all variations of the face-to-face position as acceptable, including that with the woman above. It even states that this is "the best position" for honeymoon relations because it "allows the woman to control the pressure being made upon the hymen. . . ." No mention is made of the rear approach.

A traditional Jewish rule on coital positions simply states that intercourse should be accomplished "in the most possible modest (sic) manner." An authoritative interpretation of this says that the position with the female above is considered improper.

Apart from the taboos that man has arbitrarily fastened on his own sex behavior, is there any real significance to one sex position as opposed to another?

The fact that most couples stick to what we call conventional face-to-face coitus with the man above seems to indicate that they find this most satisfactory. The Kinsey studies found that all the couples interviewed usually used this method, and that a majority of them used it exclusively. The only drawback to this position is that it does place the weight of the husband on the wife.

Thus a variation is sometimes helpful when the wife is pregnant and should not bear weight directly on her abdomen, or when the husband is so much larger and heavier as to constitute a serious burden for her to support.

Sometimes an illness may demand inactivity on the part of the husband. At such times the position with the wife above is recommended by some doctors. The lateral position, in which husband and wife lie side by side facing each other, is also recommended as restful and physically undemanding.

There are other medical reasons which suggest such variations in position. Among these are a too-short vagina, a too-long penis, or an exceptionally tough hymen. Almost any circumstance in which it is better for the wife to control the motion and degree of coital thrusting can be served by the wife-above position.

There are some other sexual reasons for recommending this position. Some marriage experts feel that this position helps the man suffering from premature ejaculation to delay his orgasm. It is also felt that it affords the woman greater satisfaction since she can control the movements of coitus. This position also affords greater body contact and stimulation to the female clitoris.

As far as conception is concerned, it is felt that the conventional position, with the woman remaining prone for some time after coitus, will facilitate fertilization of the egg. Some obstetricians feel that crouching in the knee-chest position right after coitus is even better.

As to the less-popular rear vaginal entry position, this is rarely recommended. Perhaps this is because it is almost impossible, in this position, for body or penile friction to be applied to the clitoris. On the other hand, this position makes possible manual manipulation of the clitoris, where this is necessary or desired.

Ancient erotic literature and art make much of the vast number of coital positions possible. But in actual fact, almost all of these are merely variations of face-to-face coitus. Some of them are so impossibly acrobatic in their requirements that it is doubtful if many ordinary couples could actually perform them.

The chief value of variations in position lies in the extra stimulation this can afford a husband and wife. A desire for variety is after all a quite common human trait.

Some marriage manual writers lay great stress on the importance of such variety. Write Jerome and Julia Rainer in *Sexual Adventure in Marriage*: ". . . Only a course of continuing practice with a variety of coital postures can bring genuine liberation from inhibited coital behavior, and the comfort of mind that is essential to free, joyful sexual adventure within marriage."

A more conservative Catholic view is expressed by Dr. Cavanagh: "Numerous positions are described in works on the art of love . . . but all of these are merely minor variations . . . and have no real advantage to offer except variety."

Perhaps most balanced is the view of pioneer sex educator and veteran marriage counselor, Dr. Walter R. Stokes, who writes in *Your Sex Life: The Newer Understanding of Married Love*: "There can be no objection to a certain amount of experimenting with posture in intercourse but it should be obvious that physical comfort, rather than acrobatic agility, is paramount."

**To sum up:** Position in sexual intercourse is only a means to an end. When that end—mutually comfortable and satisfactory coitus—is successfully achieved, it doesn't much matter what technique is used.

# 30. Secrets of Lovemaking
### Albert Abarbanel, Ph.D.

Specialists in marital problems seem to agree that there would be fewer unhappy marriages, and fewer divorces, if the average American husband knew how to make love to his wife. Many a marriage has been wrecked because of the husband's ignorance or awkwardness, and an unhappy percentage of married couples are losing half of the joy of living because the man's lovemaking technique is poor.

The man is principally to blame, of course, only because his role is usually the dominant one. If the average wife were running the show, she would probably make just as many mistakes.

If you recognize yourself in the cases given below, it is purely intentional. They are caricatures, but it is sometimes easier to see yourself in a caricature than it is in a portrait, particularly where an intimate subject such as lovemaking is concerned.

Carl G. is a rough-and-ready sort of man who dislikes art, classical music, salads, lace curtains and frills. He thinks of himself as a man's man, and smokes big, black cigars. When he kisses his wife he grabs her with all the grace of a grizzly bear, and proceeds to crush, maul, and smother her into a state of gasping submission. This approach we might call "sweeping her off her feet." Frequently she would like to sweep him out of the house.

Howard B. is avowedly masculine, too, but in a way more reminiscent of John Barrymore, with a dash of lifeguard and Viking thrown in. He may admit that art has something, and he may listen to Beethoven's *Fifth Symphony* and use a perfumed after-shaving lotion, but he is very, very masculine all the same. He thinks women are fascinating little baggages designed for his personal amusement, but not to be taken seriously.

When he kisses his wife he enfolds her condescendingly

and, maintaining a proper degree of detachment, reduces her to a state of infantile helplessness by means of his overwhelming personality. This might be called "the wonder man" approach. When the wonder of it wears off, his wife often wants to poke him in the eye to wake him out of his dream.

Ferdinand C. may be as big as a house, or as thin and willowy as a sapling, but he always manages to look helpless. It doesn't matter whether he likes art and music or not; he has trouble enough keeping up with his pipe, his slippers, the evening papers, or his spectacles.

He may be a big man in the office, but when he comes home he wants to be comforted. When Ferdinand takes his wife in his arms, he cuddles. There is no other word for it. It is cute, but unsatisfying. We might call that the "arousing the mother in her" approach. His wife eventually wishes she had married a man, instead of a perennial infant.

There are other types, of course, and special variations which men work out for covering up their own particular weaknesses, but they are all based on the husband's unwillingness or inability to grow up and be a man. He just can't approach love naturally, in the same way he would approach eating or breathing.

He has to hide himself behind a lot of phony aggressiveness or indifference or boyishness because he has never grown up. The crude and overaggressive man has been brutalized by life to a point where he has forgotten there is such a thing as softness and gentleness. The arrogant and supercilious man either hates women or is afraid of them to such an extent he has to keep even his wife at a distance. The excessively helpless and dependent man uses his softness as a defense against his feeling of inadequacy. He is afraid of love, or any other powerful emotion. His wife is not a love mate; she is a refuge to run to when the going gets rough out in the world.

Oddly enough, men of all three types may think of themselves as Don Juan, Lothario and Casanova all rolled into one handsome package. This is particularly true of the men who use the "sweeping her off her feet" and "wonder man" tactics.

They may even become quite promiscuous, but not because the fires of passion are consuming them. The real reason is that they are sexually disturbed, and they flit like butterflies from flower to flower seeking the satisfaction that always eludes them.

These men can't really be blamed for their shortcomings,

of course. They are merely the product of a confused culture where morality and nature have come to grips with each other in a battle to the death. We are learning only slowly that we cannot train our young to be s⟨ less for twenty years, and then expect them suddenly to flower into fully-functioning adults at the altar.

The marriage ceremony makes sex legal, but it is often too late. As many husbands and wives have discovered en route to the divorce court, legal sex, too, can be a shameful and a fearful thing.

What are the secrets of love? Is there some lost ecstasy, some will-o-the-wisp which leads millions of men and women yearly to invest in books about sex and marriage in the hope of finding a clue to its hiding place? There is, indeed, an ecstasy in sex and in a successful, sexually happy marriage.

Sex response is a powerful but delicate thing. It requires, first of all, a feeling of infinite leisure. There should be so much time that time has no meaning. A love session should have no beginning and no end; it should simply be. It should take place after the schedules of living have been met, if possible.

Fear, anxiety, anger, impatience—such emotions are poisonous to love. They foul the air; they shut off feeling; they create awkwardness; they reduce ecstasy to a sham. It is better for lovers to be simply close to each other, and to forget temporarily about sex, when powerful negative emotions are at work in their minds.

A man should make no rough or sudden gesture. He knows that his wife's response is usually slower than his; that her satisfaction is always poised, ready to flee or to come near. He knows that he must wait for her, that she must respond of her own desire.

A wise man soon learns the wonders of the delicate touch. He knows that the barest brush of the finger tips may be far more thrilling than a harder, rougher pressure. Kisses should be gentle, too, not devouring. Rough, frantic kisses speak of anxiety, not love.

A man who is afraid of feeling, or who is burdened with anger or hatred, cannot surrender to emotion. He must touch or kiss roughly, or indifferently, or like a child. He must make of his wife a slave, or a toy, or a mother. He may even make of her an idol; but he never looks upon her and responds to her as a woman.

For a normal loving husband, his wife is no mystery. Love is a natural thing. Sex and love come as easily as all of life's other functions.

# 31. Using Non-coital Sex Methods in Marriage

## Stephen Neiger, M.D., Ph.D.

Methods of achieving sexual arousal and satisfaction other than intercourse have traditionally been looked upon as "perversions" in the United States. Among these methods are hand-genital contacts and mouth-genital contacts, with the latter being more strongly tabooed.

In recent years, however, these practices have been gaining more general acceptance. Most writers of manuals still give only conditional approval to these practices, declaring that all methods of arousal are legitimate *provided* that they are directed towards (and end in) intercourse.

This shy approval reflects the continuing strength of our Puritan heritage and is in sharp contrast with the attitudes of many European peoples. These peoples accept manual and oral methods of intimacy up to and including orgasm as refined and pleasurable sources of marital variety.

It is interesting to note that, in spite of the taboos, the Kinsey investigators found that mouth-genital contacts played a part in the marriages of some sixty per cent of college-educated persons. The figures fell to twenty per cent for persons who had only a high school education and to eleven per cent for those who never went beyond grade school. In the decades since these figures were gotten, the acceptance of such practices has probably increased.

I believe that the time has come to stop treating hand-genital and mouth-genital practices as necessarily "second-class" methods in marriage. Instead, we should seriously consider their numerous advantages as at least occasional methods for full marital satisfaction in their own right.

One such advantage is variety. Another is that some women will respond with greater pleasure to the stimulation of external genitals than to intercourse. Further benefits of non-coital sex methods lie in the ease with which they can be used for satisfying a mate in situations where the other cannot fully involve himself or herself—either because of temporary or permanent differences in sexual desire, or for reasons of health.

They can frequently ease, and sometimes completely remove, certain marital problems. The most common marital problems are difficulties in obtaining orgasm ("frigidity") for the wife and erection difficulties on the part of the husband ("impotence"), as well as premature ejaculation.

Although such problems can be created by physical causes that must be investigated by a physician, the overwhelming majority are of psychological origin. Before (and often instead of) running to the psychologist's office and spending a considerable amount in fees to get "at the root of the problem," some experimentation with home remedies can often be quite rewarding.

Among home remedies, non-coital sex methods are perhaps the most useful of all. In what way can such practices help in common marital problems?

A great deal has been said even in the earlier literature about how a "dormant wife" can often be awakened through the use of non-coital sex methods. Such practices are frequently the key not only to eventually bringing a woman with reduced or completely inhibited orgastic ability to satisfaction, but also to "conditioning" her sexual system towards sooner or later responding with orgasm also to intercourse.

Similarly, in the various forms of vaginal spasm brought about by anxiety or fear, non-coital methods can often more easily induce a pleasurable response than intercourse. Often the fearful or inexperienced wife can be thoroughly relaxed by the use of these techniques, to the point where intercourse then becomes easy, because she genuinely desires it.

Much less is written, however, about the potential benefits of such methods for the male who has a problem. Let us start with the most frequent male problem, psychological difficulty in achieving an erection.

The achievement of an erection can be inhibited by emotional factors such as fear, guilt, or simply insufficient stimulation. To mention one very frequent example, the husband may worry about not being able to have an erection.

Often such fears result from some past experience in which he had been "unsuccessful"—a situation that will almost inevitably occur occasionally in most marriages. Some husbands will tend to take failure very seriously. Such men keep asking themselves, "Will it work this time?" "Will I be able to satisfy her, or will I fail again?"

Such watchful concentration on the mechanism of erection will create, of course, exactly the situation in which the response of erection is least likely to occur. The problem is aggravated by the knowledge that he will be unable to satisfy his wife.

Obviously, the husband who knows that he can easily satisfy his wife by non-coital methods is in a superior position. This assurance, along with the pleasure a loving husband will receive from seeing his wife respond to his skillful use of non-coital techniques, will often bring about strong erection. Perhaps it is almost needless to say that the female hand and mouth, if skillfully applied, can greatly help to accelerate this process.

Similar considerations apply in cases of premature ejaculation. Males of most mammals ejaculate within a few seconds after entry, but this does not matter because orgasm in the nonhuman mammalian female is extremely rare anyway.

On the average, men in our culture will tend to ejaculate in about two minutes after entry; but this time is usually insufficient for the achievement of female orgasm, which nowadays is desired by most American women.

This is why methods of delaying the male ejaculation are given so much consideration in marriage manuals. Practices of prolongation that are recommended range from anesthetizing ointments (useful in some cases) to diverting the male's attention from his own pleasure by such methods as the recitation of multiplication tables, etc.

But again non-coital sex methods offer a much superior alternative. If the husband, by the skillful use of non-coital methods, has brought his wife to orgasm one to several times (depending on her capacity), his own ejaculation can no longer be really "premature." Furthermore, many a wife who has been aroused with the help of non-coital practices, may be brought much more quickly to orgasm in intercourse.

Finally, premature ejaculation is frequently precipitated by fear. The confidence, however, that comes from the knowledge that the wife's satisfaction no longer depends on when the husband's ejaculation will occur is one of the best means to counteract this fear and thus relax the man sufficiently to delay ejaculation.

The point of view herein is put forward for discussion and is purposely provocative. There is no implication that non-coital sex methods are a cure-all for *all* marital difficulties, or even for *all* the cases of common sexual problems that were discussed. In a number of cases, the difficulty will be of a physical nature and eventually a physician will have to be consulted.

Even in many cases of genuine psychological difficulty, hand-genital or mouth-genital practices will not prove to be a practical remedy. Deeply ingrained guilt feelings and negative attitudes to sex may prevent one or both of the partners from obtaining pleasure in marital relations and a specialist may have to be consulted.

Especially in such situations, one or both of the partners may feel aversion or even disgust towards employing non-coital practices. Even in less extreme cases, the husband or the wife may find that, although they have given it an honest try, they still cannot respond to either non-coital stimulation or to intercourse. Such cases exist.

Nevertheless, many (even if admittedly not all) married couples may benefit considerably from wider experimentation with non-coital techniques, especially in the situations which have been discussed.

# 32. The Ways
# People Spoil Sex
## Josef E. Garai, Ph.D.

Everywhere we look—the popular press, films, television, advertising, and books—everything implies that sex is plain fun. And yet, more and more, counselors report that men and women are coming to them because they cannot have this fun; they do not enjoy sexual intercourse.

What many of these people fail to understand is that sex without total emotional commitment by the two partners may be a self-defeating, frustrating experience. Any activity resulting from a compulsive need becomes unsatisfactory because the relaxation from which the enjoyment of the emotional experience flows is disturbed.

Real love requires a sense of relaxation, release from excessive tension, and a playful, expectant attitude open to surprise and novel experience. The pleasure of the sexual act is increased by the acceptance of the partner as an independent individual and by the desire to explore the secret of his personality. Respect for the worth and dignity of the partner is basic to a relationship.

There are three kinds of sexual attitudes which spoil the normal enjoyment of intercourse: (1) the mechanical, (2) the competitive, and (3) the escapist approach. Each stems from a lack of basic trust in oneself and others.

The mechanical attitude is particularly widespread. People feel helpless because they are confronted by the dehumanized, super-automated, and bureaucratic structure of industrial society. They are deprived of creative jobs and feel themselves doomed to perform meaningless activity, unrelated to their human needs. Boredom creeps into their sexual activity, too. Men begin to feel like machines and sex becomes a mere memorized exercise, like a movement done by rote on the assembly line.

A sense of inner emptiness results. In an effort to hide the inability to respond emotionally, each partner accuses the other—or himself—of sexual inadequacy.

In their search for more fun and an authentic experience, these sex-mechanics go frantically through all the sex manuals to discover better techniques or positions, or other forms of titillation. But usually it is not the technique of the partners that is at fault. Dissatisfaction stems from their inability to remain in touch with their feelings and those of the partner. Since each partner remains in a different orbit, virtually "in isolation," there is no real "inter-course" but rather separate "apart-course."

The competitive attitude that prevails everywhere in our society also has its effects on sexual relations. People are all brought up to aim for certain standards of excellence. Having been graded in school, college, and on the job, they enter the bedroom with the same eagerness to get superior grades. But nobody knows what is a fair grading system for sexual performance.

Sex manuals frequently contribute to the confusion by stressing impossible goals, such as the achievement of orgasm by both partners at precisely the same time, or setting certain numbers of "normal frequencies" of sexual contacts per week for certain ages, or pointing to the need of women to attain a complete orgasm during each act of intercourse.

Such unrealistic and perfectionistic standards may provoke innumerable instances of psychological impotence or frigidity. Imagine the man who finds out that he is unable to provide his partner with an orgasm during each sexual encounter. Having read the sex manual, he may feel that he is inadequate, and his fear of sexual incompetence actually may weaken his ability to perform the sex act. Impotence frequently results from excessive concern with impossible standards of performance.

In reality, there are no standards of sexual performance that are valid for everybody. Frequency may vary according to the sexual energy of the particular partners, the conditions of lovemaking, and even the weather.

Sexual differences in arousal must be taken into account. Women usually take longer and remain at the peak for a longer period than men. Men attain orgasm more readily, while women find it more difficult to reach an orgasm each time because they are affected more easily by external interference or mood swings. However, under the best conditions, women may experience several orgasms during intercourse.

Reaching orgasm together is not always possible because the two partners may have fantasies, fears, insecurities, and guilt feelings which affect them differently. The sensitivity of each partner, the willingness to cooperate, the desire to please the other together with oneself, the male's readiness to wait patiently for the woman's response, the woman's assistance through vigorous pelvic muscle movements—all these are crucial elements in determining sexual responsiveness. Excessive concern with standards of sexual performance prevents the full enjoyment of the sexual act.

As an expression of the power of love, sex becomes the embodiment of zest and enjoyment. But when the competitive love of power takes over, sex is perverted into the expression of hostility and aggression.

Love simply exists without the need to prove its existence. It gives without demanding anything in return except the full acceptance of the gift of oneself. But the person who cannot really trust and love will seek to conceal this inability behind a façade of sexual superefficiency.

A man may try to prove his manliness by the compulsive pursuit of all women. For him, no woman is an individual in her own right. All he wants is sexual gratification—or rather the gratification of his sexual pride. He seeks to prove that he is irresistible and will go to any length to seduce the woman whom he selects as his target.

In his distorted mind, any woman who will resist his advances constitutes a denial of his manliness. He may even resort to rape when his attempts to prove his supermasculinity are thwarted. In reality, he is extremely insecure and not at all confident that he is really a man. Therefore, he must prove his masculinity compulsively.

The Don Juan among males is comparable to the nymphomaniac among women who must prove her femininity by enticing every male in sight. If sex is used to prove masculinity or femininity, the real enjoyment of the sex act is greatly impaired. The interest in the other person exists only insofar as he or she can be regarded as another trophy in the quest for "sexual success." The sex act itself becomes perfunctory. While the man is in bed with one body, he is thinking already of the next body to conquer, never taking time to explore the person who belongs to this body.

If a person is secure in his sexual indentification, he does not need to conquer every woman. On the contrary, he will seek to enter into a deep, secure, and prolonged relationship with the woman of his choice, since he knows that one absorbing and consuming relationship is much more meaningful than many inconsequential sexual episodes.

But the weak and insecure person may misuse sex as a means to dominate and subjugate the partner. This proof of superior power over the partner is the result of a basic feeling of inferiority, which can be dispelled only by assuming the dominant role. This may lead to the type of relationship portrayed in *Who's Afraid of Virginia Woolf?*, in which the partners attempt to tear down each other's basic self-respect and feelings of human dignity and equality.

This sadistic behavior is the exact opposite of a loving relationship which can occur only between equals. It is based on the master-slave relationship and is bound to deteriorate into a terrifying experience of constant humiliation and disappointment. Healthy sex needs two equal individuals who respect each other.

The third type of person who cannot really enjoy sex is the "escapist." Sometimes sexual adventures may be sought as a reaffirmation of one's adequacy after a severe setback in some important area of work or creativity. The businessman whose venture went bankrupt may seek to forget his failure by a series of sexual episodes or infidelity to his wife. The soldier who is being sent to the war may attempt to "live it up" in an outburst of sexual voluptuousness. But when sex is used as an escapist substitute for success in another area, it becomes a second choice only and the need for commitment and depth of experience is lacking, with subsequent loss of enjoyment.

We must conclude that the inability to enjoy sexual relation results from a lack of readiness to commit oneself to a total relationship of mutual trust and sharing with a person with whom one is in love. The sex-mechanic, the sex-escapist, and the sex-competitor are likely to miss or misinterpret the real enjoyment of the sexual act, no matter how often they go through the motions of engaging in it.

# 33. The Importance of Good Sex Hygiene

## Stephen Neiger, M.D., Ph.D.

Two people who share the physical closeness of lovemaking cannot regard body cleanliness as an entirely "personal" matter. The husband or wife who neglects such care must be prepared for health hazards, not only to himself but quite possibly also to his partner. In addition, he risks inspiring aversion rather than sexual desire. Aversion to mutual experiences because of habitual uncleanliness is a serious threat to marriage.

Sexual hygiene is not restricted only to keeping the genital region clean. Perspiration anywhere can be one of the greatest enemies of sex enjoyment. Fresh perspiration does not offend, of course—to many its smell is even a stimulant. Stale sweat, however, soon decomposes under bacterial action and, as most people know, causes body odor.

Individual preferences modify the rules, but as a rule of thumb for young marrieds, women and especially men who lead a physically vigorous life should bathe often. Dr. LeMon Clark points out that men who like an "invigorating" cold shower in the morning frequently neglect to take one *before going to bed*. If you are one of these men, you would do better to take your shower in the evening: the woman in your bed usually has a keener sense of smell than your co-workers.

Mouth hygiene is even more a factor in lovemaking, where kissing and love talk play so important a role. A mouth exuding the smell of onion or garlic is hardly ever welcome. Because bacteria quickly break down remnants of food not removed from the mouth, offensive odors develop. Furthermore, to introduce these decomposed particles on a partner's genitals during mouth-genital contact could lead to worse consequences. For this reason, as well as others, care also should be taken to have scrupulously clean hands.

Apart from infection possibilities, and even apart from esthetic sensibilities, there is also a fundamental psychological reason for cleanliness in lovemaking. Unfortunately, there is a strong association between filth and sex in many people's minds due to their upbringing. To be unhygienic during lovemaking may reinforce the belief that sex is dirty, and as a consequence, people may rob themselves of their own sense of dignity.

To approach sexual love with a clean, refreshed body is to proclaim the dignity of the act. It is one way to announce wholehearted respect for oneself and one's partner.

General measures of hygiene, however, may not even be enough. In bathing, the genital area is the one that is most often neglected. This is frequently due to an upbringing by parents who hesitate to direct the child's attention to the sex organs. They are afraid of making the child "sex-conscious" or of inducing him or her to masturbate. The result is that not only are the sex organs thought of as "dirty," they actually become so.

There are many good reasons for measures to keep the male sex organs clean. In uncircumcised men, a secretion called smegma tends to accumulate between the foreskin and the head of the penis. Unremoved smegma not only will produce an offensive smell, it can also create painful inflammation. It is also believed that habitually neglecting to remove smegma increases the risk of cancer of the penis.

Moreover, evidence links uncleanliness (including neglected smegma) in the husband with cancer of the womb neck in his wife. Therefore, regular application of soap and water on the penis (with the foreskin pulled down in the uncircumcised) is definitely called for.

The female organs require more attention, both because greater daintiness is expected of a woman and because her structures are more complex. She must be alert to secretions from the vagina, the area of the urethral opening where urine may accumulate and decompose, and the vulva, in which secretions tend to collect.

Cleaning the vulva is like cleaning the ear. Its shape and the inner folds of the small lips make it impossible to keep clean by merely washing with the flat of the hand. Reaching within the outer lips is necessary for an effective job of cleansing, no matter how much emotional resistance may be awakened in women who, as little girls, were taught that it is sinful.

There are good reasons for cleaning the vulva in this manner. The secretions here are active and the mucous membane is easily irritated. Unremoved secretions will not only decompose and become the source of unpleasant odors, they may also harden and cause painful local inflammations.

Whether or not the vagina should be cleaned, and if so, how often, is a matter of controversy. The vagina has natural protection provided by its own beneficial bacteria, which prevent the growth of harmful bacteria. Many authorities recommend *against* routine vaginal douching to avoid disturbing this self-protecting mechanism too often. But how often is "too often" frequently is left to personal judgment or, if concrete recommendations are given, they vary extremely.

In spite of differing points of view on the frequency of douching, experts tend to agree that water should never be introduced into the vagina under great pressure. No attempt should be made to hold the large lips together to swell the vaginal walls with water. This can force the water up into the womb and into the Fallopian tubes, leading to possible infection that can lead to sterility.

Bulb syringes with too large a nozzle also can close up the vagina and create a similar effect, as well as introduce the water with too much force. Nothing should be added to the water unless advised by a physician.

Special hygienic measures immediately before, or immediately after, marital intimacies are unnecessary. Standard measures of cleanliness are sufficient. Sexual cleanliness should be a part of general cleanliness. One's state of hygiene, it must be remembered, reflects one's opinion of oneself and one's mate, and of sex in general.

# 34. First Marital Intercourse

## LeMon Clark, M.D.

Some young people are still troubled over the question of just how to attempt first intercourse, and what may be done on the honeymoon.

Some fifty years ago, a doctor of divinity wrote a book purporting to solve most of the problems which might beset young people before and after marriage. His suggestion was that the bridegroom show his real love for his bride by foregoing intercourse for at least their first night together. Very romantically, he should take her in his arms and go to sleep.

Today I am very much afraid that this procedure might mortally offend the bride. She might well wonder what was the matter with her husband. Was he impotent? Did he find her so unattractive that he did not want to consummate the marriage by actual intercourse?

I am convinced from my own experience that fifty percent of all young couples who marry, at least those who have gone to college, have had intercourse before they married. The ceremony merely sanctifies that which has been going on for a greater or lesser period of time. First intercourse after marriage poses no problem to them.

But some young people are still distressed over the questions and problems that may arise, as the following letter testifies.

"Some marriage manuals," the letter says, "suggest that the bride, herself, grasp the penis gently and direct it into the vaginal opening. This will prevent the male from approaching from a wrong angle and thereby decrease any discomfort which the bride might suffer.

"But," the letter goes on, "other manuals claim that, if a virgin is asked to handle the penis, she will more than likely be shocked and frightened by the experience and thus cannot relax sufficiently for satisfactory coitus. I would appreciate your views as to which course to pursue on the wedding night."

In this day and age when petting and caressing are commonly carried on to the point of mutual exploration of the primary sexual areas of each other, the possibility of a bride being startled, let alone being frightened by the erect penis, is relatively remote. But there is the possibility, where intercourse has not been tried before marriage, that a tight, intact, fibrous hymen might cause trouble in attempting intercourse.

It is frequently helpful for the bridegroom to attempt very gentle manual stretching of the hymenal opening prior to attempting intercourse, using a lubricant such as vaseline.

If there is any real difficulty, a little anesthetic ointment might be rubbed gently around the vaginal opening. A tube of Nupercainal ointment or of Xylocaine ointment, either of which can be purchased at any good drug store, might be used. A wise bridegroom might provide some as part of his honeymoon equipment.

After fifteen or twenty minutes, intercourse might be attempted. The bride might very well guide the penis into the vaginal opening. Often in such cases the woman-above position is recommended, so that the bride can herself control the depth and intensity of penetration.

"Some marriage manuals," the letter goes on, "suggest that the male withdraw completely after rupturing the hymen, because continuing the act will aggravate the torn hymen and cause distress to the female. Others suggest that the husband continue with coitus after defloration, provided that deep penetration does not take place. The manuals emphasize the importance of the bridal night. I want to avoid any serious mistake through ignorance."

This last statement appears to me to be ridiculous. Once the penis is inserted past the hymen, deep penetration will certainly cause no more distress. Actually, complete insertion of the penis might serve to prevent any bleeding from a tear in the hymen, would bring about further muscle relaxation, and would undoubtedly ultimately be beneficial rather than harmful.

"The wife of one of my friends warned me to go easy on my bride during the honeymoon," the letter continues. "She proceeded to tell me that coitus was unpleasant to her during the honeymoon because they had it every day. Her torn hymen never did have a chance to heal. She admitted that the pain was not agonizing, but nonetheless uncomfortable.

"Since she loved her husband, she did not refuse him or even complain. I know that it would be difficult for me but I am willing to abstain for as long as possible if it means a happier sexual life later on."

The most important thing for a young couple to do is to keep open channels of communication. Sexual intercourse is not something that the young husband must do to his bride and something that she must accept and even learn to like, quite regardless of how she feels.

Human beings are in a difficult position. We have lost the guidance of pure instinct and have not yet learned completely to substitute rational, mental function in its place. But by understanding, thoughtfulness and consideration, and with openness of discussion, most of the problems which arise in marriage would be nipped before they became problems.

Here again information and judgment may help. If there is some tenderness following first intercourse, but it is not great, a small amount of the anesthetic ointments already mentioned, Nupercainal or Xylocaine, might be put around the vaginal opening and this would solve the problem.

The young man's statement of the information given him by his friend's wife reminds me of my own experience. The day before I was to be married, the husband of a somewhat older couple living across the street from my fiancée's home asked me to go for a ride. I knew he had something on his mind from the way he asked, and so I went.

In a very halting fashion he tried to tell me something about the problems of the first night. To save him embarrassment I hastened to tell him that I had been raised in a doctor's family and understood the problems fairly well. With great relief he accepted that.

Some time after we returned from our honeymoon, his wife told mine why he had done it. She said that she told him that if he did not talk to me, she would never forgive him. Her college roommate and best friend had had such a horrible experience on her wedding night that she never got over it. She lost all the love she had ever had for her husband as a result of that experience and had lived for years a tragically unhappy existence.

What a commentary upon the sexual attitudes of our time! Of course this was nearly fifty years ago. But how much real information can young people of today get as a preparation for marriage? I have said it before but it will bear repeating over and over again—one hundred, two hundred years from now, the people of that day will look back upon this time as the emotional dark ages. We have all the information to do better. We know enough to do better. But our culture, our attitudes, and our religious preconceptions have not let us.

# 35. Birth Control for Newlyweds
## Nathaniel Shafer, M.D.

When it comes to planning families, young couples find that this is a new, emancipated era. The fear of unwanted pregnancy need no longer disrupt sexual enjoyment and marital harmony.

At the turn of the century, birth control methods were primitive and most ineffectual. Withdrawal (coitus interruptus) and the post-coital douche were the most popular forms of contraception. Condoms were used, but their poor quality resulted in very limited protection. Occasionally a cloth or sponge was inserted into the upper vagina to block the mouth of the womb or cervix. But for the most part, the usual pattern was for young couples to have babies immediately after marriage.

The situation today is quite different. Most couples getting married now either regulate their fertility immediately or right after the first baby has arrived. Yet with all the new effective methods of birth control available, there is still a good deal of ignorance on the subject.

Too many couples still rely on inexpensive, inefficient, and generally unsatisfactory methods. There are groundless fears that certain methods will lead to cancer and other horrible diseases. There are women who borrow their friends' contraceptive pills and use them incorrectly without medical supervision.

There are women who rely on the rhythm method, failing to realize that it is quite possible to conceive during the so-called "safe" period. And some persons even use Saran Wrap instead of a condom.

There is no ideal contraceptive method. Each has its advantages and disadvantages, and the method chosen by any one couple will depend on many factors such as educational level, religious views, opinion of family and friends, doctor's attitude, social and cultural mores, cost, availability of other methods, and personal taste. But there is no doubt that for every married couple so desiring one, there is a contraceptive method that can meet their needs.

Perhaps the most talked about, if not the most widely used, contraceptive method is the new pill. The birth control pill, for the first time, offers couples a contraceptive that is virtually one hundred per cent effective. This method involves no special precautions or duties at the time of intercourse and, for this reason, has been accepted by many couples who might object to some of the other methods.

The tablets, which are begun on the fifth day of the menstrual cycle, are taken once a day for twenty consecutive days. Then the woman stops taking the pills for five days, so as to have a normal menstrual cycle. She then resumes taking them. It still isn't precisely understood how the pills work, but they somehow seem to interfere with pituitary function, producing a state which is similar to pregnancy and which, therefore, precludes further conception.

For some women it is thought that the pills do not become effective until the second month of their use. A failure to realize this is a common cause of pregnancy in women taking oral contraception without a doctor's supervision. It is thus desirable for a future bride to visit her physician and get started on oral contraception one month before her marriage date to assure a honeymoon free from all fear of pregnancy.

Birth control pills can also be used to regulate the period. So if they are taken throughout the honeymoon, the menstrual period will be postponed.

There are several popular doubts about birth control pills. However, there is no evidence to show that there is an increased incidence of cancer associated with this form of contraception, nor has it been established that such pills cause circulatory problems. The most we can say is that to date the pills have caused only minor side effects, but that not enough time has gone by to be absolutely certain about their long-range effects.

One of the disadvantages of oral contraception is the fact that the female must be completely faithful in following her instructions. If she forgets to take the pill on two consecutive days, there is a definite risk of pregnancy. And occasionally there are minor side effects such as nausea and weight gain.

The advantages of oral contraception for young couples are quite significant. Aside from its ease and reliability, most important for newlyweds is the fact it is one of only two methods that make it possible for the couple to be entirely spontaneous in their sex life while maintaining complete protection against unwanted pregnancy. The pills also regulate the menstrual period, eliminating painful or irregular menstruation.

The other contraceptive method permitting complete sexual spontaneity is the intrauterine device inserted in the womb by a gynecologist. But such devices have been found to have undesirable side effects when inserted in women who have never had children. Thus they are not recommended for newlyweds, and doctors generally will not approve their use until the couple has had their first baby.

A tried-and-true contraceptive device in use now for at least half a century without any evidence of ill effects is the vaginal diaphragm. When used with a spermicidal jelly, this method is almost one hundred per cent effective. One major objection, from the point of view of newlyweds, is the need to insert it just prior to intercourse.

A physician should decide on the proper size and correct type of diaphragm, and he should instruct the patient on how to insert it. The device is usually inserted just prior to intercourse and removed the following morning. It should never be removed, however, until at least six hours after coitus, and preferably longer.

Routine examinations should be periodically performed by a doctor to make sure the diaphragm fits properly. This is especially important after pregnancy, when there may have developed a change in the shape of the vaginal wall. Also, newlyweds should have a checkup after their honeymoon, since repeated coitus may have enlarged the virginal vagina.

Condoms—sheaths of fine rubber that fit over the erect penis—are one of the most widely used and effective birth control devices available today. Sometimes they are used in conjunction with a lubricating jelly when the female vagina is dry. Some have suggested that the condom be checked for holes and leaks before use, and it may be advisable for the female to insert a spermicide before intercourse as an added precaution.

It is important that the condom be applied before genital contact takes place; otherwise a few drops of semen, sufficient to impregnate the female, may escape. Care must be exercised when removing the penis with the condom, so that no semen will spill into the vagina.

The condom is a simple, efficient, and relatively inexpensive contraceptive device. One of its major drawbacks, however, is the possibility of its leaking or bursting. Some women find it irritating, and some men claim that it impairs sensations and interferes with pleasure.

Perhaps the oldest form of birth control, coitus interruptus, involves withdrawal of the penis just before ejaculation. Although this method requires no special preparation and places no financial demands on its practitioners, it does have disadvantages.

For one thing, sperm may be present in the erect penis even before ejaculation. Also, if the husband finds it difficult to control ejaculation, coitus interruptus may cause anxiety or nervous strain in one or both partners. This method is neither reliable nor emotionally satisfying.

The only form of birth control permitted by the Catholic Church, the rhythm method, requires that a couple abstain from intercourse during certain days of the menstrual cycle. Fertilization can occur only if the sperm meets the ovum or egg, so the danger of pregnancy exists just during the time of ovulation—when the egg is discharged from the ovary.

Couples using the rhythm method must avoid coitus during the five days before and the two days after the probable day of ovulation. This is because the ovum can be fertilized for some twelve to twenty-four hours after it has been shed, and the sperm may remain alive in the female tract for up to five days, although it probably loses its fertilizing capacity in half that time.

The rhythm method can succeed, however, only if the time of ovulation can be accurately determined. In women with regular menstrual cycles, ovulation usually occurs from twelve to sixteen days before the next menstrual period. Temperature readings are helpful in achieving a more precise estimate of the time of ovulation.

This method of contraception, which demands that coitus be suspended for a week during every menstrual cycle, requires a high degree of motivation, especially for newlyweds. But even strong motivation is no guarantee of success, since the method has inherent uncertainties. For the young couple in particular, the rhythm method is not a foolproof method of family planning.

Spermicidal preparations in the form of jellies, creams, gels, foam tablets, and aerosol foams are another type of contraception. The newer aerosol foams, packaged under pressure in a rigid container and inserted into the vagina with an applicator, are more effective than some of the older vaginal foams. Once the foam is applied, coitus may occur any time within the hour. These vaginal foams, however, are not as effective as the other contracepive devices.

To sum up: There are many kinds of birth control methods available to newlyweds and young couples. The prospective bride and groom should give serious thought to their family planning needs and should discuss these frankly. They should also consult a physician. They can then take the necessary steps to assure, through intelligent planning, a harmonious marital sexual adjustment.


# 36. Keeping Sex Alive in Marriage
## Robert A. Harper, Ph.D.


Many of the people who come to see me for marriage counseling or psychotherapy have been married ten or more years. A very common problem among the great variety of difficulties they bring to me is a sharp decline in both the frequency of sex relations in their marriages and intensity of enjoyment.

The case of the R.'s is fairly typical. In this instance it was the wife with whom I had the first interview.

**Mrs. R.:** Although I am only thirty-two and my husband only thirty-five, you'd think we were eighty. It is not at all unusual for two or three weeks to go by without any sex at all. Sometimes it is longer.

**Counselor:** What do you and your husband do together that is fun?

**Mrs. R.:** Fun? What do you mean "fun"?

**C.:** You have answered my question. Apparently you do very little if anything that you consider real enjoyment, exhilaration, excitement, *active* pleasure. Please notice my emphasis on *active*.

**Mrs. R.:** Well, we take the children to the zoo or the museum once in a while. And on a nice Sunday we take rides in the country.

**C.:** Sounds as if such things might be mild fun for the kiddies, but is it really active enjoyment for you and your husband? Do you and he have fun in these or other ways?

**Mrs. R.:** Well, no. These things are a kind of responsibility, but we've got to do some things for the children. But he and I practically never even *try* to have fun doing anything without them.

**C.:** Don't misunderstand me. I think it's fine you do these things with the children, and I suspect you might do even more imaginative things to help them to have fun. But fun for them is no substitute for fun for the two of you as a couple.

Mrs. R. and I went on to explore what might be possibilities for increasing her and her husband's enjoyment of each other. My talks with her were, of course, supplemented by conferences with her husband, in the course of which I discovered his pleasures, interests and needs.

But the point I want to make is that Mr. and Mrs. R. were really doing nothing together that was actively enjoyable to them. They found each other's company totally unstimulating —sexually and nonsexually. They in this way were unfortunately not very different from many "settled down" middle-class and middle-aged American couples.

Let me pause at this point to state that there can be a great variety of causes of lack of sexual enjoyment in marriage. Some couples never achieve sexual satisfaction either because of specific sexual malconditioning before marriage of husband, wife, or both, or because of lack of love and compatibility between husband and wife.

But where considerable sex interest and satisfaction once existed in the marriage, I have found two outstanding causes of great decline in such interest and satisfaction. The first we have just brought out and will discuss at great length in a moment: general lack of enjoyment of life *as a couple*. The second is related to the first, and it is the development of a monotonous routine in lovemaking itself.

*The very nature of life is growth and change. To the degree that anything—a marriage relationship or anything else —gets into a changeless, ungrowing rut, to that degree it loses vitality.*

It is amazing to me how so many couples settle into "an easy routine" in both the sexual and nonsexual aspects of their marriage. Anything that is familiar in all its details, easily automatic in procedure, and routine in its performance is no longer challenging, interesting, alive. Many hundreds of men and women have described their sex life to me as an invariable step by step regimen. Many couples come to do "sex by the numbers," from the same dull opening gambit on through to the mechanical routine, dropping off to sleep.

It is often the couples who find sexual life dull that are like the R.'s as far as general enjoyment in marriage is concerned. What can a couple who has found life boring do about it? Sometimes the husband and wife can revive activities that they found enjoyable earlier in marriage. If they used to like to walk in the woods, bowl, play tennis, read plays by the fireside, dance, join discussion groups, ride ferris wheels, or shoot rabbits together (or whatever) and dropped these activities "because of the pressure of other duties," such fun can sometimes be recaptured.

Often, though, old fun cannot be recaptured. Drinking beer out of a can together on the porch swing just does not have the thrill it did a dozen years ago during courtship. The couple must use their imagination to discover some new and perhaps more mature worlds of fun. New activities must be tried. New paths must be explored. New interests and new people must be approached.

I have worked with many couples on the problem of learning to like and enjoy themselves again, and I can say definitely that it works, providing they get started and *persist* in their pursuits of new enjoyments. Some have too much inertia to take the first steps. Some get too easily discouraged at not being all aglow from one or two feeble efforts. But those who carry on for a while soon find life together can still be a lot of fun.

Once life in general for a couple becomes enjoyable again, sex, too, revives. Although it should be obvious that sex interest is generally tied up with interest in the whole person, couples are often surprised that having fun in other ways helps to renew their sexual enjoyment.

In addition, however, the same imagination and adventurous explorations that apply to other life activities can be applied to sexual relations. What these will be must be worked out within the particular marriage. But one general suggestion which has proved helpful to many couples may seem too obvious to state and yet is quite apparently often overlooked. I refer to allowing *time* for making love.

As silly as it sounds, many couples seem to be surprised to find that they either ignore each other sexually or follow out some uninteresting routine. This is because they never leave any time in the day or night to pay attention to each other in a casual, relaxed, unhurried way.

Another general recommendation I make for a rejuvenated sex life in marriage will also seem absurdly unsophisticated to some people: *throw out the twin beds and sleep together in a double bed*. Being physically close together in bed greatly improves the satistical probabilities of getting sexually close together. Many a love impulse was lost, I suspect, by the necessity of a journey, however short, to fulfill it.

What, in summary then, can be said about keeping sex

alive (or bringing it back to life) in marriage? One suggestion is the application of imagination and creativity and persistence in the couple's learning to enjoy each other again (or at last) in a variety of general life activities.

A second suggestion is specific development of imaginative and varied approaches to sexual intercourse. The minimum beginnings for a rejuvenation of a husband's and wife's sexual interest and activity is to allow time reguarly for casual, relaxed, and unhurried sex relations. They should place themselves regularly in a situation (namely a double bed) where sexual impulses can be most readily fulfilled.

While some couples have much more complicated and difficult causes of sexual maladjustment or inactivity than the foregoing, there are many who would find these relatively simple suggestions all they need to make sex really fun again in their marriages.

# IV.

# PROBLEMS THAT INHIBIT SEXUAL FULFILLMENT

# 37. Fantasies in the Marriage Bed

## John B. Oman, D.D.

". . . And he ought to look just like Dr. . . . . !"

Something about the way my mother and the neighbor lady were laughing, and the fact that I was sent out to play, as I always was when adult conversation began to get interesting, made this fragment of a sentence remain intact in my subconscious until many years later when I was studying applied psychology.

I had known intuitively that my mother was not telling the whole truth when I had asked her afterwards about why the neighbors' new baby should look like Dr. So-and-so. Her carefully phrased, "Why, because the doctor is a nice-looking man," didn't fool me for a minute. Any child quickly learns to recognize the tone of voice that means his parents think he is Too Young To Know!

Now, after many years as a marriage counselor, I have come to use "Doctor X" as my own label for a type of sexual fantasizing that exists almost universally, but, when it advances to a certain degree, can lead to overwhelming and destructive urges.

I am referring, of course, to the "phantom lover" who can aggravate neurotic tendencies and who can wreck a sex life that has already started to veer off the track.

Who is the phantom lover?

Sometimes he is as vague as the "dream man" or "dream girl" every normal person secretly sketches as a mental image of the perfect, hoped-for mate. It can be a mop-topped singer being screamed and sighed over by teen-age girls. It can be the foldout picture in *Playboy*. Or maybe it appears on the movie screen, with every middle-aged woman in the audience mentally elbowing the feminine star out of the love scenes and wrapping herself in her negligée and in the hero's arms.

For that long-ago neighbor, it was her doctor.

When our neighbor conceived, it was only technically with her husband. Behind her closed eyelids, she willed the transformation of her plain and plodding husband into the all-wise and authoritative young Doctor X. Hardly the sort of adultery that could be grounds for divorce, and yet this type of transference has ended many a marriage.

While there are harmless fantasies, daydreams that help speed one through monotonous tasks, there is a distinct borderline between this and the state where the person is no longer consciously aware of the difference between fact and fantasy.

Psychiatrists define this stage as being "when the child in us convinces the adult in us that the fantasies of the child are the facts of the adult." What it means, in a life situation, is that a woman who starts out merely to admire a movie star, for example, then to imagine what it would be like to have him make love to her, may finally be unable to have sexual relations with her husband unless she visualizes him as the movie star.

The tragic final step in this may be that the transference gets weaker—that is, she can't arrange the mental transformation of her husband into the star any longer, or herself into the feminine lead opposite the star. When this happens, she will seek a stronger bond of transference—in other words, another man. This time a touchable, flesh-and-blood man.

Fantasizing is common in childhood, especially for lonely, only children. A child too isolated from other children his own age many fantasize a playmate. Often this playmate is so real to him that it is easily recalled, by name and characteristics, in later life.

Childish daydreaming which extends into adult life also includes fantasizing about career attainments ("I'll be the world's best fireman, baseball player, astronaut, etc.") with all the applause and fringe benefits. This is, of course, not only harmless, but probably beneficial in shaping a life—as long as it does not become a substitute for the real thing or does not make the individual too unhappy with the actual attainments he is capable of.

The key word is *substitute*. Fantasy must never be an enduring substitute for facts.

As in the case of the lonely, bored child, fantasizing is an indication that life as it really exists is not satisfactory. Perhaps it is not entirely satisfactory; perhaps it is not satisfactory at all.

When fantasizing is sexual, it is an indication of inadequacy or some lack of adjustment. A certain amount of fantasizing is almost automatic: a man meeting an attractive woman for the first time or even seeing one pass him on the street instinctively may fantasize for a moment on what a sexual experience with her would be like. But when fantasizing crosses the borderline of fact in the person's mind, there is trouble ahead.

Thelma V. could only attain orgasm if, instead of her healthy, clean-cut Mr. Nice Guy husband, she imagined herself being raped by a burly, unshaven, uncouth Skid Row bum.

Burt S. liked to have intercourse with the lights off, because then his mousy little wife could be imagined as a teasing, tantalizing, vibrant temptress. Interestingly enough, he always endowed the fantasy female with some conspicuous feature such as flaming red hair or a large mole on the chin.

Dorothy J. could never reach orgasm, but she daydreamed constantly of the men who could make this possible for her. Although differing from each other and from her husband, each had that certain something, that indefinable appeal and mastery that could work the alchemy of sex.

These three people have followed fantasy into a dead-end street: Thelma can't resolve the conflict of her childhood training, that sex is dirty and disgusting, with her realization that sex is enjoyable and good, so she fantasizes that she is being raped. Burt S. is struggling with a problem of impotency. Dorothy J. is an almost classic case of frigidity.

All three, if they are to be happy, must learn that a phantom lover can destroy a marriage.

Daydreaming, imagining, fantasizing—these mental holidays can refresh and inspire, but only if the line is kept carefully and steadily drawn between what is fact and what is fantasy, and only if fantasy is never allowed to replace real values, real experiences, real living.

# 38. When the Bride Is Not a Virgin

## Helen K. Branson, M.A.

"I just found out last night that my fiancée is not a virgin!" The young man before me was earnest. "Now that I know this, do you think that we should marry? Will I ever be able to trust her?"

I knew the young man well, for he was a member of a pre-marital counseling group sponsored by my husband and me at our church. I knew, too, that this couple shared many common interests and similar points of view. I also had learned through earlier private counseling that his proposed bride had gone through a period of sexual experimentation.

Could this young man trust his bride-to-be? Together we talked of his feelings about the matter. Would he have rather found out that she was not a virgin on his wedding night? Was not her telling him a sign that she trusted him? In view of her many assets, the young man decided, in conference with the counselor and his fiancée, that he could ignore her early sex experience and that their marriage could be mutually trustworthy.

By now they have been married for ten years, have three very fine children, and have built a strong and stable home.

This is not to say, of course, that virginity is not an advantage in many instances. If this girl had not been forced by her own personal qualities to learn about sex from experimentation, her finance would not have doubted her in the first place. But it does illustrate that good marriages can be built on firm grounds even when there is something in the past—sexual or otherwise—that needs to be discussed and thought through ahead of time.

Some may say that this girl is the exception to the rule, and that once a girl begins sexual relations, she loses her inhibitions in this regard. Many boys seem to have this point of view. This, however, is not a sound assumption. It involves, in my opinion, a male error in the understanding of the female point of view.

The vast majority of girls who have sex relations before marriage are not promiscuous and uninhibited. Most of them have a strong emotional attachment for the person with whom they share sexual intimacy—even though this "attachment" may be a temporary one. The fact that a woman has had sex experiences before marriage does not mean that she will not be faithful to her husband when married.

Whether the bride-to-be should have told her fiancé about her past sexual experience is another matter. Most counselors feel that it is by no means wise to do so.

In spite of the fact that our double standard of sex—which says that sex before marriage is all right for men but not for women—is weakening, it still has a strong hold on most men. A great many of them, no matter how sexually liberated they feel themselves to be, still can't accept the fact that their wives have had sexual experiences while unmarried.

Often when an engaged woman or a wife confesses to past experience, she does it out of a sense of guilt. If she does feel the need for confession, she should seek out a counselor to discuss her problems with. She should not burden her husband with them.

People must be accepted as they are without too deep a prying into their past. If they seem suited as a partner at a particular time, past experiences should not change this.

However, there is no doubt—our society being what it is —that certain problems may be created when the bride is not a virgin which may require a special adjustment.

The wise husband who knows that his bride is a virgin recognizes that sex may be new to her, and that she may require considerable emotional reassurance as their sexual life grows.

If his bride is not a virgin, on the other hand, he may fear that she has enjoyed sexual relations more with some other partner and is making comparisons. Some men may feel that they may be less adequate physically than the other partners and thus do not make as adequate lovers.

What these men need to realize is that the satisfaction which the wife receives from sex relations is based far more on *mutual affection* than it is on *physical* factors and techniques.

The wife who has had sex relations with others before marriage is frequently afraid to be sexually aggressive for fear her husband will consider this as an indication that she is not readily satisfied by his lovemaking. For this reason, the husband should never hesitate to encourage her.

He should let her know that her initiation of sexual relations is not only acceptable to him, but from time to time enhances his feelings of security. This, of course, lets him know that she is not merely submitting to his desires, but that she appreciates them enough to seek his physical attentions.

It is not so often demanded that the husband be a virgin. In fact, many women have the idea that unless a man has had some sexual experiences before marriage, he may be clumsy or crude in sex relations.

This belief also is not necessarily true. The husband may go through a learning period in sex just as she does. With her cooperation, he can learn in a very short time the things that supposedly "just come naturally."

Much worry over the "first night" is needless. Experienced or not, no person's sexual approach exactly matches that of another, and the following of natural impulses without inhibition usually results in adequate adjustment in a short time.

As the ten-year experience of the couple I have described shows, lack of virginity at marriage need not prevent a stable, happy marriage. If it appears likely that it might, the couple should postpone marriage until they can find a way of truly accepting each other completely as they are.

# 39. Sex as a Trap
## William Zehv, M.S.

Marriage counselors often treat cases of husbands and wives who perceive the sex relationship as a trap. These individuals have the distorted notion that to submit sexually is a sign of weakness.

Mr. and Mrs. I. were in for marriage counseling. Mrs. I. complained that her husband was frigid, physically and emotionally: he was stingy with affection, he lacked warmth, he initiated sex relations infrequently.

Mr. I., in talking about himself, indicated that even as a boy, to defend himself, he had to control his emotions or else others would take advantage of him. He said that soon after the wedding he realized that, unless he learned to control his sexual needs, he couldn't control the marriage situation. If he initiated sex relations more frequently, as he really would like to, he explained, "my wife will have me where she wants me."

Mr. I. contended that *all* women take advantage of men by virtue of their sex, which of course is not true at all. Unfortunately he had never learned how to give and receive affection on equal terms.

Our society is such that while we learn to be competitive, we must also learn to be cooperative, particularly in the marriage relationship, each spouse recognizing that there is a need to depend one upon the other for physical and emotional security. If a husband and wife cannot depend upon each other, whom can they depend on?

Actually, two distorted notions bothered Mr. I. First, he had the idea that frequent intercourse would sap him of his physical strength, which is of course nonsense for persons in normal health.

Secondly, Mr. I, was fighting not to admit to himself that he did have a need to depend on his wife, not only for sex, but as a general partner in a cooperative effort, which marriage is. He thought that dependence on a wife was a sign of masculine weakness, whereas actually it is normal and often a sign of character strength.

There are many myths about women using their sexual allurement to trap men. Circe was an enchantress who lured men and turned them into swine. Lorelei was a beautiful maiden who sat on a rock in the Rhine River and by her beauty and singing lured sailors to shipwreck on the reefs. Samson was infatuated with Delilah, who betrayed him.

There have always been stories of female spies using their sex to trap government and military leaders. Recently there have been articles detailing the use of women using sex to ferret out business secrets. Currently there is a profusion of novels and TV films showing how women trap their men or make fools of them.

I have had many husbands refer to such stories to rationalize their fear of the sex relationship. Unfortunately, too many men take these myths and stories too seriously. There is a significant difference between a single incident and the usual behavior of men and women.

There are also women who fear sex as a trap. In my clinical experience as a marriage counselor, I have found that there are many wives who conceive the sex relationship as a form of entrapment.

Mrs. C. was in for marriage counseling. She had many complaints: she and her husband quarreled a good deal, they disagreed on child discipline, they quibbled over finances, but mainly Mrs. C. objected to her husband's demand for more frequent sex relations.

It seemed that Mrs. C. had a need to limit the conjugal act to about once per month. She said, "Otherwise, I'm trapped. My husband will have me just where he wants me. He'll think he possesses me. I don't want to depend on anyone."

Mrs. C. was influenced by her mother, who was an extreme champion of female equality. Just as soon as her second child was old enough for school, Mrs. C. obtained a job, to which her husband objected because he earned a substantial salary. But Mrs. C. insisted on contributing a portion of her pay for household expenses.

Of course, in both cases, sex was only a symptom of disturbances elsewhere. These individuals suffered from inner feelings of insecurity and a fear of being dominated. Such fears spill over into other areas of interpersonal relations and these individuals will very often quibble and be stubborn as a false geture of strength and independence.

Mr. and Mrs. W. came for marriage counseling because after almost twenty years of marriage and two teen-age children, they were completely estranged and on the verge of divorce. Ever since they were married, Mrs. W. was stingy with affection and Mr. W. was miserly with money. The wife used sex to manipulate her husband and he used money to manipulate her. Both considered sex relations as a form of entrapment.

Mrs. W. made it plain that she submitted sexually as a favor which she hoped her husband would appreciate by giving in to her demands for money, which, by the way, he could afford. Nevertheless, he resented his wife's attitude and for years initiated coitus infrequently. Mr. W., in supporting his wife, felt that she was obligated to submit sexually. Of course, both husband and wife had neurotic and distorted notions about interpersonal relations.

Individuals who fear sex as a form of entrapment are usually afraid of their own impulses. Mr. I. feared that if he gave in to his natural need to depend on his wife, he might become too dependent on her, which clashed with his notions of masculine strength. He had to learn that a man can be masculine and still trust and depend on others. No person can afford to isolate himself emotionally because affection and warmth are deep human needs and can only be obtained through emotional involvement.

Mrs. C. feared that if she gave in to her sexual impulses, she might become "lustful." But sex is more than physical contact. It includes affection, warmth, sympathy. A woman can achieve self-realization and independence as a person, can have strong sex drives, and still be warm and sympathetic. Her fierce demand for independence was a cloak to cover up the fact that she never learned how to handle an intimate relationship such as exists between a husband and wife.

Mr. and Mrs. W. used sex as a means to dominate the marriage relationship. They had to learn that in all interpersonal relationships, but particularly in marriage, adjustment means compromise, being flexible, respecting the rights and privileges of the other.

Men and women are most vulnerable in the sex relationship because it is the most intimate human experience. Each one feels that he is giving of himself physically and emotionally as a symbol of love, as a gesture of surrender to the psychological experience of intimacy. The relationship is fragile, yet pregnant with feelings that momentarily come to the surface out of the depths of the individual. No wonder each partner feels psychologically naked and vulnerable, fearing that such surrender might be interpreted as a weakness.

But men and women hunger for such experiences and as a rule do not take advantage of the situation but gather strength from it. Nevertheless, it is a calculated risk that each individual must take, for it is a path that leads to emotional security and to marital serenity.

# 40. The Drinking Husband and the Frigid Wife

## Charles F. Mayer, Ph.D., J.D.

In the practice of marriage counseling, it is often quite difficult to determine which came first, the proverbial chicken or the egg.

The wife sometimes is firmly convinced that the conflict stems solely from one or more of her husband's faults. After a while, even the husband begins to believe that his wife's complaints are thoroughly justified.

This appeared to be the situation when Mr. and Mrs. George Harper (that's not their real name) came to my office.

George and his wife, Sandra, had been referred to me by

their physician. Actually, he did not refer them for marriage counseling; he really referred them to me to see whether I could help George with his drinking problem.

During my initial interview with the Harpers, Sandra appeared to be concerned almost exclusively with George's drinking, which she was sure labeled him an alcoholic. Moreover, she had not only won the referring physician over to that viewpoint, but she had even persuaded George to believe that he was an alcoholic.

But at the first interview it soon became very evident that George was far from having even approached alcoholism.

As we went along, in individual sessions and in joint consultations, both George and Sandra realized that the drinking problem was very likely only a symptom of more deep-rooted personality problems, rather than the basic problem itself.

When the Harpers were first married, George was an officer in the Air Force. Later, he became a civilian test pilot. Both of these fields were quite glamorous, and his ego had plenty of opportunity to expand. But after an accident he went into his present occupation—building and general real estate.

Although this proved quite lucrative, it apparently never furnished the satisfactions to his ego that he seemed to need. As he put it, before he went into his present business, he felt superior to his wife; now he is beset with many doubtful moments as to his adequacy and competence. Besides, his wife looks down upon the people he now has to associate with.

In subsequent interviews, it appeared that the marriage had deteriorated in various other aspects. For one thing, they had very poor communications; in fact, they were unable to discuss any matter at all without getting into an argument. Besides, Sandra had always been quite disappointed that they had not been able to have children.

And then it became clear to me that the real crux of their problems was a sex maladjustment—Sandra was frigid. And her inability to have children had indirectly caused it!

How had Sandra become frigid?

Very simple.

Although she was a well-educated and quite intelligent woman, she had erroneously clung to an incorrect interpretation of the tenets of the church in which she had been reared. She firmly believed that sex relations were for one purpose and one purpose only—for the purpose of procreation. Sex was not to be enjoyed. That would be sinful.

A year after they were married, her doctor had informed her that she could never bear children. If she and her husband continued to engage in sex relations merely for their personal pleasure, she felt they would certainly be dreadful sinners and would be forever consigned to perdition in the hereafter.

Sandra never asked her priest whether this was true or not. She merely condemned herself and her husband to seventeen years of sex austerity. During that time, she became gradually less and less responsive. Ultimately, she hardly ever permitted George to come close to her. Even when she did, it was quite evident that she did so reluctantly.

However, Sandra's ideas about marital sex relations were based on an incorrect interpretation of Catholic thinking, namely that the sole purpose of sex in marriage is to produce children. In fact, sex in marriage is seen by Catholics as an expression of love and unity between husband and wife as well as a means of procreation.

Writing in *Catholics, Marriage, and Contraception,* a book officially approved by Roman Catholic officials, Dr. John Marshall describes as a "misunderstanding" the sex-for-children-only interpretation. He states: "The unique and specific experience of . . . love within marriage is coitus. . . . In unvarnished terms marriage is not just an arrangement for the begetting of children. . . ."

The effect of Sandra's "frigidity" became more and more devastating to George's ego. Being of a somewhat dependent nature anyway, it was very easy for him to feel that Sandra had let him down—socially, personally, and sexually. That is most likely when his occasional drinking bouts occurred. He needed to restore his self-confidence.

George's family background, of course, had a great deal to do with how he reacted to his wife's remoteness. In talking about his childhood, George readily launched into a report of his father's strictness. George had quite often clashed with his father about drinking, church attendance, etc. "At first," he said, "the mere fact that I differed with him bothered me. But I think now you have to make your own decisions." Thus it was that he grew up expecting the husband to be the head of the family.

When I inquired how his wife fitted into this picture, he said, "She grew up under quite opposite circumstances. Her father was a mild man, dominated by his wife." George thought that his own background of male dominance had caused part of the trouble in their marriage. As an example, he cited the last argument they had had a few days ago. He wanted to visit his father's home in south Texas, but Sandra refused to go. "So," he quipped, "we compromised. We didn't go."

By this time, this outwardly successful businessman was confessing to a deep sense of inferiority which had been produced by his domineering father's criticism. He now realized why his wife's refusal to go along on the trip had become such an important issue to him. I, of course, encouraged this kind of introspection as a wise investment for the future.

Temperament tests given to both of them indicated that, whereas George was quite composed, Sandra was very nervous. Sandra was fairly gay-hearted, but George had a tendency to be depressed more frequently. At least at home, Sandra was overly active, but George was much more quiet, with a preference to be the "pipe and slippers" man. Both of them were very low in natural cordiality and in sympathetic qualities; also, they were both subjective rather than objective. Neither one of them was submissive—they were both overly aggressive, and this led to a constant contest for dominance. Sandra had a tendency to be quite critical, but George was more appreciative. Both of them, however, were extremely rigid and inflexible, to the extent that each felt "my way is the only right way."

I, of course, gave them specific instructions for modifying or eliminating some of the troublesome qualities which the tests disclosed. But most important of all, both were given a better understanding of sex, some of it so basic they should have known it when they were first married. I also had Sandra read many Catholic authors who emphasized over and over that "sex is not only a joining of the bodies, but of the mind, the soul and the spirit as well."

Apparently, they obtained excellent results from what they had learned. During the last interview with George, he reported a closer and more comfortable feeling with his wife, and he was also proud of the fact that he had had no great desire or compulsion to drink during the past few weeks.

The greatest improvement he noted, however, was in the sex area. Heretofore, he had always taken the initiative and his wife submitted quite reluctantly. But recently, she had been making all the overtures, and that pleased him immensely. For some time before that, he had even begun to have doubts as to his potency, but now he was acquiring much more self-confidence than he had ever had before.

When Sandra showed up, she was radiant. She felt that they had made great progress. In fact, she reported that they had even had what she called a "sex orgy," where she refused to let him out of bed for hours at a time. She sheepishly said,

"Dr. Mayer, I don't know what has come over me. After I talked to you, and you showed me how wrong I was on some of my guilt feelings about sex due to my incorrect interpretation of Catholic teachings, I have felt such strong sex desire for my husband that actually I have hardly been able to leave him alone for the past week."

Remember, this was a woman who thought she was "frigid" for seventeen years; yet here she was now enjoying sex, to her surprise.

And somehow or other, the resulting feeling of togetherness had opened up a line of communication about other areas of mutual interest where they could now talk to each other in an atmosphere of friendliness and understanding. They had even learned to disagree agreeably, and to look at more things in a humorous vein.

And, because George was now less tense, he did not seem to require as much drinking as he did before. At any rate, what little drinking he did did not bother Sandra as it once would have.

I agree that this may sound like a miracle, but it happens quite frequently, not only for so-called "frigid" women, but also for so-called "impotent" men—providing that they avail themselves of competent professional help in order to remove the emotional blocks which impede their ability to become sexually compatible.

# 41. Sexual Inhibition as Self-Punishment
## William Zehv, M.S.

As a professional marriage counselor, I see husbands and wives who come to me with all sorts of difficulties, including sex problems. Here I want to deal with a specific type of sex problem: the use of sexual inhibitions as self-punishment.

Mrs. B. was referred to me by her physician and she came out of desperation: she was extremely nervous, ready to jump out of her skin. She was twenty-five, married three years, and she had a child one year of age; her husband, twenty-eight, was a fireman. She was afraid that she was destroying her marriage.

Beginning with her wedding night, she found the sex act abhorrent and distasteful. Her husband was gentle and considerate. On the honeymoon, she complained that coitus was painful. Mr. B. was understanding. Later she would complain of being tired, of having headaches, of not being in the mood. Her husband respected her feelings.

But after six months of marriage, her husband was no longer understanding or considerate. He was angry and sexually frustrated. Mrs. B. then changed her tactics. She no longer rejected her husband. She yielded every time he initiated sexual intercourse. But she would become rigid and immobile. She simply couldn't relax sufficiently and abandon herself to the sexual experience.

After a while, her husband complained of her lack of sexual response. By now they were having intercourse no more than once or twice a month. In addition, they were now quarreling on the slightest pretext. As she said, they would quarrel, and for the life of her she couldn't tell how it began and what it was about.

In my office, she wept, she fidgeted, she smoked incessantly. With a little gentle urging, she talked about her marriage, her growing up. Several times she said that she wished her husband would be mean to her and beat her; then she wouldn't feel so bad. She blamed herself, saying she had a good marriage, why did she have to spoil it?

After several hours of verbal meandering and self-recrimination, she told how at age nineteen she committed her cardinal sin. She had moved away from her parents to a large city and shared an apartment with two sophisticated young women. She dated a great deal and became involved in a social whirl. She petted to extreme and was often tempted to find out what sexual intercourse was like.

Finally she gave in, largely to satisfy her curiosity. As she said, she didn't even like the young man. A single act of intercourse and she became pregnant. She then went through the traumatic experience of an abortion. Now she was punishing herself by being sexually inhibited.

Inhibition is self-restraint. It is self-imposed. Inhibition means that a person doesn't permit himself to do something, *not* because he can't do it, *not* because he doesn't want to do it, *not* because he wouldn't like to do it, but because he is *afraid* to do it, out of a sense of guilt. A sense of guilt can be conscious or unconscious.

In the case of Mrs. B., it was a conscious feeling of having violated a moral principle and therefore of being unworthy and inferior. She was obsessed with the thought: "What would my parents, my friends say if they knew the truth? What would people say about me if they knew? They would all say that I was no good, that I was a tramp; they wouldn't have anything to do with me."

There are two kinds of inhibition, normal and abnormal. In the case of Mrs. B., normal inhibition would have been to resist the temptation of premarital coitus. Abnormal inhibition for Mrs. B. is the fact that she cannot accept that sexual intercourse in the marriage relationship is normal, appropriate, and socially acceptable. The fact that she had made a mistake as a teenager should not interfere with a satisfactory sexual relationship with her husband.

It is difficult for people to realize that one is one's own worst policeman. As a child, one develops the idea of good and bad behavior, of the "good me" and the "bad me." One learns that the "good me" is rewarded, and the "bad me" is punished.

People constantly reward themselves. When a man gets a raise or a better position, he rewards himself: he and his wife treat themselves to a luxurious dinner. When a young man graduates college, he receives gifts, and he feels that he deserves them.

Similarly, when a person does something that he judges to be socially inappropriate, or if he feels that he has not achieved what he aspired to, he punishes himself. But he is not aware of it. For example, the man who does *not* get the raise he feels entitled to, or does *not* get the promotion he desires, punishes himself by feeling inadequate and inferior.

Particularly is this so in the transgression of moral and ethical principles: the individual carries with him a sense of guilt and is constantly punishing himself. Of course, self-punishment is unconscious. When confronted with the idea of self-punishment, a person will say, "Why should I want to hurt myself?" The answer is that every person has a deep conviction that the "bad me" has to be punished, and he does it very efficiently, but unconsciously.

Mr. Q. considered himself a business failure. He was an accountant earning $12,000 a year. But he had aspired to be a captain of industry. He had promised his wife that some day they would be rich and she would have jewels and furs. Now he was in his middle forties, and wealth and success had eluded him. He was suffering from periodic sexual impotency, to the distress of his wife. As he talked about himself, he said outright that, considering himself a failure, he felt he didn't deserve life's joys, surely not sexual satisfaction. He used sexual inhibition to punish himself.

Another case, Mr. A., had been unemployed for six months. For twelve years he had worked as an assistant editor for a publishing concern until it went out of business and he lost his job. Immediately his sex drive weakened and he was subject to premature ejaculations. As he talked about himself, he mentioned that he felt inadequate, *impotent*.

Sexual inhibition as a result of feelings of inadequacy, lack of success, and job failure is much more prevalent than we realize. In our American society, the prize goes to the hero, the man who is a success. The man who is a failure, or thinks he is a failure, feels that he doesn't deserve the "prize" of affection, of gifts, of sexual conquest and satisfaction.

Sexual inhibition is not something one is born with. It is acquired in the process of growing up and developing a personality. It can be resolved, either by rigorous self-awareness or by talking it over with the spouse or a friend whom one can trust and respect. If necessary one can consult a professional marriage counselor.

The single, most significant aspect in facing up to the situation is to precisely identify the conflict. In the case of Mrs. B., she had to accept the fact that, having made a mistake, no one expected her to suffer for it a lifetime.

In the case of Mr. Q., he had to closely evaluate the notion of success and failure. To be sure, he didn't achieve the success and wealth he aspired to, but an income of $12,000 a year put him in the top fifteen per cent income bracket.

With Mr. A., he had to differentiate between being unemployed and being impotent. Even without a job, he could still be a good husband, a good father, a good scout leader.

Sexual inhibition may be used as a form of self-punishment. However, one should be as just and fair to oneself as one would be to a stranger.

# 42. Good Boyfriends Can Be Bad Husbands
### Robert A. Harper, Ph.D.

A young woman was consulting me regarding her marriage of about three years duration. She had given me a general description of her background and that of her husband. She then went on to say:

"Before marriage I was sick and tired of fighting off sexy eager beavers. Besides, I had seen so many people get married on a basis of sexual attraction—they always call it love—and have their marriages blow up in their faces that I had decided I would pick me a nice, stable, well-mannered, ambitious businessman and forget about being 'sent' sexually by him. Well, I did just that and now I'm not only horribly frustrated sexually, but terribly bored in general with this nice, staid, dull successful man."

This man's greatest premarital assets, his dependability and stabilty, had, in the judgment of his wife, become his major marital liabilities. Changes in both circumstances and attitudes can transform premarital strengths into marital weaknesses (and sometimes vice versa).

The "good listener" who thus flattered your ego as you courted her can become the "drip without a word to say or an idea in her head" after marriage. The boy who is so full of fun and clever little practical jokes may seem an annoying buffoon as your husband and the father of your children.

The sweet, endearing way that Edna, at eighteen, wrinkled her nose may be unutterably annoying four years later when Edna's your wife. Good old George is cute when he's drunk? Probably not, now that he's your husband.

Take the case of Ed, the scholarly type, and Ellie, the girl who livened up every party. Ed, though intelligent, was a slow-moving, slow-thinking, and quite shy person. He was thrilled to have a girl like Ellie show an interest in him. Before marriage, he'd proudly point to her gay and carefree ways. He felt that they nicely complemented each other. So did Ellie, who liked to have "a brain" be fascinated by her.

Then came marriage, and the great fun became a drag. Ellie still wanted to rip off to a party or have people in for a "whing-ding." Ed in bed, with or without a book, gave Ellie no kicks.

Ed would usually join her in the sociability because he was afraid of losing her. He eventually lost her anyhow, though. Each was so unhappy with the other's different conception of enjoyment that both the sexual and nonsexual aspects of their life together became wholly unsatisfactory. What seemed like premarital complementary harmony turned into marital incompatibility.

As in the Ed-Ellie example just considered, traits and attitudes transformed by marriage do not have to be directly connected with sex in order to have an adverse effect on the married couple's sex life. Even relatively trivial changes in perspective about what are assets or liabilities in a mate can have important consequences in and out of bed after marriage.

An important question, then, is: what, if anything, can be done about such changes? Three procedures are helpful—one before and two after marriage.

The thing that can be done before marriage is to spend as much time as possible in as great a variety of social situations as you can with the person you are thinking of marrying. While spending this time in these various ways, stop to make an inventory from time to time.

Ask yourself such questions as the following: What kind of person is this? How well is he or she "wearing" with you? How do this person's and your interests and needs look together? Will they gear together on a day by day basis on into the indefinite future? How do the traits and attitudes he or she now shows look to you as you, in your imagination, project them a decade or so into the future?

Such a process just described will work quite imperfectly at best, but it will help a little. Just asking yourself such questions can stimulate perception and thought that in some cases can prevent gross errors in judgment about the person being considered for marriage.

But, in the most fortunate cases with the most careful persons, certain traits destined to become future marital liabilities will probably slip by at first as premarital assets. When, after marriage, you find you have misjudged the nature or effect of certain characteristics of your partner, one course of action you can take is to try to control your own attitude change.

It is sometimes possible to retain, to some degree at least, the view you had toward your mate's traits before marriage. Ed and Ellie, for example, could have worked out certain compromises to strike a balance between constant partying and complete social retreat which would have helped them to hold on to their premarital respect and liking for each other.

Another course of action after marriage is to look for unsuspected compensations for the liabilities that develop. The young woman in our first example was helped to find her marriage less dull and unbearable by taking up some new activities with her husband which revealed that he had some redeeming qualities, such as a previously unrevealed sense of humor.

His calmness, steadiness, and stability also seemed less tedious in their new hobby of sailing, as well as in parenthood, where their children found security in these traits. He also turned out not to be wholly unteachable on the matter of sex functioning: some improvement came in this area, too.

After many months of working at it, the woman said to me: "I've known three Toms, and I realize the three are as much in my attitude as in him. The first was the rock of virtue I married. The second was where the rock had changed into dishwater—the Tom I found insufferable at the time I came to see you. Now in the third Tom there is a peculiar mixture of the premarital assets, which have somewhat returned, along with a number of other assets that I didn't even know were underneath 'the rock'."

Things don't always work out so well, but it is usually possible to improve your prospects at least a little by (1) critical premarital inspection to try to see whether alleged strengths would hold up as such in marriage, (2) work to keep from changing your attitude, and (3) efforts at compromises and at searching for new strengths in your mate (and yourself) to counterbalance unexpected weaknesses.

# 43. "Uncontrollable" Sex Desires

## Robert A. Harper, Ph.D.

"I know it's wrong. I don't want to do it. I can't help it, though. I just can't stop myself. It's something out of my control."

The person who was speaking was a young man of twenty-five who had been referred to me for treatment by his family physician. He was a child molester. He claimed that his sexual offenses with young boys were a true compulsion —that is, a force which uncontrollably drove him to act against his will and better judgment.

Uncontrollable compulsions do exist, but my experience in working with patients, including the one just quoted, leads me to believe that they are much rarer than often thought. "A force outside my control" is the best excuse in the world to go ahead and do the easy or enjoyable thing, be it sexual or nonsexual, without feeling guilty about it.

If I have a bad temper, for example, but it is "uncontrollable," then I can go ahead and "blow my top" without any sense of responsibility. I can't control the uncontrollable, can I? The same goes for people who get labeled "compulsive drinkers" or "compulsive eaters." "I want to stop eating (or drinking) so much, doctor, but, after all, it's a compulsion with me."

So say many people, like my child molesting patient, with so-called sex compulsions or "uncontrollable" sex desires. Fortunately, such impulses are by no means beyond the control of the will. The will often simply needs reeducating— that is, the individual needs help in learning to control himself.

The myth about the uncontrollability of sex impulses is very widespread and deeply ingrained. Part of the reason for this is that people do not know how to reeducate or retrain themselves sexually. Another important reason is that already referred to earlier—the easing of guilt or responsibility.

In any case, people seem to accept their sex interests and activities as inevitable and unchangeable.

This fatalistic attitude is often taken not only toward various sexual deviations, but also toward such conditions as frigidity, impotence, premature ejaculation, preference for certain sexual positions, means of experiencing orgasm, desire for "lights on" or "lights off," and practically anything else in the way of a habit that they have willy-nilly developed.

Sometimes what seems to be a compulsive or uncontrollable sex pattern may really have some other hidden explanation. The individual may be (deliberately or unconsciously) using a certain kind of sex behavior as a means to an end.

Mr. F., for example, claimed an uncontrollable impulse to have sexual relations with other women. He said that he loved his wife dearly and wanted to stay married to her. But every couple of weeks, to his distress (he avers), he would find himself driven to go out, pick up another woman, and then have sexual relations with her.

As I talked with Mr. F., I realized that in many instances he had told his wife or dropped obvious clues so that she would know of his escapades. This led me to look for some other motive than an uncontrollable inner impulse.

After several sessions with him, I found that his "compulsion" was really an unconscious desire to be reassured of his wife's love. And because she went on forgiving him, she was actually convincing him she didn't care too much and didn't really love him.

When I then talked with her and helped her to see that her attitude was a major factor in his sexual adventures, she began to express disapproval of this behavior. More importantly, she began to show positive indications of her love for him. His "uncontrollable" adultery very quickly stopped.

It is only when the expression of a particular sex impulse is in some way harmful that some kind of control is needed. The individual with the so-called uncontrollable impulses can often be helped to achieve this control by (1) seeing more clearly the undesirable effects of his actions; (2) recognizing in a personal way the desirable results of controlling himself and (3) realizing that his impulses are probably coming from preferences rather than from dire needs and that he has probably convinced himself that they are "uncontrollable" in order to excuse himself.

This is where psychotherapy can help. When a strong sex desire leads to a self-defeating result (such as jail, humiliation, or marriage failure), the individual is mistakenly putting short-term ahead of long-term pleasures. Much of any program of treatment, whether it is a person's self-treatment or his treatment by a psychotherapist, calls for a recognition of the long-term happiness that can be achieved by changing bad habits. Very often the individual who is used to short-term pleasures doesn't really understand this. The personal, emotional gains of the changed course of action must somehow be hammered home, either in professional treatment or in self-treatment.

Edward B. is a case in point. He came to see me because he allegedly had a compulsion to masturbate. He proceeded to do this habitually rather than to engage in sexual intercourse with his wife.

"I love her very much, Doctor," he said, "and I find her sexually attractive. But when I start to have sexual intercourse, the old compulsion to masturbate takes over. I am impotent with her, and then I go off somewhere to masturbate."

Mr. B., as it turned out, had a real fear of failing in sexual intercourse. He had never actually proceeded with it in or out of marriage. He had to be helped to realize that his fears of not being capable in sexual intercourse were entirely imaginary and that these very fears were causing his impotence.

It was also necessary (and fortunately possible with the help of his understanding and patient wife) to make him understand the much greater delights of sexual intercourse over the "easy-way" satisfactions of masturbation. Gradually, Mr. B. was able to see and act on the understanding that his shortsighted preference for masturbation actually kept him from greater pleasures.

The "uncontrollable" became controllable once the personal advantages and the means to achieving these advantages got through to Mr. B. And so it often is with other "compulsive" persons in learning to control so-called "uncontrollable" sex desires.

# 44. Promiscuous Sex Desires

### Robert A. Harper, Ph.D.

The tendency of men to have a "roving eye" is widely accepted and joked about. Most people realize that a desire for some sex variety seems to be rooted in the male psychology.

On the other hand, it is often incorrectly assumed that most women do not have such thoughts and feelings. The traditional disapproval of such desires has even led many women to deny their existence.

The fact is, however, that many human beings—male or female—are inclined to be promiscuous in their sex desires. Despite all the pressures of society, religion and morality, there is in most of us a resistance to confining all one's sex interests to the "one and only."

In fact, the romantic belief of many youngsters that there is only one possible mate who must be sought and found has no real basis.

It is possible that some inborn tastes influence a person's sex preferences. That is, we may be biologically inclined to favor certain skin textures, eyes or hair or skin colorings, and various smells, tastes, sounds of voices, etc. But it is more likely that the attraction we feel toward certain individuals in our sexual responses comes from early associations with actual people or with storybook or television or movie figures.

Neither inborn tastes nor learned preferences, however, are apt to apply to just a few people, let alone to a "one and only." Whatever characteristics arouse a man or woman, they are likely to be found in many other members of the opposite sex. In other words, there are probably a great many individuals who could arouse us just as much—if not more than the one we happen to marry.

Few, if any, females as well as males reach late adolescence without being sexually and emotionally attracted to dozens of movie and television stars, school leaders and assorted individuals from their everyday life.

We are compelled to realize, then, that promiscuous sex

desires are thoroughly normal—biologically, socially, and statistically. They are as natural and expected as, say, the desires that millions of people have for new foods, new sights, and new experiences in other areas of living. It might even be contended that people who never experience varied sex urges are the ones who might be viewed as being "abnormal" or peculiar.

Action, however, in this as well as other areas of living, is very different from thoughts or feelings. Just because it is natural for a person to have varied sex desires, it by no means follows automatically that it is intelligent and desirable for him to act on them.

It would be quite unusual for a married man to fail to notice a sexually attractive girl on the street. He might even wonder for a moment or two how pleasant it would be to enjoy sexual intercourse with her. There is hardly a man who does not sometimes have such thoughts and feelings in the presence of a good-looking girl. But this is very different from actually pursuing the girl and making a real attempt at intercourse.

For anyone who has a marriage that is presently or potentially happy, the risk of extramarital sex relations is apt to be too high. Adultery is a high-risk undertaking for a person who is fairly happy in general and who is well satisfied with his marriage in particular. Persistence of the strong moral code that adultery is marriage-destroying and heaven-defying usually brings about serious guilt feelings and bitterness in the individual and in the marriage.

Probably only a very small percentage of men and women have truly freed themselves of deep-seated anxieties and guilt about sex relations outside of marriage. Still fewer have husbands or wives who would tolerate adultery. Where the individual himself is free of such feelings about infidelity, he may find himself concerned about being dishonest with a wife who would disapprove if she knew.

Even where both husband and wife know and approve of extramarital sexual activities, these can still drain time, energy, money, and affection from the marriage.

In my work as a psychotherapist and marriage counselor, I have met with a large number of people who like to play games with their promiscuous sex desires. They flirt, and they have "innocent" dates. They talk glibly and sophisticatedly of sex without emotional involvement. They neck and pet in dark corners.

With some of these people, nothing serious seems to happen to their marriages. Others, however, get emotionally and socially caught up in their games, and their marriages (some of which are quite desirable ones) get severely shaken or broken up.

For patients who are contemplating *acting* on their promiscuous sex desires, I have sometimes used such an example as driving an automobile on a dark night over a winding and narrow road at a very high rate of speed. One *may* get away with it, but the risk is quite high. It is only if you don't value your marriage in the one instance, or your life in the other, that the risk is not going to be too great.

To live successfully in society, we must consciously suppress many acts we would like to perform—such as getting out of the hot, tight, itchy swimming suit at the beach in order to swim and sun comfortably in the nude. Or such as machine-gunning into silence our musically untalented neighbor who is practicing shrilly on his clarinet.

To deny that we have the desire to cavort in the nude or to brutally silence our neighbor or, perhaps, to make mad love with our favorite movie star is silly. Human beings do have such feelings and thoughts. And you and I are human beings.

*To sum up*: Promiscuous sex desires are normal, natural, and expected, and should be freely faced and accepted in oneself, one's mate, one's children, and others. But, like many other ideas and impulses we have, not acting on them is usually best if long-term happiness is our goal.

# 45. The Retreat from Sex

### John B. Oman, D.D.

"How can I make love with a man with such disgusting personal habits?"

"By the time she gets her hair up in rollers and a layer of face cream on and her teeth brushed and her toenails clipped, who could be in the mood?"

"She drinks till she's unconscious. . . ."

"He's got his bottle; he doesn't need me."

"Since we got the twin beds. . . ."

"He's even had a *kitchen* fixed up in his office. I hardly see him at all now."

These are all flags identifying an army of people retreating from sex.

It's a strange phenomenon in this age when sexual happiness is avidly pursued, sexual accomplishments saluted, unlimited information on sex is available, and men and woman are living longer and more healthily, with extra years of vigorous sex potential to enjoy.

Why then are people anesthetizing themselves with alcohol, making themselves unlovely with a barricade of habits ranging from unpleasant to irritating, taking refuge in work, washing, kids, headaches, hobbies?

Gwen smiled as she said, "I remember when we graduated from high school, somebody wrote alongside Bill's picture in my annual, 'May all your troubles be little ones.' Of course they meant kids. Very funny. But our troubles have been little ones—only they add up to an awfully big total. You see, they are such *little* things that I can't even talk to him about them . . . but they keep bothering me and there keep being more."

Asked to be a little more specific, she continued, "Well, he picks his nose. And he scratches his head. In just one spot. He digs at it . . . like monkeys I've watched at the zoo. And he whistles. The same tune . . . just three bars of it. Loud. And you wait, knowing that any minute he'll whistle them again. Or maybe he won't, and that's even worse!"

"Do you love him?" she was asked.

"Of course. But I can't go on like this. I get more irritated with him every day and . . ."

"And every night?"

She blushed. "Yes. That's really why I'm here. The way I feel doesn't stop when we go to bed."

At this point, the problem was to find out which partner was using the irritations to retreat from sex. Was it Bill? Was he avoiding sex by a series of habits which he could sense were irritating Gwen? Or was Gwen using these flimsy excuses to hide a lack of sexual feeling for Bill?

It was felt that the best way to get at the truth would be for Gwen to confront Bill with her complaints, as tactfully as possible, but without disguising how she was reacting. She did.

Bill was embarrassed and apologetic. He promised to make a special effort to stop doing these things. And he did. But their sexual life was no better. When Gwen admitted this, it was clear that she was the partner retreating from sex.

Under thorough questioning, the real, underlying cause of the difficulty emerged. Gwen's mother, an ultra-fastidious woman (who was probably frigid, judging by Gwen's description of her) was convinced that Gwen was marrying beneath her. She referred to Bill as "unmannered, coarse, no background." Sex was never discussed by mother and daughter—that would be the ultimate in coarseness.

Gwen was unable to throw off her mother's influence. Feeling guilty about sex, her subconscious began trying to bail her out of this situation (which Mother wouldn't approve of) by proving that Mother was right—Bill *was* coarse and unmannerly. When Gwen realized what she was doing, she made a gradual, though eventually complete, change to become Bill's loving wife.

Vernon, a man of sixty-one, was seeking the cause of impotency. A thorough physical exam had revealed him to be in excellent health, but still his problem remained. He wondered if some hormone or a special food might help restore him to his former virility.

But, other than the psychological value (people think they're being helped and this removes the mental block and presto! they *are* helped) sex foods don't help; neither do hormones. The famed Mayo Clinic physician, Dr. Walter C. Alvarez, wrote recently that in most cases the man still has plenty of the male hormone substance in his blood and that, after sixty, a man's failure to perform sexually is, in many cases, due to his wife's "lack of interest or cooperation."

The retreat from sex again. Counseling with Vernon's wife would help to awaken her to her fault here. And, for Vernon, the advice is, "It's never too late in life for courtship—the interest, attention and caressing that may serve to reawaken sexual desire in his partner."

Phyllis, a thirty-four-year-old widow who had just remarried, had difficulties of quite another variety. "I'm married to a . . . to a . . ." She groped for the words. "Whatever it is, all he thinks of is sex . . . nearly every night. There must be something wrong with his glands."

This is a fairly common misunderstanding—the person who thinks she's married to either a sexual athlete or a sexual 4-F merely because the mate's sexual desires are different from her own. This subject has been developed by such experts as Dr. Donald Hastings who has pointed out that there are varying degrees of sexuality within the norm.

Encountering a sexual appetite so much heartier than one's own may provoke a retreat from sex. That is, a person may be so overwhelmed that he or she recedes from desiring less sex to little sex to no sex at all. This is a development which, obviously, must be counteracted as early in the marriage as possible.

A woman is in a more favorable situation because she is able to accommodate her husband at any time (with such exceptions, of course, as certain stages of pregnancy, menstruation, or ill health). A man faced with a ravening sexual demand by his wife may have an ever-increasing problem, however.

Some men with a low sex drive may become almost asexual. The husband with far less sexual interest than his wife may retreat from sex into hobbies, his work, psychosomatically-induced heart attacks, over-drinking, or even alcoholism —or, at least, into a twin bed!

But the mating of a highly-sexed woman and a moderately-and-less sexed man is by no means hopeless. The wife can almost accomplish miracles if she is willing to do more than her share toward solving this problem. First, she must never be critical. She must be loving, nonpressuring, alluring and patient.

The wife must remind herself that her husband may be harboring vestiges of the centuries-old fear of women that persists even today in many an immature male. Hopefully he outgrows such legendary apprehensions as the vagina containing teeth or other castrating equipment—myths found in the history of almost every culture in the world. But he is still normally fearful of the unknown, wondering what to expect, what to do, what will happen.

The childhood of every male influences his sexual life mightily. Rejection, overdependence on his mother, too-harsh discipline by his father—all may make him apprehensive about testing his sexual ability. After all, the wife has no problem about performance; he does.

It is his responsibility to achieve an erection, sustain it, and produce in his wife an orgasm. The responsibility, the fear of failing, the energy required—all for an estimated *one hour* of orgasm a year—no wonder a man with low sex-power retreats!

But the pleasure and power of consistent sexual relations can't be measured in a mere totaling of seconds of blissful sensation. The healthy happiness to be achieved this way is worth planning and working for.

# 46. Unexpected Sex Problems Created by the Pill

## John B. Oman, D.D.

The Pill, which promises new freedom and security for the enjoyment of sexual relations, is a real blessing for many married couples. But to the surprise of some men and women, its very success has given rise to a new crop of marital complaints.

Use of the pill can make intercourse much more spontaneous and "spur-of-the-moment." Many of the methods which men and women have been forced to use, and found unpleasant and inhibiting, are now unnecessary. All in all, the pill has undoubtedly lessened sexually-based tensions for most couples using this method of birth control. But there have been exceptions serious enough to warrant attention and study.

For example, the pill has uncovered a rather large number of low sex drives which, up to this time, were hidden by the fewer opportunities for sex and the other complications of taking birth control measures.

Men who claimed to be shortchanged on sex when following the rhythm method, for instance, where they abstained from relations for as long as two weeks out of the month, suddenly found that they had more opportunities for sexual enjoyment than they knew what to do with.

Myra and Glenn illustrate this paradoxical new problem. At forty and forty-one, respectively, they were entering into what could be a golden phase of their sex life. The early problems of childbirth and rearing were over. They had few economic pressures. What happened to their sex life couldn't be blamed on worry and tension.

During her annual checkup, Myra's doctor advised her to start taking the pill. After being rather reluctant to start with, Myra began to see definite advantages to the pill. She and Glenn had had some problems over the years—her periods were irregular and had an annoying habit of coming on suddenly if she became overly tired or worried.

Half-jokingly, Glen accused her of "having the curse twice a month just to avoid sex." On some occasions, too, when they had to pause in lovemaking to employ a birth control device, it seemed to break the spell of their mood.

Now, after a few months on the pill, Myra rather blushingly admitted that she seemed to be more passionately attracted to her husband than even in the early years of their marriage, so she welcomed the new freedom. It looked as though sex might become as regular as TV-watching for them.

But now it was Glenn who pleaded fatigue, or a headache. Or he would stay up at night watching the late show, raiding the refrigerator, and reading mystery stories, instead of going to bed with that look in his eye.

When Myra became more demanding, finally asking bluntly why he was avoiding her, Glenn began going back downtown to the shop after supper, not returning home until late. Far from being convinced by the excuse of work, Myra began to suspect—and accuse—Glenn of having another woman. His denials only infuriated her. It looked as if this marriage was headed for divorce, so the two decided to see a marriage counselor to help them cope with their new problem.

Counseling didn't provide a complete solution to the problem; it never does. Couples must work things out themselves on the basis of suggestions made and insights arrived at.

Once Myra realized that Glenn was not meeting someone else secretly, not using his sexual energy outside his own bedroom, she became more understanding. And, although her desire for sex remained higher than it had before the pill, it did settle down.

"I just never felt so free before," she said in one counseling session. "I guess I got carried away. I wasn't thinking about anything but sex!"

Instead of being overwhelmed with too much of a good thing, until it looked like duty with a capital "D," Glenn began to respond more warmly. "Sure I like steak 'n apple pie—but not three times a day," he grinned. "We had to make some adjustments, just like newlyweds. We are having sex more often than we did before the pill and we enjoy it more, now that we understand each other's attitudes."

In my own experience as a counselor, I have often found one aspect of sexual activity to be at odds with much that has been written about intercourse, its art and its practice. It is something that the use of the pill highlights even more than before.

Most textbooks on the "how's and why's" of lovemaking stress *romantic moods, spontaneous relations,* and so forth. Let your husband *seduce* you, wives are told. Make love when the spirit moves you.

But some men hate this kind of love life! They like the very things the sex manuals tell them should be taboo in marriage—a definite pattern for love. And, surprisingly, some women feel the same way, a rather large number, as a matter of fact.

Before the pill, George and Libbie made love on Thursday nights and Monday afternoons. They managed to keep that evening clear and his job allowed him enough leeway so that he got home that afternoon each week. Libbie used a diaphragm for birth control purposes, but she hated using it "because it was messy."

George thought it sometimes interfered with the ultimate in pleasure for him, too, but their level of gratification was very high, they said, and it was the most reliable birth control item for them.

Along came the pill. Libbie no longer has to deal with a "messy" or uncomfortable preparation. If they want, she and George can roll together in drowsy warmth before they get up in the morning. Or they can have sex relations when George comes home in the afternoon, and on just *any* night when they hop into bed. Many other couples have delighted in just such freedom and expansion of their sex lives as a result of the pill.

Not George. George liked things just the way they were. In the first place, he is just a nice, ordinary guy—not a great lover. In addition, he hates it when he is put on his own in romantic matters. Books tell him, for example, that he should look for that gleam in his wife's eyes and should rouse her slowly. Well, George can't read signs like "a gleam in her eye." Furthermore, Libbie doesn't always have time for all the preliminaries either.

George liked the pre-pill way. He knew what to expect. He had (what textbooks have often warned against) a sex routine and schedule. He and Libbie could *count* on intercourse on Thursday night and Monday afternoon.

Romantic souls might cry out that love shouldn't be that way. I can only answer: for some people, it works. Indeed, for some persons like George (and Libbie), no other system will work. George has peace of mind when he knows in advance what he'll be doing. He likes knowing he'll have sexual relations on Monday afternoon each week, just as it gives him security to know he'll be in his office chair for Tuesday conferences at 10 a.m.

These two cases typify many others of a similar nature. There have also been other pill-prompted problems. Not all involve reluctant men either. For one thing, some women have found their sex drives to be notably *reduced* after starting the pill. This may be on an actual physical basis.

Will the pill stimulate or complicate a couple's sex life? There are no pat answers. It is a question each couple must solve on an individual basis, in the light of their own temperaments, desires, needs, and backgrounds. Every advantage the pill offers will also involve new conditions that must be weighed by each couple in order to safeguard their sexual relations and their marriage.

# 47. How Pregnancy Affects Marriage
## LeMon Clark, M.D.

Some years ago, I was caring for a young woman during the course of her first pregnancy. In this relationship between doctor and patient, I ordinarily develop some feeling of rapport between the two of us. In this case it was utterly impossible. She never relaxed, even for a moment. Her attitude could only be called very "stand-offish."

The day of delivery arrived and she gave birth to a very nice baby girl. Three weeks later she came to the office for a checkup and two weeks after that for her second and last checkup. As I always do at the second checkup, I asked, "Do you want to talk over the question of birth-control with me?"

"Oh, no," she said, quite tartly, "That won't be necessary."

That aroused my curiosity and I could not drop the subject at that point so I asked why it would not be necessary.

"Oh," she replied. "My husband is suing me for divorce."

"Well," I said, "how can you youngsters fall in love, get married, have a baby and get divorced all in one year?"

"When I was pregnant," she replied, "I didn't feel like having sexual intercourse, and didn't see why I had to. My husband says I have never been a real wife to him, and so he is suing me for divorce."

That dialogue tripped a trigger in me that really set me off. I gave her a tongue-lashing as to her selfishness, her stupidity, her utter ignorance of what marriage meant such as I have seldom given any patient. She broke down and sobbed and cried and I didn't care. I never expected to see her again. I only knew that she left town and went to the far West, Arizona or Nevada.

Three years later, she came back into the office carrying a six-month-old baby, with the three-year-old I had delivered trotting along between her and her second husband. She was in town on a visit and wanted to stop in to thank me for what I had done for her by opening her eyes as to the meaning of marriage. With her present husband, she was supremely happy!

This was, of course, an extreme case, but a very real one. Loss of sex desire when a young woman is pregnant is a fairly common occurence. Undoubtedly, among the contributing factors to the frequency of divorce in those cases where the bride is pregnant at the time of marriage are the stresses and strains resulting from pregnancy so early in marriage. The young couple have no chance to learn to live together before their lives become more complicated.

Some men find it hard to share the attention of their wives even with their own offspring. One evening my wife and I stopped by to see a young doctor and his wife and their baby, which I had delivered a few weeks previously. We found the young mother sitting in a chair in the kitchen nursing the baby with tears streaming down her face. The young doctor was in the living room patently sulking. The young mother finally, in a whisper, sobbed to my wife, "I don't know what to do. They both want to be fed at the same time."

Even before the baby is born, from the very early days of the pregnancy, there may be problems. Some women are nauseated during the first ten or twelve weeks of a pregnancy. The smell of food makes it worse, so it is difficult for them to prepare meals. Where a woman resents the pregnancy because she did not want it to occur so soon, there is further difficulty. At best it will be only a few months before she will not be able to get up and get moving as easily and enthusiastically as she did before she was pregnant. The husband may feel hemmed in by circumstances.

Money problems immediately become of some concern. A pregnant woman should go to the doctor regularly and there will be the doctor's and hospital bills to pay all too soon. Financial circumstances will be especially aggravated if they are also paying a substantial amount each month on the furniture they purchased on a time payment plan.

After the birth of the baby, routine habits may be markedly disrupted. It will be impossible to run off to a movie at a moment's notice, or to a friend's house for bridge or anything of the kind. Weekend trips are sharply restricted.

The young mother, herself, may be troubled by her conflicting feelings towards her baby. She knows she should love her offspring. But when the baby cries and cries, when her sleep is disturbed night after night, when she has what seems to be mountains of soiled, messy diapers to wash, she may not be too sure that she does love the baby. Guilt over this feeling of questioning her love for the child and guilt over her resentment towards the whole situation may make her more irritable and unreasonable. She is angry and upset over the whole affair and then is more upset and angry over the fact that she is upset and angry.

A condition similar to pregnancy is created by one of today's most popular birth control methods, the "pills." They work as a method of contraception by preventing ovulation, the release of the egg from the ovary each month. They do this by keeping the young woman in a state of pseudo or false pregnancy.

Her breasts commonly are somewhat fuller (frequently to the delight of the husband), she tends to gain weight if she is not very careful about her diet, and in some cases she may suffer a considerable loss of sex desire. This may not become apparent at first since freedom from worry over possible pregnancy serves to offset it. But some time later, two to four years after the start of taking the pills, some women may lose their sex desire.

A recent case in point is a patient of mine who had been on the pills for two years. I knew her quite well before she and her husband left the local university and moved away.

A few weeks ago they drove back here to see me. Emotionally she was a very stable young woman, but she was literally in tears over her situation. She said, "I always used to love to go to bed; we had a wonderful time together. But now I literally cringe when he touches me."

I told her to stop the pills and inserted an intrauterine device, the so-called Saf-T-Coil, which I consider the best of them all, and she reported a week ago that she was quite back to normal.

When birth control is used in the early days of marriage, how long should it continue? There are, of course, many factors which may enter into consideration. How old is the bride? If under twenty she would be wise to wait until she is twenty or over, for both her own health and for her offspring. What is the economic situation? Is the young husband still in college? If so, with his wife working he may be able to finish his education. If she has to stop work because of her pregnancy and he has to drop out of college, he may literally blame her for his failure to complete his education.

How long should pregnancy be postponed? Not too long. If a young man gets into the habit of having all of one woman's attention and devotion, he may find it very hard to share her attentions with someone else even though it is his own child. Planning to have a baby two to three years after marriage is probably wise.

As in all other aspects of married life, common sense, cooperation, self-discipline and judgment are necessary in pregnancy planning.

# 48. The "Pregnant" Husband

## Isadore Rubin, Ph.D.

Shortly after learning that his wife was pregnant, a young husband experienced attacks of nausea resembling "morning sickness." In the months that followed, he had strong sensations of fullness in his abdomen as though he, too, were carrying a child. Finally, at the end of nine months, when his wife went into labor, the husband too was wracked with so-called "bearing down" pangs.

Odd as it may seem, pregnancy symptoms among new fathers-to-be are not a rare phenomenon. A recent British study, for example, suggests that one out of nine prospective fathers shows signs of the mysterious malady, and studies in the U.S. show an even higher figure.

In any event, this curious phenomenon, which today we call the "couvade syndrome," has been reported many times down through the centuries. There is word of it from Greece as early as 60 B.C. It is mentioned by that famous medieval explorer Marco Polo in his *Travels in China*. It pervades lit-

erary history, particularly English literary history. Francis
Bacon, essayist and statesman, knew of it; and the Elizabe-
than dramatists Dekker and Webster referred to it in their
plays.

The word "couvade" is derived from the French verb
"couver," which means "to brood" or "to hatch." The term
was first used by anthropologists to designate a series of related customs connected with childbirth. These customs,
found among many primitive peoples, require that the father
of a child, at or before its birth and for some time after the
event, should take to his bed, submit himself to a diet and
behave generally as though *he,* and not his wife, were under-
going the rigors of the confinement.

In its classic form, the husband observing the couvade
takes to his bed and pretends to be lying-in, sometimes imi-
tating childbirth, even to the point of rolling about and
groaning as if in labor. While in bed, the husband is pam-
pered and fed on dainties, and receives the congratulations of
his relatives and friends. Often, in such cultures, the women
go through a minor physiological labor process, and simply
deliver the baby without much fanfare.

One view of couvade, as found among primitive tribes, is
that it represents an example of the practice of sympathetic
magic. The husband simulates his wife's childbirth in order to
protect her from harm. By pretending to be *her* at this critical time, he hopes to direct the influence of evil spirits away
from her and on to himself.

But couvade among the primitives is one thing to explain.
Couvade among modern Western man is quite another and
more difficult phenomenon to account for and remains, to a
large degree an intriguing medical and psychological mystery.

Yet it is possible to understand something of the mechanism of the couvade syndrome, according to psychiatrist Ar-
thur Colman of the Langley Porter Neuropsychiatric Institute
of the University of California Medical Center in San Francisco. "We realize now," he says, "that men are, in some
sense, part women. As a matter of fact, the differences between the sexes are really remarkably small, despite the obvious anatomical differences. Men seem to be capable of
mimicking many of the psychological changes of pregnancy
—much as women are quite able to mimic some of the better
known masculine psychological characteristics."

One study was carried out among Army servicemen whose
wives were pregnant. It was discovered that about 60 per cent
of the husbands displayed some striking symptoms of pregnancy. These symptoms included large weight gain over the

same period that the wife was pregnant, early morning nausea, and fatigue. Some of the men experienced the typical "baby blues"—they actually became depressed after the child arrived.

The question naturally arises as to whether such behavior represents a "healthy" reaction on the part of the husband. Dr. Colman says there are almost no data to answer the question in any scientific way. He feels, however, that for a husband to experience some of the pregnancy his wife is going through may well be part of the process of accepting the fact that he is going to be a father.

"As a matter of fact, the more 'unhealthy' reaction to a pregnancy is probably when the husband takes no part in it whatsoever. This is altogether too common. Partially this is fostered by our modern obstetrical-medical care which is, of course, most interested in the wife. Often the husband is completely out of the picture. If he is seen by the physician or nurses, it is only briefly. Furthermore, it is rare for the husband to be included in the labor room, and rarer still for him to be allowed into the delivery room."

The enforced separation of husband and wife at delivery occurs at the time when the man is about to have a child belonging to him as much as it does to the wife who physically delivers the baby. One husband who felt neglected described his impression of his wife's pregnancy: "I felt as if the new baby was something between my wife, her mother, and the obstetrician."

For one reason or another, many husbands simply "take leave of the family" at the time of their wives' pregnancy. This is particularly true toward the later months, Dr. Colman notes, and immediately after the baby is born.

In a series of interviews with normal pregnant women at the San Francisco Medical Center, Dr. Colman learned, to his amazement, that a considerable number of husbands were "taking off." One of the expectant fathers went on a trip with a local college band for three months, scheduled to return about the same week the baby was due. Another took a sudden interest in cars, and his wife reported that she never seemed to see him any more since he was "always tinkering with his automobile."

More drastic reactions are the total alienation of the husband—to the point where the arrival of the child and the increased attention demanded by the infant is a starting point in the dissolution of the marriage. Psychiatrists can often trace marital discord directly back to the special complications which began to occur when another demanding individual suddenly arrived on the household scene.

A psychiatric study reported by Beatrice Liebenberg at the American Orthopsychiatric meeting in March of 1967, confirmed the notion that "pregnancy and parenthood is a crucial time for the male as well as for the female." About two-thirds of the expectant fathers developed pregnancy symptoms, and many experienced emotional difficulties of various kinds. Some men experienced the pregnancy as a severe test of their masculinity; for some it was a period of heightened dependency.

What preventive measures can be taken to help keep a family together when the baby arrives?

"To insure that the parents function as a unit after the child is born," says Dr. Colman, "every effort must be made to involve the man in the psychological plans of the woman."

One of the most crucial preliminary tasks is the matter of public enlightenment regarding some of the reactions of the so-called "pregnant male." It should be made clear, for example, that identification with the feminine qualities of the wife is common—even, in fact, to be hoped for. This would help allay the anxiety that may come with the "unknown"—with the misunderstood aspects of the husband's reactions to pregnancy.

The second major step is for the wife to encourage the participation of the husband in the entire cycle of pregnancy. According to Dr. George Schaefer of the New York Hospital-Cornell Medical Center, the expectant father should have access to his wife's doctor for discussion of sexual problems, emotional disturbances and factual questions about labor and delivery.

"Many obstetricians," Dr. Colman notes, "are beginning to approve of the idea of bringing the husband into the delivery room. If the husband can take it, I think it is highly advisable to be in on the first sighting of the new child."

It is Dr. Colman's opinion that a reexamination of the present system of obstetrical-medical care is required. Standard medical procedure, he says, is for the child to be kept away from the mother for from twelve to twenty-four hours.

Even after that, the child is brought to the mother perhaps every four hours, stays for a half-hour feeding, and then is brought back to the nursery.

As to the father, he is usually allowed to visit only while the baby is in the nursery—and this means looking at his child through a glass partition for the first five days. In effect, the modern maternity ward is a sort of woman's world, run by nurses. The father, when he comes to visit, may feel out of place in this exclusively feminine society.

The upshot of all this is that the family is continually separated. The husband is isolated from the wife and baby. The wife is isolated from her husband, and communicates with the child only at certain specific times.

At any rate, doctors are increasingly recognizing that expectant fathers can no longer be ignored during the difficult period of pregnancy and the early days after delivery. Their emotional and other problems must be given careful consideration.

# 49. How Resentment Turns Wives Cold

## Vernon W. Grant, Ph.D.

In ten years of marriage counseling, I have many times been asked the question: "Does sex often create marital problems?" I usually answer: "Yes, but much more often, marriage creates sex problems."

By this I mean that an unsatisfactory sex relationship is more often than not a reflection of problems in nonsexual areas of the marriage. Here, for example, is one housewife's statement:

"My husband has accused me of being cold sexually, but it is not true. What happens is that we will have an argument about something that leaves me resentful. A few hours later it's bedtime and he wants sex. I'm still simmering inside and I say I'm too tired or just not in the mood. Or else we have sex but I don't respond the way I usually do. He can't seem to understand that the trouble is not with sex itself."

Something else he probably can't understand—and a great many other husbands with him—is that there is a difference in sex psychology here. The sexual impulse in the male is more readily separated from other emotional states. Just as a man can enjoy a prostitute not only without affection or respect, but even with contempt for her personally, he can enjoy his wife sexually despite unresolved emotional tensions.

For most women it is a different matter. For them, sex is much more a part of an emotional relationship that must be close, warm, and "right" if she is to be sexually receptive.

There must be no emotional barriers in the way if she is to share the experience fully.

There are occasional exceptions to this rule, as to most others concerning human emotions. There are women who can "take sex like a man" and detach the experience from other feelings which might be unfavorable to sex. But it is safe to say that there is a general sex difference here.

One of the areas of marriage from which emotional conflicts may transfer to sex is the closely related one of nonsexual affection. For most men, any kind of physical expression of affection is likely to become sexually stimulating. But there is a different kind of "lovemaking" that is understood much better by women than by men.

This "love outside the bedroom" is different in quality from sexual excitement. I've heard women say, a hundred times and in one way or another: "I need a lot of affection, of the tender and romantic kind. About the only time my husband is affectionate is when he wants sex. It makes me feel as if that's all I mean to him. So I get frustrated and a bit resentful."

Some of this resentment may not wear off quickly, and the husband later complains that his wife seems "a bit frigid at times."

Much is written about frigid wives, little about a certain kind of frigidity in husbands. It is usually referred to as undemonstrativeness. Such men tend to feel awkward and self-conscious in expressing tender feelings, either physically or verbally. Said one: "My mother never kissed or hugged me except maybe when I was going away on a trip. She seemed uncomfortable when I would try to show affection."

These men are inclined to be somewhat abrupt in their approach to sex, and their wives complain: "He wants it right away. There is no courtship or personal feeling. He makes me feel it could be just any woman in bed with him. Then he wonders why I'm not enthusiastic." The wives may be starved for nonsexual affection, and the resulting resentment then affects their attitude toward sex.

The term "infidelity" usually suggests a sex problem in the sense that it implies probably dissatisfaction of some kind with the marital relationship. The sex disloyalty then endangers the marriage. In my experience, the sequence is more nearly the reverse. That is, a nonsexual conflict leads to infidelity, with the sexual phase essentially secondary.

Here again, an excerpt from a case history illustrates the point. The wife is an attractive and intelligent brunette of twenty-four whose husband has filed for divorce because she was sexually intimate with another man, following a drinking party. Her account follows:

"The way this began had nothing to do with sex. Bill had been either staying away from home evenings or watching TV all evening when he did come home. There was no companionship. I felt I was just a housekeeper, cook and mistress. I did not feel needed as a person and I did not feel that I was an interesting person. The night of the party, this male acquaintance was very attentive. He made me feel attractive and even a bit glamorous.

"I hadn't had any of that kind of treatment for years. The sex part was not really important. I don't remember much about it but I do remember thinking: 'The way Bill has been treating me, he probably wouldn't give a damn.' Yes, I was bitter. It was mostly revenge."

The *motive* to infidelity is usually assumed to be sexual. In reality it is more often an "ego" motive. One of the mates has become vulnerable because the marriage has ceased to provide satisfaction or the need to feel needed, to feel valued. Next comes an encounter in which he or she is stimulated by admiration, has the experience, perhaps for the first time in years, of being an exciting personality. Sex may eventually enter the relationship, of course. My point is that it is rarely primary.

Insecurity in one of the mates, with failure on the part of the other to realize it, may lead to a sex problem. In one of my cases the husband doubted his adequacy as a lover and felt that his wife had little respect for him in this sphere. This was not true, but she was not aware of his sensitivity.

When, on several occasions, she truthfully protested that she was too tired for intercourse, her husband interpreted it as personal rejection. He became increasingly anxious about his emotional hold on his wife, and before long began to experience episodes of impotence. The problem was successfully treated by convincing him that he had misinterpreted his wife's behavior, and by helping her to become more aware of her husband's need of reassurance.

It is at times surprising how far from the sexual area the actual source of sexual conflict may lie. One woman made a derogatory remark to her husband in the presence of the children. He repressed his resentment at the time, but confessed that several days later he allowed himself to be rather brutally inconsiderate of her feelings during intercourse. It is, of course, common knowledge that in the reverse situation the wife may take revenge on her husband by sexual denial.

In another instance, a wife acknowledged that she sometimes did this even when her husband unknowingly caused her to feel humiliated because of her relative lack of formal education. She admitted: "I know it isn't fair, but sex is the one place I have the advantage because it's harder on him than on me when I refuse him."

There are, beyond question, many marriages in which a sexual maladjustment is a primary problem. Marriage manuals deal with such as these in considerable detail, with emphasis on the elementary psychology of effective mutual stimulation. More attention is needed, I think, to the many ways in which factors outside the sex relationship may directly or indirectly cause strain and frustration in the sexual side of marriage.

# 50. Husbands Who Are Not Interested in Sex
## Clifford Allen, M.D.

Sex is such an urgent mattter for most men that they find the unmarried state nerve-wracking. Premarital sex has the anxieties of possible pregnancy and venereal disease, and most men fear the "shotgun" marriage. It is then a great relief when they are able to marry. Now, at least, they can have sexual relations with the woman they love. When two people can live together, nothing need limit their intercourse.

It comes as a surprise to some people that there are many men who are not very sexually excitable. They may enjoy sex for a short time and then lose interest, or they may never be aroused by their mate. Sometimes sex continues at a low level, and sometimes unwillingly.

Now there is no doubt that sexual intercourse varies in its urgency according to the person. Whereas one man feels the need for intercourse once or more daily, another may ask for it only once a month. In most younger people, however, the need comes two or three times a week, though naturally as men grow older they feel less desirous.

What are the factors which may prevent or diminish a man's sexual interest in his wife? We mean here, of course, emotional or psychological factors. The overwhelming majority of young husbands who lose interest in sex do so for nonphysical reasons.

First, we must exclude the obvious causes. Intercourse is

an act of love. If the man is not in love with his wife—if, for example, he has married her not because she attracts him, but beaause she is wealthy, or can promote his social position —then obviously he will not show the same enthusiasm which he would feel for someone he loves.

Again, if the husband has a mistress, or if he was in love with someone before marriage and still pines for her, then his wife is not likely to arouse him.

I once treated a girl who had recently married and felt so aroused that she had intercourse daily with her husband. Then, suddenly, she lost all sexual interest and developed anxiety symptoms. Investigation showed that she had been in love with a man other than her husband before she married.

He went abroad and she felt that all was over. Then she married and all seemed well until the first man wrote and said that he was coming back to marry her. It was this which destroyed her sexual feeling for her husband. Obviously, such a situation can happen to the man as easily as to the girl, with similar results.

A common cause for lack of interest in the wife is when the husband has some serious psychosexual abnormality. Probably the commonest to cause such trouble is when he is consciously homosexual or sadistic.

Some homosexuals feel that marriage might "cure" them, and there are women so ill-advised and so ignorant as to feel that they might be able to change their husbands. Surely, they argue to themselves, a loving wife will give him greater pleasure than the men he meets casually in bars or public toilets.

Unfortunately, this is not so and although I have seen many men who married and whose marriage was destroyed by their homosexual orientation, I have never seen one who was able to develop a normal marriage. This does not, of course, mean that the homosexual must never marry, but he should only do so when he has had adequate treatment and his psychiatrist says that he is capable of being a normal husband.

Again, the sadist may be sexually aroused only by actually being cruel or by thoughts of cruelty. A gentle, kindly wife (unless he can hurt her in some way) is not likely to arouse him. Indeed, he may actually enjoy the idea of frustrating and hurting her by the refusal of intercourse. Similarly, the masochist cannot be aroused by his wife because she is unable to understand that what he really wants to stimulate him is for her to be cruel to him.

These are the more obvious factors and include such extreme cases as transvestism, transsexualism and similar things. The greatest number of men who show no sexual interest in their wives do not show such obvious abnormality. The usual picture is something like this:

A man goes out with a woman for some time and finally, probably at her suggestion, they drift into marriage. On their honeymoon there is a certain amount of intercourse, but not very much. Then, on return to their normal life, there is less and less sex. Their life becomes a pattern: the husband either returns from work, has his food, sits and reads the newspaper, or watches the television until it is time for bed.

Or else he starts going around to the saloon, or billiard hall, and spends his evening with his friends. His wife, in either case, feels neglected and bored. She may accept it and settle down to this husband who shows no interest in her, either up and about or in bed; or, as sometimes happens, she find someone else and the marriage breaks up.

Why has this happened?

I think that often in such cases, the husband is *unconsciously* homosexual and has drifted into marriage either because he feels that it is the thing to do or because the wife has pressed it on him. Once the marriage has settled down, he returns to his old habits without consideration for the wife. He is leading a bachelor life in his marital home. His interests are for other men and his wife is often regarded as a housekeeper or a nagging nuisance who wants to intrude into his private life.

There are, of course, many other reasons why a man's sexual interest may diminish. For example, when a man develops a neurosis, he often loses his sexual urge. Supposing, for example, that he has trouble at his work, a superior who bullies him or something of the sort. He grows so anxious that he develops neurotic headaches or a similar neurosis. He loses interest in his wfe because of the neurosis and complaints from her will only make things worse. The cure naturally lies in his obtaining a transfer or another job.

In general, anxiety lies behind cases of impotence where the man is physically normal. The trouble is that anxiety may make him fail on one or two occasions and then he develops a vicious circle: anxiety makes him lose his erection but the loss of his erection leads to further anxiety lest it will happen again. This further anxiety makes him fail again and so on round and round.

Many men who lose interest in their wives have had this sort of thing happen to them and after a time they fear to try lest the apparently inevitable failure occur again. Complaints from the wife increase the fear and they dare not attempt what other men find so enjoyable.

Sometimes the anxiety has to do with the man's job. I can remember a very typical case I saw shortly after the end of the last war—that of a partner in a stockbroker's firm. This poor man spent his time worrying over what might happen to the shares. He worried all the time, buying every edition of the newspapers, listening to the news on the radio and mulling over their significance every minute. He started to get neurotic, could not sleep, could not concentrate and felt ill and tired all day. Not surprisingly, he lost all sexual interest in his wife.

A wife, too, may have much to do with how her husband feels, and we must not absolve the wife completely from the situation in which the husband loses interest. There are many women who think that marriage is the end of the efforts to attract the husband and, as people say, "let themselves go."

They become slovenly, dress carelessly and slop about all day in a dressing gown, and never see that their hair is dressed well, their frocks are neat or such minor matters as their nails attended to. The result is that the man, who has been working all day with fastidiously-dressed women, may be disgusted and revolted by his wife. He cannot rouse sexual interest in her.

Again, some women cease to be interested in their husbands when they have children and concentrate all their affection on them rather than on their mates. The husbands feel this and reciprocate.

How can we avoid this sad situation in which the husband has no sexual interest in the wife? Firstly, I feel that no woman should ever marry a man who is sexually abnormal unless he has had treatment and is considered cured. Marriage does not cure psychosexual abnormalities. Men should marry women for love and not for money or social position.

A wife will be a fool who marries a man who appears more interested in the company of other men before marriage (when he is usually on his best behavior) instead of wishing to spend all his time with her. Neurosis should be treated and not neglected in the hope that it will clear up in time, particularly if accompanied, as it usually is, by impotence or diminished sexual feeling.

The wife who neglects her husband for her children is lucky if all she can complain of is his lack of sexual interest in her—she often loses him altogether.

All this may sound obvious but it is astonishing how many

marriages are broken up because of obvious things. Happiness in sex is not something gratuitous but is earned by affection, attractiveness, and willingness.

# 51. Why Women Resist Contraception
## Hugo G. Beigel, Ph.D.

Many people will rely on the most primitive and notoriously risky methods to prevent pregnancies, even though they really do not want children at the time.

Uncounted numbers of females—married and unmarried —fear the consequences of unprotected intercourse, but still cannot or will not take the necessary precaution. Some of them actually own a contraceptive but consistently refuse to use it. We are not here talking about women who have religious or ethical objections to birth control.

This resistance is particularly conspicuous if the couple's decision not to have children is not just a question of convenience but is dictated by necessity. Unmarried girls know very well that a pregnancy will adversely affect their future and may, in fact, even endanger the relationship with the unwilling father.

Other women have been warned by their doctor that pregnancy may jeopardize their health or even their lives. Nonetheless, many of them stubbornly resist the only rational solution to protect themselves against conception. They have dozens of excuses when they finally confess their "bad luck" to the doctor or inquire secretly after an abortionist.

The truth in practically all these cases, however, is that, to them, the contraceptive device or pill has become the symbol for something that rouses stronger anxieties than the fear of pregnancy.

Take the story of Barbara. This young woman sought help in a very disturbing situation. She came from a devoutly religious and strict home. She had always tried to retain her parents' love by being a "good girl" who obediently did what she was taught to do. Her older brother, by contrast, worried her parents by his willful ways. Barbara fortified her position by occasionally informing on him.

Once her brother had used a "dirty" word. Barbara pretended to be terrified and reported him. Once, when he was eight and she six years old, he showed her the organ that distinguishes boys from girls. Barbara screamed. The parents came running. The boy was beaten and the girl was pacified with sweets and candy, and was allowed to sleep in her parents' bed for two nights.

At the age of twenty-one, Barbara married and moved to another state. Friction developed because she wanted to visit her parents every second weekend. After six months she declared that she could not go on living with her husband. The parents objected to a divorce until Barbara hinted that her husband was a pervert who had asked her to "do unspeakable things with him."

Barbara was a pretty divorcée and many men took her out. But they also made sexual demands on her. When these consistently met with a "no," one after the other withdrew. Eventually, Barbara made the acquaintance of a man who showed more patience. But even he indicated that a prude was not for him. The young divorcée, now twenty-four years old, became frightened at the thought of losing him.

A girl friend advised her to buy a contraceptive. Barbara hesitated, but eventually she went to a doctor and had a diaphragm fitted. Yet when she returned home, equipped now for all eventualities, she was overcome by crying spells which were followed by a deep depression.

In this state, I saw her for the first time, heard her story and the wild fantasies with which she upset herself from session to session: that she was pregnant; that people on the street looked at her in a strange way; that they thought she was a prostitute; that she was a homosexual—for her the most contemptible of all human states.

Barbara's breakdown was caused by a conflict she could not resolve. Her emotional dependence on her parents' approval urged her to get married as quickly as possible, yet the manner in which she hoped to achieve this goal ran counter to the primary condition of her parents' love: that she must remain a good girl. This condition she was about to violate. The possession of a contraceptive became the symbol for it.

Barbara took flight into sickness; others punish themselves for the violation of rigid moral rules with whch they have been brought up in different ways. Thus a woman had four abortions in three years, because, as she said, she was "too lazy" to take precautions for her protection. Neither pain, nor anxiety, nor expense convinced her that she could *not* rely on good luck.

Another woman, pregnant against her will, argued that it was so "unromantic" to interrupt kisses and caresses to make herself ready for intercourse. When she was told that she should make the necessary preparations before the husband came home, she replied, "I did that once. But then he did not come near me."

Other women in similar situations retorted with indignation, "If I had to be ready for him all the time, I would feel like an object that he can take or disregard at will." Or: "It is the man who has all the pleasure; why can't he take the responsibility?"

Such arguments leave no doubt about the real feelings of these women. They resent the man's "privilege" and protest against their own female role.

Sometimes the resentment involves not so much the sex roles as the husband himself. Reasons are manifold: she does not love him; he does not spoil her as her parents did; he is not willing to change ideas and attitudes the way she wants him to change them; she does not share his sexual desire; and so on.

These wives do not necessarily deny themselves to their husbands, but they "forget" to prepare themselves, cannot find the contraceptive in a hurry, discover all of a sudden that it is worn out or give what other plausible excuse occurs to them. Since as a rule husbands do not carry condoms on them once the wife has agreed to use a contraceptive, they must either forego their gratification or return to a method that is less satisfactory to them. The contraceptive thus becomes an instrument of revenge for whatever the wife feels hostile about.

But not every man yields peacefully. One woman, Joyce, claimed that she disliked the sex act because it gave her only unpleasant feelings. She played the game that we mentiond above over and over. One day, the husband had enough of her excuses. He said he didn't care whether she got pregnant or not and took her despite the fight she put up.

The wife wept and sulked and spoke of divorce. I asked her why she made such a fuss about it. Had she not gotten what she wanted? All her dreams indicated that she wanted to be taken by force. She had obviously aimed at this by her game with the contraceptive.

She was very angry at me. But at the end of the session she relented and confessed that at the occasion of the "rape" she had, for the first time, experienced an orgasm.

This woman was sexually so inhibited that she could not allow herself sexual intercourse unless she was forced into it.

Even when she was willing, any attempts at foreplay froze her feelings. And the application of a contraceptive went against her conscience. To her it symbolized the impermissible compliance with forbidden sexual desire.

Among the most frequent excuses given by those women who resist using the diaphragm is a dislike of "poking around" in their own genitals. This uneasiness can, in practically all cases, be traced back to the threats or punishment with which their parents conditioned them as children against masturbation.

Optimists have said that the pill and the intrauterine devices will do away with this resistance. Our experience is that this is true only to some extent. For where the resistance is caused by an unconscious fear of sex—as in most instances it is—only a fundamental change in attitude will solve the problem.

Gynecologists and others working in the field of birth control are well aware of the equivocal feelings women have. For this reason, it is an accepted thesis that a method is only as effective as a woman's willingness to use it. Most failures are by the person, not the device.

# 52. Men Who Fear Women

### William Zehv, M.S.

I have always been impressed by the many husbands who manifest a fear of their wives. These husbands indicate subtly but surely that somehow they perceive women as the dangerous sex.

Such husbands find themselves in a bind: on the one hand they are impelled by a need for sexual gratification; on the other hand, they feel reluctant and apprehensive about the sexual relationship.

One husband summed it up quite well: "Sometimes I wake up during the night, on fire with sex desire. And there is my wife, lying next to me. All I have to do is to touch her, fondle her. And yet I hesitate and debate with myself: Should I or shouldn't I?

"I know that the chances are that she will agree to intercourse, that she may even desire it, but the one chance in a thousand that she may say no, that she may reject me, terrifies me. I almost feel as if I'm in some kind of danger."

Mr. and Mrs. T. were in for marriage counseling. Married fifteen years, with three children, they were at odds over almost everything. At the root of their conflict was their sex relationship. Mrs. T. resented the fact that her husband could never initiate intercourse at the proper opportunity. Mr. T. admitted frankly that somehow he felt apprehensive in making love to his wife. He felt that he had to be devious, that he had to trap her into it; he would therefore wait till his wife was asleep and then he would fondle her and arouse her. As he said, "Otherwise, I was afraid she would make it difficult for me, she might tease me and tempt me till I was so aroused, I'd have to beg her for it and afterwards I'd feel humiliated and ashamed."

More men than we are aware of have conflicting feelings about the female sex. A woman perceived as a mother is thought of as pure and sacred; a woman perceived as a sex object is somehow considered tinged with sin and danger.

Mr. and Mrs. G. came in for marriage counseling. There were times when Mr. G. wouldn't initiate sex relations for five and six months at a time. And if his wife ever made overtures indicating sex desire, it would frighten him and he would crawl away or even jump out of bed.

Mr. G., it seemed, was never at ease with women except when he was drunk, and he couldn't approach his wife sexually except when intoxicated. But the doctor had warned him to stop drinking. Thus, the months he was sober, he and his wife lived as if they were sister and brother.

Mr. G. told how during his teenage years, his father had impressed him with the notion that a woman was of the dangerous sex, that he should beware of falling into the clutches of the "wrong" woman who would use her sex to dominate him, to use him for her selfish ends; that women are not to be trusted; that sexual intercourse saps a man's strength; that he would be better off if he never married.

It is rather ironic that women, too are sometimes carried away by such superstitions and caution their sons against the wiles of women who would entrap them and subjugate them.

Mr. M. was a bachelor of thirty-nine. He had been engaged three times and each time he had managed somehow to escape from going through with the marriage. On the first occasion, a week before the wedding, he simply disappeared.

Several years later, he again became engaged. But he couldn't face up to the task of setting a wedding date, and out of sheer exasperation, his fiancée broke off the engage-

ment. He waited quite a few years before he became engaged
a third time. But the very thought of being engaged plagued
him and he soon found an excuse to sever the relationship.

Now he was in for counseling because, as he said, he was
thirty-nine years of age, there was a woman he was romantically interested in, and the idea of marriage appealed to him.
But he didn't want to go through the emotional tortures he
had previously experienced.

Mr. M. was literally brainwashed by his mother into a fear
of women. Whatever reasons the mother had for disparaging
her own sex, her influence upon the son was tragic. As a
child, as a teenager, and as an adult, Mr. M. was constantly
showered with anecdotes of the selfishness, unfaithfulness and
the domineering character of women. If a boy and girl of
their acquaintance married, the mother would smile know-
ingly and whisper that the girl had entrapped the boy; if
there was a divorce, she would hint that the wife had destroyed the marriage; if they met a woman who was a shrew,
she would whisper, "See, that woman is leading her husband
by the nose."

Each time he became engaged, his mother found fault with
the girl and slyly hinted that he was being entrapped. On one
or two occasions, Mr. M. took courage and asked his mother
how she knew, and her response was, "I'm a woman. I
know."

It took a considerable amount of time for Mr. M. to realize and appreciate what a neurotic woman his mother was
and that her fear of women had nothing to do with him and
his relation with women.

Of course, the fear of women has a long history that has
continued to this day. Eve as the mother of mankind is respected and even venerated. But Eve as the spouse of Adam
has been pictured as the evil instrument of the devil, as the
source of original sin, as responsible for the fall of man and
the expulsion from Paradise.

That women were the dangerous sex was quite widespread
among primitive people: for a woman to touch a man's hunting or fishing gear, or his weapons of war, was taboo. A man
was not to have sexual intercourse before hunting or going
into battle: coitus was believed to be debilitating.

There is a myth of women possessing a vagina with teeth
that cut off a man's penis. Almost two dozen versions of this
myth have been found among tribes in various parts of the
world, from North American Indians to Siberian tribes. Even
in this day and age, psychiatrists have reported patients who
thought of the vagina as a wound, as a mouth devouring the

penis, and have equated coitus with death, the man dying in the female organ.

In recent years, women have entered business, industry and the professions in great numbers, to the extent that some women have become a competitive force to be reckoned with by men. With a husband and wife both working, it can become a source of profound disturbance if the wife should earn more or be more successful.

Mr. U. came for counseling. He had just been offered a new job with more money and greater prestige—a sure indication of success. But he was fearful about accepting it because he would have to work under a woman boss. He had never really been at ease with women. He recalled that, even at college, competing with a coed made him feel uncomfortable, less masculine. As he said, for no rational reason that he could think of, he was a little afraid of women.

The important thing for men to realize is that these myths and irrational fears are entirely unrealistic. There may be some women who are castrating and demanding, but not all women are so; there are shrews, but not all women are so. There are exceptions to the rule, but that does not invalidate the rule, which is, that by and large, most women are pretty realistic and want a pleasant and amicable marriage.

Mr. T. had to learn that if he confronted the sexual situation and talked it over with his wife frankly and openly, he would have found that she was willing to cooperate. With Mr. G., his alcoholism involved many psychological factors. However, in his attitudes toward sex and women, it was important for him to reevaluate the horror stories that his father had told him, and realize that very likely his father had thus expressed his own fears and anxieties. Mr. M., for his part, had to accept the unpleasant fact that his mother was neurotic and that the basis for her fears of women had nothing to do with him. And Mr. U. had to accept the fact that successful businesswomen were now more prevalent and he simply had to adjust to it.

When men's fear of women is put into rational perspective, one cannot help but conclude that women are not the dangerous sex and men have no need to fear them.

# 53. Using Sex for Nonsexual Reasons
### Edward Dengrove, M.D.

When one thinks of sexual activity, it is commonly assumed that its aim is sexual pleasure. This is assumed even where odd sexual events take place, such as exhibiting oneself, or peeping, or child-molesting, or rape.

This is only partly true. Dr. Lionel Ovesey writes that there are at least three things to keep in mind when considering sexual activity: sexual pleasure, power play, and dependency need.

Consider the power play shown by a rapist. He has a need to dominate the woman by force and to make her submit; this is more important to him than even the sexual experience itself.

Dr. Ovesey describes the case of a thirty-year-old man who had felt a constant, unreasoning resistance growing toward his wife, and a gradual loss of sexual interest in her. He found it necessary to be drunk in order to carry through his more and more infrequent sexual approaches to her. It was then that he decided to enter psychiatric treatment.

His mother had been a domineering, overprotective and affectionate woman who set exorbitant standards for performance. His father rarely showed any interest in him. His childhood was a nightmare of failure, recrimination and exhortation to do better. He suffered lifelong feelings of inadequacy, inferiority and lack of confidence. He had trouble in the Army and trouble on his jobs.

He frequently thought that he might be homosexual, or that people thought him effeminate. But he did not engage in homosexual acts. Encouraged in treatment, he overcame his failings, became more and more bold, and underwent a boost in self-esteem and self-confidence. Heterosexual interest returned, and so did his potency.

Other psychiatrists have written of similar cases in their practice, and have used nonsexual means to treat patients with sexual problems. Dr. Leo Alexander writes of a twenty-three-year-old, highly intelligent college senior who, since coming to college, found himself unaccountably compelled to submit to homosexual relations whenever solicited by fellow students.

He experienced the homosexual acts as hostile and degrading assaults in spite of the resulting physical satisfaction, as one might experience a horror movie. It was particularly distressing because he was in love with a girl back home and hoped to become engaged to be married.

After three years of a losing battle against this, to him, distasteful submissiveness, he became increasingly despondent and depressed and fell behind in his studies. For this reason he saw a psychiatrist.

It was discovered that he was the illegitimate son of a rich and powerful father who exposed him to unreasonable tyranny. His submissive pattern became established very early in life.

Encouraging him to be an assertive, aggressive person enabled him to reject a homosexual advance for the first time, and thereafter he gradually recovered. The doctor never had to mention the words "sex" or "homosexual" at any time.

The nonsexual use of sex is not confined to human beings. Two scientists, in a study of the male squirrel monkey, observed the display of penile erections by one male to another as a means of exerting and establishing his dominance.

It has been said that masterbation in children may sometimes be the expression not only of sexuality but also of anxiety. In the same way, adult intercourse may sometimes be the expression of anxiety, its frequency being not so much robust as compulsive. This means that a person does not always engage in sexual relations for the pleasure of the act alone, but also to please others, to perform one's duty, or to prove one's masculinity or femininity.

A young female patient, who engaged in frequent sexual relationships outside of her marriage, told me, "I need to feel like a wanted woman. My husband doesn't know how to make me feel like one." She felt the need to punish him by her extramarital adventures.

The famous psychoanalyst Erich Fromm writes of the Don Juan as a person who does not feel strong enough as a man because emotionally he has remained a child. He tries to compensate for this lack by the exclusive emphasis on his male role in sex. He adds that when the paralysis of masculinity is more extreme, sadism (the use of force) becomes the main or perverted substitute for masculinity.

Dr. James M. Toolan studied depression in children and noted that in many adolescents and adults, sexual acts are a method of relieving their depressed feelings. "Such a person frantically seeks contact with another human being by means of sexual intercourse," he writes, "the only method of relating that he knows. Quite often . . . this activity produces only further depression and guilt, which once again he attempts to relieve by further sexual acting out."

Masturbation in psychotic patients may result, through the achievement of a high degree of sexual pleasure, in blocking pain. Dr. W. E. Marchand describes the case of a young male schizophrenic who was seen masturbating almost continuously, whether in the ward dayroom or in bed. This was new for this patient.

Asked why he did it, he replied, "It is good for me . . . It takes my pain away." What pain? "The pain up here," he answered, as he put his hand to his upper abdomen. X-ray studies revealed the presence of an active duodenal ulcer, and the masturbation stopped soon after the ulcer was treated.

In his classic *Studies in the Psychology of Sex*, Havelock Ellis observes, "Masturbation is in the main practiced for its sedative effect on the nervous system. The relaxation that follows the act constitutes its real attraction . . . . Both masturbation and sexual intercourse should be classed as typical sedatives."

Psychologists have long known that there are two phases to any sexual event. There is the exciting, driving, uphill progress toward a climax; and then the more abrupt, satisfying decline with a sense of relaxation and sleep. The relaxation after the sexual act may be no less satisfying to a person than the frenzied approach to it, and may well be one of the major reasons for sexual relationships, even though we are usually unaware of it.

# 54. The Wandering Husband
## Robert N. Whitehurst, Ph.D.

American family sociologists and other professional people interested in family behavior have long held that extramarital relations are usually examples of neurotic and immature behavior.

The fact that this kind of behavior could be logically expected from a great number of males in certain parts of

American society seems not to have occurred as a serious thought to most of these professional people.

One can make a good case for the normalcy of adultery when we look at certain aspects of American life. *To say this, of course, does not mean that one is either condoning or advocating adultery.* What is important is to explain and understand it.

One of the important problems overlooked by many of those who try to explain the sexual wanderings of husbands is the different rates and ages at which males and females reach their maximum attractiveness to the opposite sex.

For males, the age of maximum attractiveness occurs much later than for the female, roughly (in my opinion) at an age from forty to forty-five. This is the age at which he has ordinarily accomplished at least some measure of success in his occupation, he is likely to have some excess money (which in our society is a real source of power), he may be more poised and sure of himself, and most important, he has not lost his attractiveness to young females.

For the female, her maximum age of attractiveness is between the ages of twenty-two and thirty-two. Those things we highly value females for in our culture tend to change in ages beyond this.

The major point here is that the maximum attractiveness of the two people who may become involved in an extramarital affair reaches the maximum probability between the male and female just described. If we grant that certain other conditions also prevail, we can then suggest that it is neither deviant nor neurotic for these kinds of people to become sexually involved with each other.

Other research in the social sciences show that (contrary to our folksy belief about comradeship and deepened communication as length of marriage increases) marriages do wear thin with time and even the best of relationships cannot sustain continued high-level involvement of both partners except in rare cases.

In general, both husband and wife are likely to find outside interests taking up more and more time as length of marriage increases. One of the adaptations of the husband is to increasingly spend more time on his job where he often has opportunities to meet young and idealistic females who may inspire him much as did his wife in years gone by.

Although he probably has lost much of his idealism in the daily struggle for survival, he is quite likely to identify with the young female who often has an abundance of verve, enthusiasm, and lust for life. Since the male often in reality starts out without lecherous intent in his relationship with this female, it is difficult to consider him as neurotic or immature because in the end he becomes sexually involved with her.

This final bit of sexual behavior could as logically be seen as a mere extension of some of the other normal learning processes in which he has indulged over the years. The point is that by this time in his life he has become an expert in justifying and explaining away questionable business ethics (which sometimes appear to be necessary for survival) and it is just an easy step to rationalize and explain away his involvement with his secretary, bookkeeper, or what-have-you.

There is likely to be a real transfer of his recently acquired views of the business world into his personal world. To call his business behavior abnormal or neurotic (when these have clearly made him successful) seems to miss the point. He is a success by current American standards. To then call him neurotic or immature because he takes advantage of his status seems likewise ill-conceived as a scheme of explanation.

The sexually-wandering husband in this instance is just extending the more ordinary definitions to cover sexual behavior. Since extramarital sex is so often available and so attractive to him (and to her), it seems peculiar to consider this as deviant behavior. Of course the behavior is deviant from the middle-class view of morals, but from the point of view of the scientific observer, this behavior might logically be expected. Not only might it logically be expected, but we might expect more of it in the future.

In reality, the sexual involvement of the male may have relatively little to do with his marriage, but more to do with the availability of willing females. It isn't that he doesn't appreciate his wife and family; it is just that as a male he finds it expedient to wander sexually.

The probability of his wandering is increased by his status, age, money, manliness, and availability of the young female, who is likely to reject her own age-group of males as immature or unsophisticated. He has in the course of time given up many of his idealistic views of both the world and himself. This makes his wandering relatively easy for his conscience to handle.

It is probable that a great many extramarital affairs begin for nonsexual reasons. Through time and sharing of many important bits of work experience and meanings, this nonsexual relationship often turns into a sexual one. It is extremely difficult to view this type of behavior as rooted deeply in personality problems of the individuals so involved.

Rather it seems more rational to see it as a natural outcome of the operation of parts of our society; a bit of behavior which is often regrettable to wives but is at any rate behavior which can be understood not as pathological, but normal. As such, extramarital sexual expression may or may not lead to the destruction of a marriage relationship. It depends on the meanings attached to behavior by the parties involved.

Our standard interpretations do not ordinarily consider the positive implications of sex behavior outside of marriage. Research has often been oriented toward the demonstration of the negative consequences, not any positive ones.

Our American middle-class view of marriage and morals has led to a highly constricted viewpoint of certain aspects of sexual behavior. We have often assumed that self-seeking of gratification is necessarily destructive to marital relationships. It is posible to show that on many occasions precisely the opposite might be true.

We need in our society an increased awareness of the possibility of viewing sexual behavior from many vantage points not yet explored. It is time we take a new look.

# 55. Should I Tell My Wife I Have Gonorrhea?
## Robert L. Rowan, M.D.

*Should I tell my wife that I caught gonorrhea?* This tragic question is now being asked of the doctor with increasing frequency. The answer is a difficult and disturbing challenge. It requires a knowledge of the disease and an honest evaluation of the problem.

Gonorrhea is a venereal disease caused by a germ. This germ is spread by sexual intercourse. Thus when a man is infected with gonorrhea or any other venereal disease, he immediately endangers his wife. The only way he can be sure that he will not infect her is to avoid sexual contact with her.

And suppose he has already had relations with his wife and thinks he might have infected her? Or perhaps he is not sure but would still like to be on the safe side? *The only safe procedure is to get his wife to a doctor and have her tested for gonorrhea (and treated if necessary) as soon as possible.*

From a health point of view, experts in the field of medicine and public health believe that—regardless of the difficulties involved—it is important for the wife to be informed. They point out that where this is done skillfully—with the aid of the doctor or a public health investigator if necessary —the marriage relationship need not be seriously damaged.

However, there is no doubt that the husband with gonorrhea faces a difficult marital dilemma. The final decision, which rests with him, will no doubt be painful. But whatever he does, he must see to it that the wife is not infected, or is treated quickly if she is. This is especially important since gonorrhea is even more serious for his wife than for him.

The male and female respond differently to the disease. This is easily understood when the difference in the anatomy of the male and female genital system is considered. In the male, the disease enters the urethra or urinary canal of the penis. It usually incubates for two to eight days. A discharge or drip then develops from the urethra and burning or pain upon urination starts. The tip of the penis becomes red and irritated. Though the incubation period is usually two to eight days, the first signs of trouble can start sooner than forty-eight hours or later than eight days.

The symptoms of gonorrhea are usually pronounced, except in cases where the patient has had gonorrhea before. Patients who have had the disease before will not develop as many symptoms the second time, or the symptoms will be much milder. This is important, for when a patient catches gonorrhea a second time, he will often disregard the symptoms and not seek medical aid.

He thinks that he does not have the disease because the symptoms are not as severe as he remembers them to have been the first time. Often, the discharge will be minute in amount or will only be present in the morning upon rising.

*The most urgent requirement is to seek medical aid at once.* The urethral discharge or drip is loaded with gonorrhea germs. The discharge is highly contagious and sexual contact is almost sure to spread the disease to the sexual partner. Having intercourse with one's wife is sure to give her the disease. Whether one tells one's wife or not, it is obvious that one should not infect her by having intercourse with her at this time.

The doctor will always take a smear of the discharge. It is best not to urinate immediately prior to going to the doctor, for it will often wash away some of the discharge. Most cases of gonorrhea have a discharge that is continuous even after urination.

When the discharge is present, the doctor will take the smear by spreading some of the material on a glass slide. The material is permitted to dry and then the slide is processed for study. A stain is applied to the slide and then removed. This stain affects certain germs.

Another stain is them applied after various intermediary steps prepare the slide for the second stain. This second stain also colors different germs. When the process is completed, the doctor examines the slide with a microscope. He looks for the characteristic appearance of the gonorrhea organism.

These germs stain red and look like two small beans placed back to back. They are usually found inside of pus cells produced by the body. They can be outside the cells in a very early stage of the disease or at a very late stage.

Once the diagnosis of gonorrhea is made, the physician starts treatment at once. The patient is warned of the extreme ease with which the disease is spread. It is possible to spread the germs to one's own eyes, and therefore good hygiene should be practiced.

The hands should be carefully washed after urination or handling of the genitals. Sexual intercourse must be avoided. The patient is told of the possibility of having syphilis as well as gonorrhea. If he caught gonorrhea, there is a chance he was exposed to syphilis at the same time.

Syphilis will often require more time to make itself known. Careful observation for the chancre or sore of syphilis must be undertaken. Blood tests for syphilis must be done monthly to assure the diagnosis as early as possible.

Early treatment is essential. This is why, if a man thinks he may have infected his wife, he must tell her for the sake of her own health. Otherwise she will not see a doctor for treatment.

Penicillin is considered the best drug for treating gonorrhea. It is excellent for the treatment of the disease but it has many problems associated with its use. Many gonorrhea germs have become accustomed to it and are resistant to it. They are no longer destroyed by its presence.

Some patients have become allergic to penicillin and will develop a reaction to its use. In these cases, other antibiotics must be used. In all cases, complete treatment is necessary and frequent checkups are required to see if the disease has returned.

If the patient's wife has caught the disease, it is essential that she be treated. If the wife is not treated and cured, she will reinfect the patient again and again so that even if he is cured, he will just catch it repeatedly. This is called "ping pong," and refers to the passing of the disease back and forth between two people.

The wife may have the disease and show no outward signs. Women can have gonorrhea and have very few symptoms or none at all. At times the disease in women will cause them to become sterile. The disease will produce a severe infection in women and an inflammation develops with fever and pain. The disease in women often develops into a very serious condition.

With all these factors in mind, the patient in consultation with the doctor should decide what the best procedure is in relation to his wife. The emotional pains caused by the situation are severe but the effects of the disease are worse. The protection of others from the ravages of gonorrhea is a moral obligation.

# 56. Wife-Spanking

### Lester Dearborn

I have before me a headline from the magazine section of one of the well-known newspapers which reads, "Should Wives Be Spanked?" Next to it is one of Ann Landers' syndicated question-and-answer columns headed, "Spanked Wife Likes It; Needs Helping Hand."

The first letter in the column concerns an attractive, well-to-do housewife in her middle thirties whose husband spanks her "when she deserves it." She says: "I usually feel a lot better after it is over." The letter-writer, a friend of this woman, concludes: "Is something wrong with him—or with her?"

The columnist's offhand answer is that "a woman who tolerates a spanking is as sick as the man who gives her one" and dismisses them both contemptuously as "physical kooks."

I have long been interested in sadomasochism as a factor in marriage and have come across hundreds of cases in which one mate is treating the other sadistically. There is a great deal of evidence in many of the instances that there is complementary masochistic response. In other words, as in the letter cited above, both the spanker and the spanked enjoy it.

Seldom has there been published any adequate explanation of this type of behavior. As a result of this lack of information, such couples find it difficult to maintain their self-respect and overcome the effect of having to label themselves as "abnormal."

It is important to note that the subject is not a new or unheard-of phenomenon.

It has been mentioned in letters to newspapers, articles in journals, and illustrated by drawings for a number of years. Books have been written entirely around the theme of spanking and have been published in English, German, and in French, going back a considerable length of time. One classic in this regard is *The Romance of Chastisement* published in 1876.

As in the examples cited above, many newspapers and periodicals have conducted a correspondence on the subject in their advice columns. The answers they have printed are often of a humorous nature, showing that the letters were not taken seriously.

Certainly some of these letters may be fictitious, many of them records of fantasy. But whether fact, fiction, or fantasy, they show an erotic interest in which the author associates pleasure with pain, humiliation, shame, exhibitionism, or some fetishistic interest.

The frequency of wife-spanking has impressed me to the extent that I have discussed it with my colleagues. While some of them have reported that in their counseling they have also recorded a number of such experiences, I have always felt that most of them took the information rather lightly, probably with doubts as to its having any important significance.

My experience leads me to believe that the subject of wife-spanking is worthy of far greater study than psychiatrists and counselors have been willing to give it.

All too often, professionals in various fields are ready to label behavior which they do not understand as "sick" and "abnormal" without engaging in the research and analysis which is necessary. Their dogmatic conclusions are sometimes the results of their feelings rather than of their knowledge.

Many people, too, are so fearful of the word "sadistic" that they cannot be open-minded in assessing the effects of any behavior so labeled and dismiss it as unworthy of proper and unbiased research.

It is for these reasons that I believe that it is of value to report my information concerning the successful marriage of a number of couples who, when they first came to me for counseling some years ago, referred to spanking as part of their married life, both for discipline and for sexual stimulation. I have selected five such cases from my files.

Recently, a Sunday supplement described a group of women who were active in social welfare work. One of them, a very active participant, I immediately recognized as a former client of mine some fifteen years ago. At that time she displayed a tremendous amount of interest in sadomasochistic episodes in her married life, including exhibitionism built around the punishment episodes in which her husband spanked her.

She got a great deal of satisfaction out of this. Invariably it led to a later experience of sex which was wholly satisfactory, with a positive orgasm release on her part. I have evidence that this type of relationship was continuing up to at least three years ago.

This couple are well known in their community; she is very active in church work and social situations; he is a professional man who has advanced considerably in his scientific work; they have four seemingly well-adjusted children, one of whom is now in college. Certainly there is no evidence that this type of behavior has led to any unresolved emotional conflicts.

In another case that I have kept in contact with, the husband is also a successful professional man; they have three children, one has just finished college. From the very beginning of their marriage, the wife has submitted to bare-bottom spankings on the part of the husband after various methods of preparation. The wife says her marriage has been extremely happy, admitting some of the usual ups and downs that every marriage has to face.

The third case is of a young woman who wasn't married until thirty and who was quite sure she wasn't going to be because she hadn't met the right man. A date with a man she had claimed she didn't care much for but whose invitation she had accepted for an evening's entertainment, led to his chiding her for something and threatening her with a spanking.

Noticing her reaction to it, he saw to it that she got the spanking. Her statement to me was, "When I received this, I knew I was in love with him." A follow-up of that marriage shows that it has continued apparently very harmoniously! The husband and wife work closely together in a business in which they have a common interest but in which he plays a dominating role, a role which is accepted and desired by her. They also have had a well-rounded family life and have raised four children.

The fourth is the case of a girl who had several lovers and was undecided which to choose until one night one of them, being provoked with her, turned her over his knee and gave her a really sound spanking after, as she said, "uncovering the necessary area." As a result of this spanking, she made her choice saying, "This is the kind of man I want to live with." That was all of twenty years ago, and a follow-up shows the marriage is still going well.

The fifth is a young woman who was having a lot of conflict with her husband; she had discovered he had had an extramarital affair, as a result of which she came for counseling. She disclosed she was unhappy with him because he wasn't dominating enough, didn't make decisions, etc.

At this time he decided that, since the marriage wasn't going to succeed, at least he would have the saisfaction of giving her what he had always wanted to, a good sound spanking. He did this and found a different reaction than he had anticipated, so on several occasions he repeated it. They reported to me that things had been going along fine ever since. That was some seven years ago.

When we think of the thousands of people who were burdened with feelings of guilt, were punished, and many of them put in mental hospitals for no other reason than that they masturbated, and compare that attitude with what we know today, we can't help being aware of the fact that our attitudes regarding any form of sex behavior may well be the result of ignorance. Such ignorance can only be dispelled by the proper type of research. We should be extremely careful about using labels which very often do no more than express our own distaste for what we don't understand in others.

# V.

# OVERCOMING
# IMPOTENCE AND
# FRIGIDITY

# 57. Impotence Can Be Helped

## G. Lombard Kelly, M.D.

Impotence has long been neglected in medical teaching and research, although its cure is of the utmost importance for the maintenance of a happy marriage.

We may define it as the inability to achieve and maintain erection of the male organ so that it can accomplish intromission into the vagina and remain there long enough for normal sexual intercourse. In cases of frigidity in wives, only one partner completely suffers the lack of sexual gratification, but in cases of impotence, neither partner can have normal satisfying intercourse.

Medical men who should know believe that over ninety per cent of the cases of impotence in younger men result from emotional causes—*that is, they are not due to bodily disease*. One investigator found that fewer than one per cent of more than 120 cases of impotence were caused by disease. (Such figures do not include glandular deficiencies in older men.)

It is amazing to what an extent the emotions can inhibit the sexual function. It is also nearly incredible what simple things can often clear up the imagined difficulties.

As an example of this, I should like to cite the case of a young man who came to my office with the complaint of impotence. I simply lectured him on the anatomy and physiology of the process of erection and told him that his trouble was purely emotional. I gave him absolutely no medicinal treatment.

Not long after this, his semi-frigid wife came to me with the complaint that I had overtreated her husband and that he was so potent that he was about to run her out of the house. She insisted that I give him something to lessen his prowess.

I explained that I had not given him any medicines at all and suggested that she take appropriate treatment in order to enable her to welcome her husband's advances.

Of course, most cases are not this simple.

In the medical treatment of impotence, the first steps are to obtain a careful history and to give a thorough physical examination. Such conditions as blood, vitamin or thyroid or other glandular deficiency must be ruled out, along with other harmful conditions.

If the underlying factors causing impotence are physical and can be corrected, the impotence as a rule will disappear. This depends of course upon the nature of the disorder.

The next step which I have generally followed is a preliminary treatment with sedatives and stimulants. One part of the nervous system, when excited, *inhibits* the activities of the reproductive organs, thus interfering with proper erection. Another part of the nervous system *stimulates* erection.

Thus, in cases of impotence, giving a sedative to calm down the nerves which inhibit erection and a stimulant for the nerves which produce erection should aid in producing erection.

If preliminary treatment with sedatives and stimulants fails, it must be determined if the patient is producing the normal quantity of male sex hormones. To determine if the amount put out daily is below normal, it is necessary to send a twenty-four-hour specimen of urine to a clinical laboratory.

If the quantity produced is considerably below normal, improvement may result from treatment with *testosterone* (male hormone). In the great majority of patients, however, especially in the young and middle-aged groups, hormone production will be found to be within normal limits.

If a man desires to stop thinking he is impotent, he should try to learn something about himself, how he is made and what makes his genital apparatus tick. He should know the structure of the erectile tissues and how their filling with blood causes the distention of the penis that he knows as the phenomenon of erection.

He should understand that if the blood flows out as fast as it enters, there can be no erection—that it must flow in faster and reach a state of equilibrium that will keep the organ firm and tense.

It is, however, not enough to understand just what the structure of the erectile tissue is. One must also know how and why the organ behaves as it does—*and why under certain conditions it does not behave that way*. This requires a study of the physiology of erection and the play of the emotions on certain nerves, some of which, as mentioned earlier, can produce erection, and some of which can prevent it.

Not infrequently, the attitude of the wife, or her appearance or demeanor, will be the principal deterrent factor. This brings to mind the case of a middle-aged man who found the clue himself. I agreed with his diagnosis when he asked: "Doctor, do you think the trouble could be my wife?"

"How do you mean your wife?" I asked.

"Well," replied, "lately she has been drinking heavily and she looks terrible!"

Distaste for one's partner is sometimes the cause of temporary impotence. Emotions of fear, worry and the like can also overcome the stimulating nerves and inhibit erection. With a feeling of calm, brought about if necessary by a suitable sedative prescribed by one's physician, and with stimulation of the erectile nerves by still another medicine, also prescribed, an excellent erection often can be achieved.

The best hope of overcoming impotence, particularly in older men, rests on full cooperation on the part of a loving wife. A slow and tender manipulation will—after two or three or sometimes ten minutes—bring about a most capable reflex erection. This requires practice and teamwork, for if the wife does not slow down the fondling on signal, her partner may get well beyond the stopping point and reach ejaculation.

Every doctor who has handled cases of impotence has always been questioned about the use of possible mechanical devices to obtain and maintain erection. Some of these devices are obtainable legally, others only by black market methods.

The only satisfactory device of this kind, in medical opinion, is a precision-made device produced by a leading manufacturer of surgical instruments in London. Known as the Coitus Training Apparaus (CTA), this device can enable the patient to have intercourse satisfactory to himself and his wife, although the penis is not fully erect.

This device has been found useful because it gives the patient confidence: he feels he can always enter the vagina and remain as long as he desires or as long as his wife wants him to.

It is important to note that the device is sold only to physicians and is dispensed only by them. In order to serve its purpose, this apparatus must be accurately fitted in person. It cannot be done by mail. Preferably, the device should be used in conjunction with psychological treatment to eliminate the causes of impotence.

Impotence is a disorder that plagues untold numbers of men—young and old—in our country. *Fortunately, the vast majority of them who think they are impotent actually are not and need only proper education and encouragement with simple treatment for overcoming their handicap.* In the more stubborn cases, intensive medical or psychological treatment, resort to hormones when indicated, or application of mechanical means in order to break the vicious cycle, may have the required curative effect.

# 58. The Wife's Role in Overcoming Impotence
## Eugene B. Mozes, M.D.

A middle-aged married woman consulted me about what she thought was pelvic trouble. Examination revealed there was nothing wrong with her, and her complaints were so vague, her answers so evasive, that it soon became apparent her condition was due to something else.

Sure enough, more questioning brought out that her symptoms had started just at the time when her husband became impotent, and they became gradually worse as he kept failing at each attempt at sexual relations.

She insisted that marital relations were unimportant for her. However, since her husband had begun to blame her for his failure, and as the bitter mutual accusations and bickering threatened to wreck their marriage, she was seeking reassurance that his impotence was in no way her fault.

Naturally, I wanted to hear the husband's version of it. As his story was unfolded, it became apparent that the fault was largely hers.

A few months before, the husband had been transferred to the night shift on his job. The wife now would not allow marital relations except in the morning when he came back from work, rather tired. Although he tried, he was unable to perform the act, and his condition became even worse as time went on. Yet his wife still insisted that was the only time she would allow it.

When he wanted to bolster his self-confidence with a cocktail or two, his wife strenuously objected and forbade him to drink anything at all. In this instance, at least, that time-worn excuse of every husband—lack of cooperation—was certainly true. When the wife was prevailed upon to change the schedule, the husband no longer had the slightest difficulty in being fully potent.

In direct contrast to this is the story of a forty-seven-year-old husband who for the past year or so had failed each time he tried, until his wife refused him altogether, knowing what the result would be.

Then one afternoon, the couple was preparing to go to a reception. As the wife was putting on her dress in the presence of her husband, he suddenly was fully aroused by seeing her half-undressed. Instead of impatiently refusing him as she had before, she allowed him to have marital relations at that time. From then on the husband no longer had the slightest difficult with potency.

Certainly it would be a mistake to think that every case of impotence is caused by the attitude of the wife. The root of impotence usually lies in psychological disturbance of the husband himself. Nevertheless, very often without even being aware of it, and in a subtle way, the wife may contribute to the failure of her husband.

But even if she has nothing whatever to do with the cause of impotence, she can do a good deal to help him overcome his handicap, or at least to help achieve sexual satisfaction for both.

It is a fundamental trait of the masculine makeup that a man takes tremendous pride, although not always expressed, in his sexual ability. Because of the role he must play in intercourse, he needs complete confidence in his virility.

So important is this self-confidence to a man that he will rarely admit, even to himself, that he has "lost his manhood." So he will at first find excuses for his failure in external circumstances: he has been working too hard lately, his heart is not as good as it used to be—as a matter of fact, anything that will save his pride.

Such excuses may work for a time. However, sooner or later he has to admit, if only half-heartedly, that he is incapable. Then comes the worst jolt to his masculine pride. He feels completely inadequate in satisfying his wife.

And it is here that a wise wife can be of tremendous help to her husband. She must try not to show by word, attitude, or gesture, no matter how unsuccessful her husband's attempt has been, that she regards him as sexually inadequate.

In most cases, the sexual relationship has become of secondary importance to the average middle-aged women, replaced by interest in other aspects of married life, including her role as a mother. But most men who become impotent as a rule develop an almost obsessive preoccupation with sex.

The more often such a man fails, the more desirous he is to prove his virility. And it is this suddenly aroused interest in sex that particularly annoys the average wife. She should understand, therefore, that the seeming oversexedness of such a middle-aged husband is actually a defense mechanism by which he is trying to prove to his wife and to himself that sex is still the central part of his life.

But it is much more than sympathy and understanding that the wife can offer to help her husband. Most women, despite their modern upbringing, still hold to the old idea that sexual initiative belongs to the male alone and that the woman's role is one of passivity and acquiescence.

Nothing discourages a husband more than seeming coldness on the part of his wife. Naturally, she need not be bold and brazen. Nevertheless, she can give expression in many subtle ways that she is taking full part in marital relations and, even more, that she derives full sexual satisfaction.

A gradual approach, always important for a complete union, is even more important for a man who has increasing difficulty in achieving erection. Yet most middle-aged couples feel almost ashamed to indulge in loveplay. And it is in this regard also that the wife can tremendously help her husband.

There is hardly a man who is not aroused by direct genital touch. But the husband must learn not to attempt the act at the very first feeling of arousal. He will be more successful in achieving full erection if he gradually builds up to full arousal before making any attempt at insertion. In this regard the wife can help a good deal if she is not overly prudish.

It is unfortunate that most women have some really fantastic ideas of what is normal in sexual relations. As a rule, they regard even the slightest deviation from what they consider "normal" as some sort of horrible perversity. The simple fact is that anything that contributes to mutual satisfaction is normal if it does not involve cruelty.

There are certain coital positions that greatly facilitate intromission when potency is not at its highest. If the wife bends her knees or elevates the pelvis by means of a pillow, insertion is often much easier. There are many excellent books written on sex techniques that couples who are troubled by this problem would do well to read.

Above all, both husband and wife should dismiss any prudish notions and discuss their most intimate problems quite frankly. By doing so they can discover for themselves particularly favorable physical conditions that help achieve the desired end.

Inability to achieve intromission is not the only problem of the impotent husband. Sooner or later, he will begin to worry that he is now inadequate and that he is unable to satisfy his wife. Such a worry is likely to aggravate his condition by contributing to complete loss of confidence in himself as a male.

And here also the wife can be of tremendous help to her husband. Most husbands still believe that the wife derives satisfaction only from sexual intercourse. Even in this modern age of sexual enlightenment, many husbands are ignorant of the fact that the center of sexual arousal for the woman is the clitoris and the area surrounding it—the vulva.

It is always a matter of surprise to the physician when he finds that his women patients are equally ignorant in this regard. The physician will explain that manipulation of the clitoral area can not only bring on arousal but also can lead to complete sexual gratification.

It is always important for the wife to remember that the husband who feels inadequate needs stimulation which she can provide only if she takes pains to appear attractive and desirable to him, both in the physical and psychological spheres. Such an attitude can also do a good deal to prevent his becoming impotent later in marriage.

If, as in the majority of cases, the real cause of impotence is of a purely psychological nature, ultimately due to loss of confidence and later to a sense of inadequacy, it is obvious that the wife can do a good deal to help her husband over this temporary disability. For in most instances the trouble is only temporary.

However, in order to do this she must first of all cast aside any prudishness.

# 59. Premature Ejaculation and Fear
## Robert A. Harper, Ph.D.

"I am so highly sexed, Doctor," the young man who was consulting me said, "that I reach orgasm before I can perform coitus with my wife."

"If you thought the cause of your quick ejaculation was being oversexed," I said, "I doubt very much that you would be here in my office. It obviously reduces both your own and your wife's enjoyment of sexual relations for you to ejaculate prematurely. Anxiety or fear or guilt or a combination of these closely related problems is causing this problem and it *is* a problem."

"But I read in one of Kinsey's books that quick ejaculation is normal. Kinsey says something about other mammals being very fast."

"Yes, Kinsey does say some presumably reassuring things about the matter. But whatever Dr. Kinsey thought about it and whatever other mammals may find satisfying in the way of sexual behavior, most human beings react as you and your wife do about premature ejaculation: it is a difficulty to be dealt with and overcome. Let's try to find the source of your problem."

Three basic fears often lie at the root of premature ejaculation, and another fear tends to keep the problem alive once it has started. The three basic fears are:

● Fear of sex itself, as something wrong or dirty or in some way undesirable;

● Fear of women in general or of one woman in particular;

● Fear that the man's own masculinity and virility may be inadequate.

After premature ejaculation occurs (often as a result of one or more of these causes), then the fear of its happening again is reason enough for it to happen again and again, even if the original cause or causes have been removed. It is a vicious circle very similar to the problem of the person who stutters or stammers, whose *fear* of stuttering or stammering is sufficient to make him do so.

Take, for example, the case of Fred. He demonstrated an interesting combination of all these factors at work. He had been brought up by a strong, dominating, prudish mother and a weak and henpecked father. His earliest memory of anything sexual was a severe spanking at about the age of five for urinating outdoors in the presence of a neighborhood girl who showed great interest in his penis.

All through childhood and adolescence, his mother reinforced the idea of sex feelings and relations as being something nasty. The image Fred had of women in general derived from his mother in particular: cold, controlling, and best avoided. And his picture of himself was unmasculine and unvirile—a weak person who needed to get away from these dominating women.

In some ways, Fred is a rather extreme example, but some degree of these factors can usually be readily observed in the background of men with the problem of premature ejaculation. Why do some men with this sort of upbringing develop other problems (such as complete impotency or homosexuality)? Part of one of my conversations with Fred may help to answer that question.

**Fred:** If I'm so afraid of sex and women and my own masculinity, why am I not too afraid to get an erection at all?

**Dr. Harper:** That cannot be answered absolutely, but some of the ideas I have run along the following lines: (1) Your basic sex drive may be stronger than that of a man who, with similar experiences, is completely impotent. (2) Some of your negative experiences about sex and women may not have hit you as intensely, or you may not be as sensitive to them, as some other males with similiar upbringing. (3) Premature ejaculation may function unconsciously as a method of expressing more resentment or hatred toward women. An impotent man may be even too frightened to begin to express hostility to his wife.

**Fred:** Is all this just guess-work?

**Dr. Harper:** Not entirely. I see some evidence in your case for what I say, but certainly no overwhelming proof. The fortunate thing, however, is that you can be helped to overcome these fears even without understanding exactly how they operate. By working with you I can help you to believe that sex is fun, that women (or at least *some* women) are delightful and enjoyable, and that your masculinity is beyond dispute.

This is what in fact I did in working with Fred. I helped him to argue against, to actively dispute and remove the nonsense in his mind about sex, women, and his masculinity. I helped him to develop new beliefs about these matters.

I also pointed out to him that experimentation with position in sexual intercourse can be helpful both physically and psychologically. Some positions (such as woman on top, side by side, and others which each couple can try) may give less intense stimulation to the penis than whatever is the customary position. And, from the psychological standpoint, a new position may help to develop a new habit: namely, lasting a longer period of time.

Meantime, however, with Fred as with others who suffer from premature ejaculation, we also had to work to overcome the secondary fear: that is, the fear of the experience itself. This fear goes something like this: I have ejaculated prematurely in the past; it may happen to me again (even though I am working to remove the original causes); wouldn't it be awful, terrible, dreadful, etc., if it happened to me again!

So, then, with that kind of fear, it often does happen again regardless of how successfully the original causes have been removed.

The only antidote for this built-in continuation of premature ejaculation which I have found helpful in working with patients is to counteract it with something of a casual, so-what, the devil-with-it attitude. If the cooperation of his wife can be obtained (as it could in the case of Fred), that helps a lot. Otherwise, the wife often reinforces the man's anxieties and feelings of self-blame.

The so-what attitude is tied in with instructions to approach sexual relations as just play, or fun. The couple is taught to enjoy each other in every way they can think of without concentrating on sexual intercourse.

They are also encouraged to proceed with lovemaking *after* the man's ejaculation. Very often erection can be maintained or reachieved after ejaculation, and even greater sex enjoyment thus obtained.

Does such a program work? Yes! I have found that in a very large percentage of cases the men who are willing to work at it can overcome the problem of premature ejaculation. The ones who fail are those who give up early.

# 60. New Ways to Overcome Premature Ejaculation

### Edward Dengrove, M.D.

Premature ejaculation is problably the most common of male sexual problems and one of the greatest causes of unhappiness in marriage.

There are two forms of this condition. The involuntary ejaculation of semen immediately after introduction of the penis into the vagina, or so soon afterward that the female has no opportunity to reach orgasm, is one form.

A more serious form is one in which ejaculation occurs *before* the penis is introduced into the vagina.

The man who is unable to delay ejaculation and thus complete a sexual union satisfying to his wife and to him, soon begins to feel inadequate. Each failure leads to the expectation of another failure. This creates a state of tension which makes successful intercourse unlikely.

The majority of cases of premature ejaculation are caused by an overly sensitive male sexual mechanism. Ejaculation is a reflex, the response to intense sexual stimulation. When the male's sexual mechanism is supersensitive, this reflex mechanism is unusually rapid; the body's response is swifter than the man wants it to be.

The hypersensitivity may be a physical one; the head of the penis may be so extremely sensitive that orgasm occurs almost as soon as the organ touches the female genitals.

It may be an emotional one; both the man who is intensely passionate and the man who harbors some mild anxiety about sex may be unable to tolerate intense sexual excitement, except briefly.

For many years, physicians have been searching for an effective treatment for premature ejaculation. Various methods have been tried, with varying degrees of success.

The young man who is overly excitable and ejaculates quickly has no real problem, since he can repeat the act within a short time. The second intercourse will generally last longer. For other men, however, solutions have been sought.

Anesthetic ointments have been helpful to some men. Applied to the glans penis before intercourse, they make that organ less sensitive and able to withstand longer contact with the vagina.

Tranquilizers have been useful in some cases, hypnosis in others, and men have been taught—or have taught themselves—all kinds of tricks to distract them from the sexual act and thus, perhaps, delay orgasm.

One patient of mine found doing complicated mathematical problems in his head a good delaying tactic. Another would silently recite the alphabet backwards.

But these methods were not completely successful, or they were successful with some men and not with others, or they worked only temporarily.

Now, however, physicians have found a new approach to this major sexual problem, an approach which gives vast promise of cure.

This treatment, too, is based on the theory of desensitization. But it does not require use of a pharmaceutical or psychological desensitizing technique at the time of every intercourse. Instead, it aims at permanenetly curing premature ejaculation by retraining the man's pattern of sexual response so that a greater—and more usual—amount of sexual stimulation is needed to trigger the ejaculatory reflex.

There are a number of methods of using this retraining technique. All are simple: they sound almost surprisingly simple. All can be used by any husband and wife who are willing to cooperate to overcome the problem. And—perhaps best news of all to those whose marriages are made miserable by the problem of premature ejaculation—improvement is rapid.

The first method takes what we may call the *active* approach. It was developed by Dr. James H. Semans of Duke University School of Medicine.

This method requires the wife to stimulate the male organ manually until the husband becomes aware of the sensation that immediately precedes ejaculation. He then signals his wife, who immediately ceases the stimulation.

When the sensation has disappeared, the wife again resumes the stimulation; again, her husband has her halt when he feels the sensation which tells him ejaculation is about to occur.

Repeating this procedure establishes a pattern of sexual response in which intense stimulation is tolerated and ejaculation is delayed. Soon, the man finds himself able to postpone ejaculation almost indefinitely.

Because ejaculation occurs less quickly when the male organ is wet than when it is dry, Dr. Semans advises the man to lubricate his organ with a bland cream when repeating the desensitizing technique.

The second, or *passive* approach, was developed by Dr. Joseph Wolpe, a practicing psychiatrist and a leader of a new method of treatment called behavior therapy.

Dr. Wolpe noted that impotence and premature ejaculation were often caused by anxiety or fear of the sexual situation. This anxiety is very easily stimulated. The man who is exceptionally fearful that he will not be able to perform intercourse successfully, for instance, may be so sensitive to any sexual situation that merely kissing the women he desires arouses this fear and triggers the ejaculatory reflex.

Desensitizing the man to these situations so that they were no longer so very disturbing enabled him to tolerate them without ejaculating prematurely, Dr. Wolpe found.

Unlike the Semans' technique, Dr. Wolpe's method does not require the wife to stimulate her husband actively. As a matter of fact, it insists that nothing at all be done to increase his sexual excitation and that no sexual demands be made of him.

The recommended procedure is for the husband and wife to engage in sexual closeness without either expecting intercourse. In bed, they are to indulge in only as much sexual activity as the man can tolerate without anxiety. He is to do only as much as he really feels like doing, and no more.

Because there is no set goal he must reach, no level of sexual performance he must attain, the anxiety he feels about sexual situations is lessened. As he becomes more relaxed, he is able to indulge in more intense sexual embraces without becoming anxious.

Dr. William H. Masters and Virginia E. Johnson, whose clinical work in this area is of great importance, advocate a method similar to Dr. Semans'.

They suggest that the male be manually stimulated by his partner for short controlled periods with stimulation withheld at his own direction as he feels ejaculation is imminent. The shaft of the penis should be well lubricated to reduce sensation.

This technique, they point out, will frequently fail and ejaculation will occur. However, the husband and wife should be encouraged to continue this method until the male's obviously improved control can lead to the next step in treatment.

The next step, according to Masters and Johnson, is for the

wife to assume a superior position and later a nondemanding side resting position.

As this period of training continues, the couple is given help in handling any of their emotional problems.

These techniques clearly require the complete cooperation of the wife, and her utmost patience. They will not work unless she is willing to help, unless she remains affectionate and encouraging and refrains from criticizing or making sexual demands.

In the method advocated by Dr. Semans, the procedure is to interview the husband and wife separately to explain the technique and give instruction in its use, and then to see both together to make certain the instructions have been completely understood. After a few weeks, the man and his wife are interviewed again so that progress can be evaluated.

Dr. Wolpe recommends that the husband explain the situation to his wife, quoting the doctor if necessary.

With the use of either technique, premature ejaculation may accidentally occur, of course. The couple is advised to expect this. Because they no longer regard it as a sign of failure, it does not create tension or arouse the man's feelings of inferiority.

If premature ejaculation accidentally occurs during the procedure, Dr. Semans advises that all further efforts be delayed, except that the husband is to manually stimulate his wife until she reaches completion. He considers that helping the wife achieve sexual relief is something the husband must do if he is to get her continued cooperation. With the Wolpe method, the man is not required to perform any lovemaking except that which he freely desires.

There is one further word. These approaches to the treatment of premature ejaculation work only in certain cases. Sometimes, premature ejaculation is a sign that all is not well with the patient's general health, and attention to the man's general well-being solves the problem. Sometimes, it is a symptom of a deep-seated fear or hatred of women. In such cases, psychiatric treatment is necessary.

Every man suffers from premature ejaculation at one time or another in his sexual life when he is worried, or fatigued. There is even a form called "honeymoon impotence" which occurs on the wedding trip, when both husband and wife are tired, tense and apprehensive.

If premature ejaculation occurs infrequently, and if there are long periods of satisfying sexual relations between the occasions on which it does occur, there is no problem.

# 61. Women Who Can't Enjoy Sex

### Hugo G. Beigel, Ph.D.

Some women just do not like sex. Their insensitivity to sexual intercourse can range from revulsion and disgust to joyless tolerance and indifference. Generally, such wives are unresponsive to their husbands' advances, and sometimes they avoid sexual relations as much as possible.

Some women with this problem try frantically to "get into the mood" and thus to achieve an orgasm. But even though there may be a will, there is not always a way.

Take Mary, for instance, a girl twenty-six years of age who was rather "broadminded" in this respect. She felt that women should enjoy the same sexual freedom as do men. She went "steady" with a man and permitted him every intimacy, including coitus, but she never experienced an orgasm except when she masturbated. This "unjust" limitation annoyed her.

During the mutual sex play with her lover, she worked herself into considerable excitement, but as soon as intercourse began, she sobered. The spell was broken, desire and all the good feeling ebbed away. She lay there passively, bored and angry with his slow and labored progress.

While consciously Mary wanted to be a wife and a mother, unconsciously she had always striven to be a boy. She liked to please her man and to be cuddled by him, but the contact of sex organs reminded her of the humiliating fact that she was a female and had to remain one forever.

In the relatively few instances in which physical causes—lacerations, sores, or inflammations of the genital tract—make intercourse painful, physicians have advised their patients to content themselves with petting. There is, indeed, no other way out until the malady is cleared up.

But in cases of emotional frigidity, that is, in the great majority of cases, it is no solution at all. Sexual coldness is most likely to yield to an attack on basic emotional problems. Generally speaking, psychotherapeutic treatment should be sought if at any time in her past the woman has experienced orgastic sensations, whether in dreams or through masturbation.

The only requirement for psychotherapy is positive motivation: that the woman wants to get rid of her frigidity. She must also be ready to divest herself of the character "armor," the rigid anti-sexual sentiments that she uses to save her from temptations, feelings of guilt, and fear. Sometimes, hypnosis is a useful part of treatment.

Thus Mary, in the case mentioned above, discovered the repressed causes of her sexual coldness in hypnosis. When she was four years old, a boy was born into the family. All of her father's love and attention, formerly hers, seemed to turn to the newcomer.

Three years later, mother came home with another brother from the hospital. Father was overjoyed. Mary was forbidden to go near the baby. Secretly she sneaked up to the room where the intruder slept, took him out of the crib and beat him mercilessly. Then she broke down, crying and sobbing.

Punished for her disobedience, she decided that only if she were a boy could she win back her father's love. She competed with her brothers and outdid them in every male activity, and tried to suppress everything that struck her as feminine in herself, including her sexual feelings and her responsiveness.

Men often feel challenged by a woman's sexual indifference. They cherish the illusion that their vigor and skill will make the woman love sex. The outcome rarely justifies their conceit. Indeed, in some instances, the good man's failure causes him further trouble.

To give an example, let us consider a man, thirty years old, who was very proud of his many sexual adventures. All of a sudden he found himself impotent. The rather boastful account of his success with women indicated that his conquests served as compensation for a deep-seated insecurity regarding his manliness.

He quoted repeatedly the phrases girls had used to praise his prowess—until "this thing" happened to him. He did not know to what misfortune the change could be ascribed. In treatment, a recent conquest that he had "forgotten" to mention revealed the source of the anxiety.

For several weeks he had dated a girl who resisted his charm. When eventually he presented her with an ultimatum, she confessed that she loved him and that she was ready to do anything he desired, but that she had no pleasure from intercourse. She feared that her lack of passion would disappoint him. He laughed and promised that after a night with him she would know the joys of sex and would want them again and again.

It didn't work out that way. He showed all his skills, but

when he was through, the girl said: "Nothing." Rather mock-ingly, it appeared to him. He was angry with her. In the morning, he decided to save his honor by another attempt. But he could not even produce an erection.

The double failure on top of his boast upset his preca-riously balanced self-confidence. To make things worse, when he tried to reassure himself in the arms of more cooperative partners, the frightening impotence reappeared.

This is an extreme, of course. And it is true that one or another woman has found in an extramarital relationship the gratification which she could not achieve with her husband. These cases are classified as pseudo-frigidity. The woman *appears* to be insensitive because of her partner's incompatibil-ity, or she dislikes her spouse, or she needs more precoital stimulation.

In other instances, the woman gives the impression of sex-ual coldness because the one and only approach with which her husband ever confronted her frightened her, or it was un-comfortable, or even painful.

Some women find the sex position preferred by the man degrading. But they are not familiar with other possibilities or they regard their own ideas as perverted. If there had been some playing or experimenting, the couple may have hit upon a solution satisfactory to both.

An improved technique of stimulation may thaw the in-difference that has been mistaken for insensitivity. However, technique is no panacea. If a man harasses his wife with his pettiness or gives her reason to suspect his fidelity, he cannot expect a bit of good technique to bounce her into ecstasies.

Besides, women who consider sexual feelings unworthy may tolerate intercourse as an inevitable accompaniment of marriage, but not the play that is meant to stir their excite-ment. To minds still crowded with the ghosts of childhood prohibitions, erotic play is undignified and debasing.

There is considerable hope that time, a loving and patient husband, or perhaps psychotherapy can help some women to acquire the courage to express without shame sexual wishes of their own. Not a few have found that, put into practice, this "forward" behavior not only gives them the desired satis-faction but delights their husbands as well.

# 62. Women Who Can't Reach Orgasm

## Aaron L. Rutledge, Th.D.

The following letter from a young woman expresses a worry of many wives who want complete sexual satisfaction, but who find that their bodies will not respond.

"Dear Doctor: I have been married seven years and have two children—seven months and six years old. In all this time I have not had an orgasm and I am beginning to wonder whether I would know it if I had. I wonder if there is something wrong with me but my doctor says there is nothing physical.

"My husband has really tried to please me within the last two years and nothing really seems to help. The only enjoyment I get is through manual clitoral stimulation and even then it feels so good I honestly feel that I cannot take any more and make him stop.

"His latest effort is discussing sex with me. This excites him and he thinks that if I would talk about it, it would excite me also, but it just does not. I would appreciate anything you can tell me that would help."

For a moment, compare this woman with other women caught in the same dilemma. There are still wives who continue to believe that sexual satisfaction is for the male of the species and give little attention to their own failure to respond. So long as an individual woman actually accepts this, she may experience little difficulty about her failure to reach orgasm. If she does not get sexually excited, she does not have to pay the price of disappointment and tension.

But the woman who wrote this letter has obviously let her failure to respond, and her disappointment, become known to her husband. Like many women, she has either feared or longed for evidence of some physical reason for the inadequacy of her response. She chose to face up to this by getting a medical examination which eliminates any physical basis for her difficulty.

Once a woman has learned that there is no medical reason for her lack of orgasm, particularly if she has read much on the subject, she quite often gets the impression that it is all the fault of the husband. After all, the sex manuals indicate that the female of the species is a delicate instrument which, if played correctly, will respond in beautiful melodies.

Many women complain that the husband does not know of their unfulfilled needs, does not care if they have actually told him, or is inept in knowing how to stimulate and satisfy. Some complain that he will not read a book and others that the husband did read a book and then tried to apply instructions in such a mechanical way that she felt like an adding machine. In this dilemma, it is not unusual to find women who refuse to talk about the issues but secretly resent the husband because he does not "understand how I feel."

Although the efforts of the husband of this letter-writer have seemingly been ineffective, she shows no distaste for her husband, nor any inclination to blame him. In fact, he has attempted many of the things that do sometimes actually work.

He has tried and keeps on trying, but she still cannot respond. He has been married for seven years to a woman who cannot respond sexually with any sense of adequacy, in spite of the fact that he has seemingly worked ardently at this for the last two years. Yet, he continues to be devoted to her needs as well as determined to meet his own needs within the marital relationship.

This woman has been willing to permit her husband to try to satisfy her manually, and she adds a very interesting comment: "Even then it feels so good I honestly feel that I can't take any more and make him stop." This is a not unusual phenomenon.

First of all, the sex manuals have put so much emphasis on the man's stimulation of the female clitoris as the one possible way of satisfying her sexually that some gross errors have occurred. Yes, the clitoris does provide the greatest concentration of sex cells of any part of the body. But the truth is that too intense stimulation of the clitoris can actually become quite "painful," so much so that the woman literally has to reject it.

It is interesting that in masturbation almost no woman stimulates the glans (head) of the clitoris. She may touch it occasionally to begin with but she usually contacts the entire pubic area. She does stimulate the clitoris but usually along the sides of the shaft or body of the clitoris, not the glans.

The more generalized stimulation of the whole pubic area, getting close to but not concentrating too much on the clitoris, seems to get the most desirable response. In fact, although the glans clitoris becomes quite prominent and evident during early sexual stimulation, if it is simulated too directly it actually seems to withdraw within the clitoral hood of tissue.

The gentle tugging of the hood of the clitoris and the sheath along the clitoris, which comes about through penetration of the vagina and the penile movements, coupled with pressure against the whole clitoral area periodically or continuously, seems to provide the best stimulation for woman. Too much stimulation of the clitoris actually makes continuation to ultimate climax impossible for many woman, despite the sex manuals.

But another look is needed at this matter of "feeling so good that I must make him stop." Many a woman has found that when she actually tries to make herself have an orgasm, it is more difficult than when she just forgets the climax and proceeds in the manner which provides the most direct satisfaction. Then it is that orgasm is more likely to come as a spontaneous climax to the combined physical and emotional excitement of making love.

But other women do get tremendously excited during sexual play or intercourse, enjoy it to the fullest up to a point, but then just at the very peak of excitement they just quit. Even if the partner continues, this woman sort of "turns things off." She lets down and fails to go on to an orgasm.

The why of this can range all the way from simply not knowing much about her bodily response, or not knowing how to continue the peak of excitement until the spontanous release occurs, to a total inability to trust herself to break the energy barrier and have a climax. An orgasm which comes at the height of spontaneous sexual abandon can cause the momentary loss of control, possibly momentary unconsciousness, which is frightening to certain women.

Very often this has to do with deep-seated lack of confidence in self, mistrust of self, or a mistrust of men that simply will not let the woman commit herself wholeheartedly to this basic experience of nature in which she lets go and loses herself. Perhaps it can be oversimplified by saying that, "never having found herself, she doesn't dare the risk of losing herself."

Having tried many things, as in the case of the above letter, it is a wise woman indeed who seeks professional help for her problem. It is an equally wise man who sees the wisdom of such assistance for his wife, and for himself.

# 63. Lack of Sex Sensation
## Donald W. Hastings, M.D.

Doctors use the term "sexual anesthesia," which means lack of sex feeling, to describe a number of conditions. A common example is the situation in which the man does not feel pleasure in the head of his penis when it is in the vagina during coitus. A frequent result is that erection is lost.

This type of difficulty may occur only under specific circumstances. For example, it may be present with his wife but not with another woman (and vice versa). Or it may be present during intercourse but not with masturbation. In such a case the "anesthesia" is due to emotional causes. Often it is a symptom of the man's attitude toward the woman.

Sometimes this term is used to describe the circumstance in which the male loses his erection for a psychological reason. For example, if during the course of coitus the wife talks about household matters, indicating that her mind is elsewhere, the husband may find that his erection vanishes.

"Sexual anesthesia" has also been used to describe the condition in which there is not enough sensation at the head of the penis to keep the erection in force. One reason for this may be the use of a condom. The rubber acts as an insulator, and its smooth slippery surface does not give as much friction to the head of the penis as does the moist surface of the vagina. (This has a simple remedy: use another method of contraception.)

Sometimes the vaginal muscles are too relaxed to afford a "grip" on the penis. Such vaginal "looseness" invariably is the result of childbearing, particularly if a tear or laceration has occurred in the muscle floor of the pelvis during the birth of a baby.

Such "looseness" is usually more pronounced under the influence of sexual excitement and hence may not be as noticeable to the physician during his examination as it is to the husband during intercourse. The prescription of special exercises for the muscles surrounding the vagina often helps. In other cases surgery may be needed.

When a person loses interest in his spouse, or in any other sexual partner, it is not correct to describe it as sexual anesthesia. While this can represent boredom with sex after years of sexual intercourse, it more often happens (in my experience) because the person, man or woman, has developed a mild depression and is suffering a reduction in all of his interests, not only his sexual ones.

This is a common situation, and the depressed person may notice a greater loss of sexual interest than in other areas. The male may be impotent and the female frigid during the course of a depression. This may last weeks, months or years.

Invariably such a depressed man notices, upon self-examination, that his interest in work, golf, hunting, and other things is also reduced. The mildly-depressed woman finds that she is not interested in house, children, and social activities. Formerly this person probably led an adequate sexual life. There is a marked difference between the sexes here. The female can permit coitus whether she is interested or not. For the male this is an impossibility: without arousal he will not have an erection.

Much has been written about "vaginal anesthesia," "clitoral orgasm," and "vaginal orgasm." Over fifty years ago, Freud described what he thought were two different kinds of orgasm in the female. During childhood and early adolescence, he felt that the seat of sexual sensation was the clitoris (hence "clitoral orgasm"), but that if the woman were to become mature, the seat of sexual excitement had to transfer from the clitoris to the vagina (hence "vaginal orgasm").

If this transfer did not take place, the vagina was, Freud thought, "anesthetic" and the woman frigid, no matter how readily she might experience "clitoral orgasm." Recent research has shown that Freud was mistaken.

Actually the clitoris and labia minora (inner lips) are the most sensitive sexual areas throughout all of life. The inside of the vagina is in fact quite insensitive and minor surgery can be performed upon it without anesthesia. The importance of mentioning this lies in the fact that if a woman had heard of this old theory of Freud's and did not experience what she thought was a "vaginal orgasm," she might foolishly consider herself frigid or neurotic.

Alcohol or drugs can reduce sex sensation. While relatively small amounts of liquor may cause the average man or woman to be somewhat more active sexually, and to derive perhaps a greater pleasure from it, alcohol in excess is known

to reduce sexual feeling. On occasion it can even result in
ejaculatory impotence. This is a condition where, although in
full erection and engaging in active coital movements, the
male cannot reach orgasm and ejaculation.

Other drugs, such as sedatives, narcotics, or "pep pills"
may do the same. A number of the newer tranquilizer drugs
are capable of doing this too, or of producing impotence or
reduced sexual drive. An unusual condition in the male, orgasm without ejaculation, has been reported as well.

The physician follows this rule of thumb about drugs: if a
person's previous sexual pattern changes during the course of
drug treatment, he suspects that the drug may be causing the
change. If it is not mandatory that the person be on the drug,
he stops it for several weeks to see if the normal sex pattern
returns. If it does, it is a fairly safe guess that the drug produced the change. A patient should not be reluctant to tell his
doctor of a change in his sexual pattern when he is taking a
drug, regardless of what kind of change it may be.

Although it is rare in men, women have a frequent problem resembling the ejaculatory impotence just described.
While sexually aroused and having intercourse, and while she
and her husband do everything possible, the woman cannot
reach orgasm. This has nothing to do with drugs and is the
commonest sexual problem of the female. (In the male it is
just the opposite. His most frequent problem is how to prevent arriving at orgasm and ejaculation too quickly.)

This female problem is called "orgasmic impotence." It can
be considered as a type of sexual anesthesia. It is thought to
be due to too strict childhood discipline with respect to pleasure in general and sex pleasure in particular. In other words,
such a woman is too inhibited to reach orgasm.

To sum up: "Sexual anesthesia" is a general term that includes a mumber of sexual difficulties. Diagnosis of the particular type of difficulty is necessary before any treatment can
be given. The person who has such a difficulty can be of
great aid in the diagnosis and treatment if he reports frankly
to the physician the details of his sexual life.

# About the Authors

**Dr. Albert Abarbanel,** a psychotherapist and marriage counselor, is co-editor of *The Encyclopedia of Sexual Behavior,* and co-author of *An Assault on Civlization* and *What Every Woman Should Know About Marriage.*

**Renee** and **Conrad Adams** are the pen names of a married couple who write from their own experience.

**Dr. Clifford Allen,** a well-known British psychiatrist, is author of *A Textbook of Psychosexual Disorders, Modern Discoveries in Medical Psychology,* and *The Sexual Perversions and Abnormalities,* and co-author of *The Problem of Homosexuality.*

**Dr. Ben N. Ard, Jr.,** is Professor of Counseling at San Francisco State College and President, Northern California Association of Marriage Counselors.

**Dr. Hugo G. Beigel,** formerly professor in the Department of Psychology, Long Island University, is a consultant in personal and sex problems and secretary of the Society for the Scientific Study of Sex; he is the author of *Sex from A to Z,* and editor of *Advances in Sex Research.*

**Helen K. Branson,** a member of the southwest faculty of the University of Idaho Extension Program, teaches courses in psychology, marriage and sociology.

**Ralph Branson** is a sociologist specializing in family relations.

**Dr. LeMon Clark,** gynecologist and authority on sex education, is the author of *101 Intimate Sexual Problems Answered* and other books; he is also editor of *Sexology* magazine's Question and Answer Department.

**Lester W. Dearborn** is a Fellow of the American Association of Marriage Counselors and Director of Counseling Service in Boston.

**Dr. Edward Dengrove** is a well-known medical author and psychiatrist in private practice in New Jersey.

**Dr. Josef E. Garai** is Associate Professor of Psychology, School of Humanities and Social Science, Pratt Institute.

**Dr. Vernon W. Grant,** head of the Department of Psychology of the Summit County (Akron, Ohio) Mental Hygiene Clinic, is author of *Psychology of Sexual Emotion.*

**Leonard Gross** is Associate Editor of *Sexology* magazine.

**Dr. Robert A. Harper** is in private practice as a psychotherapist and marriage counselor in Washington, D.C. He is a former President of the American Association of Marriage Counselors, as well as former President of the American Academy of Psychotherapists. He is author of *Marriage, Psychoanalysis and Psychotherapy: 36 Systems,* and co-author of *Creative Marriage.*

**Dr. Donald W. Hastings,** Chairman of the Department of Psychiatry and Neurology of the University of Minnesota Medical School, is the author of *Impotence and Frigidity* and *A Doctor Speaks on Sex Expression in Marriage.*

**Dr. G. Lombard Kelly** is a former Professor of Anatomy and former President of the Medical College of Georgia. He is author of *Sex Manual* and *So You THINK You're Impotent.*

**Dr. Charles F. Mayer,** a marriage counselor practicing in Dallas, Texas, is a well-known lecturer and author on law, marriage, and psychology. His syndicated newspaper columns include "What's Wrong with Marriage" and "For Love or Money."

The late **Dr. Eugene B. Mozes** was a gynecologist, Coroner of Stark County, Ohio, and author of *Sex Facts and Fiction for Teen-Agers, Living Beyond Your Heart Attack,* and *High Blood Pressure.*

**Dr. Stephen Neiger,** founder and Executive Secretary of the Sex Information and Education Council of Canada, is a Fellow of the Society for the Scientific Study of Sex and co-editor of the *Journal of Sex Research.*

**Rev. John B. Oman** is Founder and Director of the Counseling Center of the Wesley (Minn.) Methodist Church and also conducts a training program in group psychotherapy at the University of Minnesota.

**Dr. Robert L. Rowan,** a New York urologist associated with St. Vincent's Hospital, has published articles reporting his findings in various medical journals.

**Dr. Isadore Rubin,** Editor of *Sexology* magazine, is the author of *Sexual Life After Sixty* and co-editor of *Sex in the Adolescent Years: New Directions in Guiding and Teaching Youth*.

**Dr. Aaron L. Rutledge** is head of the Counseling and Psychotherapy Program, Merrill-Palmer Institute, Detroit, Michigan, and past President of the American Association of Marriage Counselors.

**Dr. Nathaniel Shafer,** a New York City specialist in internal medicine associated with Beth Israel Hospital, was formerly a consultant with the U.S. Public Health Service and Chief of Cardiology at the Valley Forge Army Hospital.

**Mrs. Lee R. Steiner,** a practicing marriage counselor, is founder and President of the Academy of Psychologists in Marital Counseling, conducts a weekly radio program, and is the author of many books including *Romantic Marriage: The Twentieth Century Illusion*.

**Richard Stiller,** a former Associate Editor of *Sexology* magazine, compiled and edited *Illustrated Sex Atlas* and *Illustrated Sex Dictionary*. He is now Associate Director of the Information Center on Population Problems.

**Dr. Walter R. Stokes,** now retired after over thirty years of psychiatric practice, is a Fellow of the American Association of Marriage Counselors and a distinguished pioneer in sex education and marriage counseling. He is author of *Married Love in Today's World*.

**Dr. Clarence A. Tripp** is a psychologist and psychotherapist in private practice in New York City.

The late **Dr. Kenneth Walker,** an eminent British surgeon, was author of *Marriage* and *The Physiology of Sex,* and co-author of *Sex and Society* and *Sexual Disorders in the Male*.

# 236      About the Authors

**Dr. Robert N. Whitehurst** is Associate Professor of Sociology at Indiana University.

**William Zehv,** a psychologist and marriage counselor, and a former instructor in psychology at Los Angeles City College, is now studying for his doctorate in New York City.

## SIGNET Books of Special Interest

☐ **ON LIFE AND SEX by Havelock Ellis.** A wealth of sound and practical advice from a noted expert on how to enrich love relationships. (#T3556—75¢)

☐ **THE HUMAN BODY, by Isaac Asimov.** An up-to-date and informative study of human physiology, which also includes aids to pronunciation, derivations of specialized terms, and drawings by Anthony Ravielli.
(#T3706—75¢)

☐ **YOGA FOR AMERICANS by Indra Devi.** A complete six-week home course in the widely recognized science that offers its practitioners a vital and confident approach to the pressures and tensions of modern living.
(#Q3661—95¢)

☐ **A READER'S GUIDE TO MODERN MEDICINE by Dr. A. G. Dally.** A well-organized reference which gives concise and comprehensive descriptions of all major functions and malfunctions of the human body.
(#Y3920—$1.25)

☐ **JOGGING, AEROBICS AND DIET: One Is Not Enough—You Need All Three, by Roy Ald with a Foreword by M. Thomas Woodall, Ph.D.** A personalized prescription for health, vitality and general well-being based on a revolutionary new theory of exercise. (#T3703—75¢)

## SIGNET Marriage Manuals

☐ **HUSBAND AND LOVER: The Art of Sex for Men by Robert Chartham.** A frank, authoritative guide describing in clear, everyday language the sex techniques every man should know in order to achieve a happy and satisfying marriage. (#T3293—75¢)

☐ **MAINLY FOR WIVES: The Art of Sex for Women by Robert Chartham.** An outspoken guide to the sex techniques that every woman should know to achieve a satisfying and mutually happy marriage. (#T3772—75¢)

☐ **SEX CAN BE AN ART by Charles E. Cooke and Eleanore Ross.** Boldly breaking away from the stereotyped patterns of sexual practice, the authors examine the full range of love techniques in a handbook designed to bring the delights of new experience to sexual relationships. (#Q3347—95¢)

☐ **THE POWER OF SEXUAL SURRENDER by Marie L. Robinson, M.D.** A leading psychiatrist and psychoanalyst tells women how they can overcome frigidity through self-knowledge. (#Q4410—95¢)

☐ **HONEST SEX by Rustum and Della Roy.** A straightforward discussion of the role of sexual intimacy as an expression of love. (#Q3857—95¢)

## SIGNET Marriage Manuals

☐ **SEXUAL LIFE AFTER SIXTY by Isadore Rubin, Ph.D.** The first work to demolish the misconceptions that hinder a full, healthy, and satisfying expression of sexuality in the later years, based on the latest research.
(#T3156—75¢)

☐ **LOVE AND ORGASM by Alexander Lowen, M.D.** A distinguished psychiatrist examines the physical and psychic conditions and effects of complete sexual satisfaction, presenting a revolutionary view of the role of love in sex. (#Q3227—95¢)

☐ **PREGNANCY AND BIRTH by Alan F. Guttmacher, M.D.** A handbook for expectant parents by the Director of Gynecology and Obstetrics, Mount Sinai Hospital, New York. (#T3446—75¢)

☐ **LIFE BEFORE BIRTH by Ashley Montagu.** Vital information for the mother-to-be to increase her chances of bearing a normal, healthy baby. Introduction by Dr. Alan F. Guttmacher. (#T2690—75¢)

☐ **PEOPLE IN LOVE: A MODERN GUIDE TO SEX IN MARRIAGE by Claire Rayner.** A marriage manual that covers a life-span of sexual problems, emphasizing the physical, emotional and psychological facets of a sexual relationship, both within and without the framework of marriage. (#Q4330—95¢)

---

# After 366 years of silence, a dictionary speaks!

World Publishing's brand new Second College Edition of the famous Webster's New World Dictionary has a special LP record which actually speaks phonetic symbols to you. So when you look up a word, you know exactly how it should sound.

And you'll know exactly what the word means because this dictionary isn't written in the usual dictionary-ese. It uses clear, easy-to-understand American English.

It's the dictionary that took 56 authorities 15 years to prepare. Webster's New World Dictionary of the American Language.

**WORLD PUBLISHING**
TIMES MIRROR

---

## ORDER FORM

The New American Library, Inc.
Box 120
Bergenfield, N.J. 07621

Gentlemen:

Please send me_____copies of WEBSTER'S NEW WORLD DICTIONARY at $7.95 each (Thumb Indexed—$8.95 each).

I am enclosing my (check) (money order) for $_____to cover the cost of the above order.

NAME_____

ADDRESS_____

CITY_____STATE_____ZIP_____
(please type or print)